NGING

ROSSLYN CHAPEL REVEALED

ROSSLYN CHAPEL REVEALED

MICHAEL T.R.B. TURNBULL

SUTTON PUBLISHING

First published in the United Kingdom in 2007 by
Sutton Publishing, an imprint of NPI Media Group Limited
Cirencester Road · Chalford · Stroud · Gloucestershire · GL6 8PE

British Library Cataloguing in Publication Data
A catalogue record for this book is available from the British Library.

Hardback ISBN 978-0-7509-4467-0
Paperback ISBN 978-0-7509-4482-3

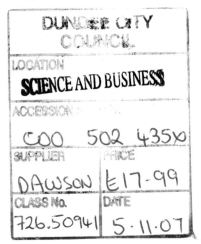
Typeset in Garamond.
Typesetting and origination by
Sutton Publishing Limited.
Printed and bound in Great Britain.

To the Earl and Countess of Rosslyn
and the Episcopal Congregation

The north aisle, Rosslyn Chapel, drawn by R.W. Billings, from his *Baronial and Ecclesiastical Antiquities of Scotland* (Edinburgh: William Blackwood & Sons, 1852).

Contents

Acknowledgements   xi

1   *The Landscape of Midlothian*   1

2   *The History of Rosslyn Chapel*   47

3   *Visiting Rosslyn Chapel*   92

4   *Varieties of Speculation*   131

5   *Contemporary Attitudes*   156

6   *Castles and Houses*   173

Epilogue   218

Appendix I   Priests in Charge   221

Appendix II   Useful Addresses   222

Notes   226

Index   236

Sculptor Lawrence Baxter (centre) with stonemason J. Lawrence Tweedie in the Lady Chapel during restoration work for David Bryce, 1862. Note the carvings removed from their location and placed on a seat at the rear. (By permission of the Royal Commission on the Ancient and Historical Monuments of Scotland)

Acknowledgements

Tackling a project such as Rosslyn Chapel has been such a wide-ranging (but very rewarding) activity that it is not possible to thank the many long-suffering people who have so readily and so generously shared their expertise and opinions – often at very short notice. Although many are already credited in the notes and picture captions, I would like to extend a special note of gratitude to the following:

Ken Bogle, Marion Richardson and Alex Fitzgerald of Midlothian Local Studies, not merely an archive but an agent of personal and social regeneration to its many users, for their ever-cheerful willingness to share the highs and lows of investigation.

Archbishop Mario Conti; Robert L. Cooper, Curator, Grand Lodge of Scotland; my former teacher at Edinburgh College of Art, William J.L. Baillie, CBE, past president of the Royal Scottish Academy, for uncovering a photographic treasure; the Bathgate Family for their kindness; Stuart Beattie, lately director of the Rosslyn Chapel Trust, for his support; Dr Jim Bewick for matters theological; Brian Caulfield for opening my mind to the properties of stone; Dr Jim Craig for sharing his research on Rosslynlee; the Revd Janet Dyer for answering my many questions in such an illuminating fashion and her husband, Dr Adrian Dyer, for his botanical insights; Dr Brian Moffat for sharing his extraordinary botanical research at Soutra Hospital; John Wexler and Marie Cope of Edinburgh University Graphics and Multimedia Centre for their willingness to go that extra mile in helping me to achieve the best possible quality of pictorial illustration; the Revd Michael Fass for his eloquent enthusiasm; the Revd John Halsey and Canon Roland Walls for allowing me to share their spirituality and sense of community; Dr Ewan Hislop for his geological suggestions; Historic Scotland for allowing me to photograph Glasgow Cathedral; Jim Shields; Joe Lang for sharing his deep knowledge of the chapel and its construction; Professor Fred Last for explaining how climate affects the growth of trees; the Episcopal community of Rosslyn Chapel and the Revd Joe Roulston for welcoming me to their dignified services; the monks of Sancta Maria Abbey, Nunraw, for providing the inspiration in my treatment of the religious and choral life of Rosslyn Chapel; the Scottish Tourist Board for answering my questions and providing advice and assistance; Winnie Stevenson of Roslin Heritage for sharing her knowledge of the chapel and village; Simpson and Brown (architects) for so generously allowing me access to their reports on Rosslyn Chapel; Chris Hall, sculptor, for teaching me how stone carving is close to godliness; the stonemasons and apprentices at St Mary's Episcopal Cathedral Workshop Ltd, Edinburgh, for providing me with the experience of watching stone being worked; the patient and ever-helpful staff of Rosslyn Chapel; and Adrian Bloore for redrawing the chapel ground plan. Finally, Christopher Feeney, Hilary Walford and Jim Crawley of Sutton Publishing, without whom this book would not have been written.

Every effort has been made to obtain permission for reproduction and to make due acknowledgement. The Author apologises if anyone's copyright has been accidentally infringed and can be contacted care of the Publisher. Unless otherwise stated, the photographs in this book are the work of the author.

The North Esk River – rocks at the Lynn. (Bryce Collection by permission of Midlothian Library Service)

CHAPTER 1

The Landscape of Midlothian

MISCONCEPTIONS AND PRECONCEPTIONS

All over the world the words 'Rosslyn Chapel' conjure up visions of conspiracies and an undercurrent of mystery. Instinctively, we imagine secrets lost in a bewildering tangle of symbols like some spiritual Sudoku to which someone might eventually provide the illuminating answer, if only the puzzle could be solved. But the true attraction of Rosslyn Chapel and its story lies in the insight it offers into the political, cultural and ecological development of medieval Scotland and the deeper answers it provides to contemporary society's hunger for meaning. As the Revd Michael Fass, Episcopal priest in charge at Rosslyn (1997–2006), observes in a bulletin displayed inside the chapel: 'Our prayer ministry is about turning the curiosity which surrounds the place into wonder at God's loving purpose for all His people by responding to the deep longings for meaning, for peace and for comfort which visitors express in the prayer requests that they leave with us.'

If only, like the Rosslyn Chapel Trust (which in the early twenty-first century is engaged in removing the white cementitious paint well-meaningly but unfortunately applied to the interior of the chapel in the 1950s), we could succeed in unpeeling the layers of beguiling conjecture that still cling to its venerable stones, we might find the true story of Rosslyn to be more compelling than fiction.

Today, Rosslyn Chapel stands naked before the visitor. Thanks to the public gangway that runs under the temporary protective canopy, visitors are able to peer in close focus at the building's most intimate and elevated areas normally accessible only to surveyors or steeplejacks. While there have been those who, in pursuit of the Holy Grail or other legendary but largely undefined lost treasures, may have seriously contemplated splitting open the Prince's (Apprentice) Pillar with a sledgehammer, bulldozing the ancient foundations of the chapel or even drilling deep into the sand-covered vaults far below, the venerable chapel still remains what it always was – a fifteenth-century Christian church, extravagantly decorated, it is true, but none-theless essentially a cherished and living place of communal worship and not merely a museum displaying a bewildering cornucopia of dead symbols.[1]

The pages that follow explore the landscape in which the chapel was built; we see how and why it was constructed and view the chapel itself in detail. In later chapters the persuasive but often over-imaginative theories that successive authors have developed to explain the structure and symbolism of the chapel are examined. We visit some of the unique institutions and communities in and around Roslin, before examining the landscape and features around Rosslyn Castle, Roslin Glen and in the Pentlands. Finally, we focus on the astonishing explosion of tourism at and around Rosslyn Chapel and Castle.

TOPOGRAPHY AND ENVIRONMENT

Wrapped tightly around Rosslyn Chapel, the picturesque and leafy Roslin Glen is a time capsule of natural beauty in mid-southern Scotland where the visitor can encounter the strangely familiar and the curiously unexpected. Midlothian, which once also included the City of Edinburgh, still constitutes an oft-forgotten southern flank of the capital. Dominated to the west by the rolling Pentland Hills beloved of writers and poets, with large swathes of open country, farmland and abandoned coal mines, Midlothian is a place of hidden valleys – a land of surprises. As one might expect, authors both popular and academic have argued over the purposes for which Rosslyn Chapel was built and the reasons for its location, but there is little doubt that the surrounding landscape, and Roslin Glen in particular, were key factors.

One vital ingredient of the chapel's mystery is the quality of its constantly renewed environment. According to a 1998 Scottish Wildlife Trust (SWT) management plan for Roslin Glen Wildlife Reserve (which extends for 114.6 acres), the area in which Rosslyn Chapel stands is one of a series of related and unique environments. Over the centuries the steep sides of Midlothian's river valleys prevented widespread woodland clearance, and, although there have been a number of later but limited attempts to manage the area, Roslin Glen today is 'a remnant of the woodland cover which was once the principal vegetation type of lowland Scotland'.[2]

Roslin Glen retains the greatest number of ancient, semi-natural woodlands in the Lothians. Moreover, the glen is special in that it offers the most

The North Esk river near Rosslyn Castle. (Ingle Series: early twentieth-century postcard)

varied mixed deciduous woodland of oak, ash and elm in the district and is a unique habitat, stocked as it is with plants now increasingly difficult to find elsewhere in Scotland. In addition, some 50 species of birds have been recorded in the reserve as well as 218 species of ground flora, among them great woodrush, wood sorrel, dog's mercury, ramsons and opposite-leaved golden saxifrage and including the rarer rough horsetail, great horsetail, wood sedge, pendulous sedge and wood melick.

The SWT reserve also falls within the Roslin Glen Site of Special Scientific Interest (SSSI), formerly so designated principally for geological reasons, but which today includes all the most important woodland habitats of the valley of the North Esk River, managed by Scottish Natural Heritage.

Without doubt, the craggy landscape from which Rosslyn Chapel emerged – with the North Esk River running through a rugged and sloping channel, surrounded by natural springs – is a natural time capsule, its identity preserved over the centuries by the inaccessible nature of its glacial-fluvial valleys, carved out by the melt waters during the latter part of the Ice Age. The inviolability of its steep and rugged valleys

has meant that timber extraction was always difficult and, moreover, that the larger farm and domesticated animals were also actively discouraged by fencing from straying there, potentially to their deaths.[3]

It was the geology of the area, however, that was crucial for the building of the chapel, with freestone widely available for intricate carving and sturdy construction. And there were other deposits in plenty – with the North Esk River flowing almost at its centre, a seam of coal runs south-west to north-east across the whole county from Carlops to Musselburgh.

Indeed, Midlothian coal was a feature remarked upon by the Italian diplomat and man of letters Aeneas Silvius Piccolomini (the future Pope Pius II), who came to Scotland in 1435, some nine years before the construction of Rosslyn Chapel began. An Italian scholar and diplomat, Piccolomini (then still a layman) was sent to Scotland by

The exposed sandstone outcrops overlook the channel of the river.

Cardinal Nicholas Albergati in the autumn of 1435 on an undercover mission to persuade James I of Scotland to launch an attack on England and so help end the Hundred Years War with France.

Fruitlessly as far as his principal mission was concerned, Piccolomini spent the winter of 1435–6 in Scotland but noticed with incredulity (among the other strange features of what he regarded as a barbarous country) that priests outside the local churches handed out black stones to the poor, who burned them for cooking and heating.

Midlothian stone was a consistent feature of local construction. In his *General View of the Agriculture of the County of Mid-Lothian* (1795), George Robertson (*c.* 1750–1832) commented that 'Limestone is . . . abundant', adding that 'Freestone is also

King James I of Scotland. (From William Drummond, *The History of Scotland* (London: Henry Hills, 1655))

Gnarled and twisted sandstone dominates the river path.

had in great plenty', 'Granite, whinstone, etc are to be had in every parish in the county, and are applied to building as well as paving of streets . . . Millstones are produced in the parish of Penicuik, likewise petrifactions (fossils), and beautiful specimens of marble.'[4]

Key to the eventual construction of Rosslyn Chapel was the local abundance of sandstone, especially freestone – a highly versatile sandstone because of its density. Describing the Roslin sandstone series (millstone grit) of the Mid-Lothian Basin, *The Geological Survey* (1910) notes: 'On the south side of the Sherrifhall fault they strike along the valley of the North Esk by Lasswade to Hawthornden and Roslin, where the massive coarse red sandstones in the upper portion of the series are almost horizontal and form picturesque cliffs on each side of the river.'[5] Geology not only determined construction methods and materials but would also, over the following centuries, prove a valuable scenic attraction for the development of tourism.

Laid down in layered deposits, these sandstones were widely available for building purposes, but it was the availability of compacted freestone, a tightly grained sandstone with no layering that could be cut in any direction, that would enable the squads of stonemasons at Rosslyn Chapel to indulge their creative skills so spectacularly, skills that were placed at the service of the passionate religiosity of the chapel's founder, Sir William Sinclair.

There is a venerable literary tradition that records how, when a member of the St Clair family dies, a curious phenomenon takes place in Rosslyn Chapel – the outside of the building seems to be on fire. This may be a characteristic of the red freestone used in its construction. Heat affects the luminosity of stone, and so the red Rosslyn freestone, much of it already stained by rust from the nodules of iron oxide that the freestone so liberally contains, would tend to glow in sunshine, whether early in the morning or late at night, in summer and in winter.[6]

Hence, the lines of the archaeologist and academic Sir Daniel Wilson (1816–92) taken from his poem 'The Queen's Choir' (1853), with their biblical comparisons, may not be completely the product of poetic licence:

> Roslin chapel, tipped with living fire
> Seen through the foliage, seemed like that divine
> Vision, when Horeb desert's leafy shrine
> Was with the visible gaze of God illumed
> And the bush burned with fire.[7]

In his 'The Lay of the Last Minstrel' (1805) Sir Walter Scott, almost fifty years earlier, had written 'Seemed all on fire that Chapel proud'. It was a tradition well known to Scott, as he had lived only 3 miles away at Lasswade and would often have seen the chapel for himself and heard its history.

In his massive four-volume folio *The Baronial and Ecclesiastical Antiquities of Scotland* (1845), Robert W. Billings has the most vivid and personal description of the phenomenon:

Rosslyn Chapel, seen from the north. (From James Grant, *Edinburgh Old and New* (London: Cassell, Petter, Galpin, 1880?–1883?))

It happened to the present writer, one clear evening, to be walking in the neighbourhood of Rosslyn, when he was startled from thinking of other things by the appearance, through the branches of the trees, of what seemed a row of bright-red smokeless furnaces. It was a fine setting sun shining straight through the double windows of the chapel; while otherwise, from the particular point of view, its influence on the horizon was scarcely perceptible. The phenomenon had a powerful effect on the vision; but it was more that of ignition than of sunlight, from the rich red which often attends Scottish sunsets. Though the setting sun doubtless pierces through many other double ranges of windows, yet perhaps there were few which, a couple of centuries ago in Scotland, could have rendered it with the same remarkable effect. It may be observed that the position of the building is the most appropriate that could be chosen, had the builder desired to produce that effect.[8]

From earliest times, in spite of (or perhaps because of) its scenic beauty, the pressures on the landscape around Roslin Glen and its ecosystem were considerable. From around the year 1400, the forests in Scotland were systematically denuded. Over the next two hundred years timber was ruthlessly felled to build houses, to make furniture, tools, carts, yokes and trestles, as well as to supply fuel for domestic heating in the form of charcoal, which was also a vital ingredient for smelting metal and making gunpowder.[9]

In one respect, Roslin Glen's picturesque scenery was preserved by its having been at one time protected as part of a royal hunting-ground where the sport of kings enjoyed a privileged, if savage status. In one of his historical works recording the complex and important history of the St Clair family, Fr Richard Augustine Hay, writing in the late seventeenth century, notes that before 1153 Roslin was 'a great Forrest as also the Pentland Hills and a great part of the country about, so that there did abound in those parts a great number of harts, hynds, deer and roe with other wild beasts'.[10]

Around the same period, protection of the land was also a consequence of the development of feudalism achieved by the introduction of 'sherriffdoms', first seen in the Lothians between 1151 and 1200.[11] Hay tells us that, in the reign of King William the Lion, Sir William Saintclair was Sheriff of Lothian.[12]

While the name 'Midlothian' seems to have first been recorded in the fifteenth century, the terms 'East', 'West' and 'Mid' were used in a general way to refer to loosely defined areas of the Lothians. According to a number of nineteenth-century maps as well as the *Statistical Account* (1845), the 'County of Edinburgh' was also, confusingly, known as 'Midlothian'. Moreover, 'Midlothianshire' was the term used for a collection of parishes, of which there were some thirty-seven during the eighteenth century. The 1801 Census of Midlothian also numbered several parishes, such as Penicuik, Stow, Temple and Inveresk, not included today in the county borders as established by the 1947 Local Government Act, which gave the county authority the right to use the name 'Midlothian'. For many years afterwards the administrative headquarters of the County of Midlothian was located in an imposing building in

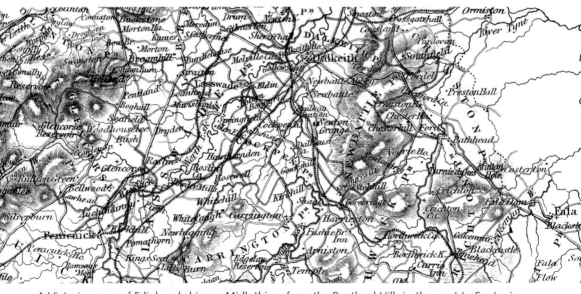

A Victorian map of Edinburghshire or Midlothian, from the Pentland Hills in the west to Soutra in the east.

Edinburgh at the corner of the High Street and George IV Bridge, which can still be seen to this day.[13]

However, in the early medieval period it was the Church, principally through its strategically situated monastic foundations, that brought not only industrious order to the landscape and culture to its inhabitants, but also social stability and leadership in some key aspects of technological innovation, such as improved drainage and the introduction of more effective agricultural machinery such as the heavy mouldboard plough.[14] A mere 6 miles from Roslin, Newbattle Abbey was part of an extensive network of monastic farming and mining enterprises that exploited the land and its resources through lead and coal mines (Newbattle Abbey being reputedly the first coal mine in Scotland), salt-panning, wool production and tree planting; the abbey itself would be periodically endowed by the St Clair family.[15]

Located just south of the important market town of Dalkeith, Newbattle Abbey was founded in 1140 by King David I (1124–53) and his son Prince Henry (d. 1153), with the first monks arriving there from King David's earlier foundation at Melrose. Although there must have been immediate provision for temporary structures, construction of the abbey church and its associated permanent subsidiary buildings did not start until almost half a century later. The abbey church itself was finally dedicated on 13 March 1233.

At Rosslyn Castle, the Saintclair family appreciated the contribution that the monks made to the local economy and to society in general; and Sir William, the founder of Rosslyn Chapel, would also have taken note of the architecture of the ecclesiastical buildings, and in particular the fact that the roof of the choir was high,

Newbattle Abbey. (From George Aikman, *The Mid-Lothian Esks and their Associations* (Edinburgh: David Douglas, 1895))

King James II of Scotland. (From William Drummond, *The History of Scotland* (London: Henry Hills, 1655))

while the side aisle roofs were low so as to allow light to penetrate through the clerestory – a feature of the architectural design at Rosslyn Chapel.[16]

An important legislative change in the status of Roslin took place in 1456, when King James II granted a charter to elevate Roslin into a burgh, giving it the right to erect a mercat cross and to hold Saturday markets and an annual fair every 8 October (St Jude's and St Simon's Day). Recognition as a burgh meant that trading could lawfully take place from open stalls set up in designated parts of the town, with the sale of each type of commodity being separated – the sale of linen was allocated a pitch away from that of fish, and that of meat away from salt, for example.

The land around Roslin Glen was also quickly developed into sections for different activities, with enclosed areas, and there was even some evidence of early industrialisation. By 1476, when Sir William Saintclair drew up an agreement with his son Oliver, we learn that Roslin had not only a castle, a chapel and a burgh but parks, woods, stanks (ponds) for fish and mills.

In the century following the start of the construction of Rosslyn Chapel (1440s), Midlothian as a whole continued to grow in importance. In his *Britannia*, the English historian and anthropologist William Camden (1551–1623) writes that what was known as 'The Sherriffdom of Edinburgh, commonly called Midlothian' had become

the principal Shire of the Kingdom; and is in length 20 or 21 miles; the breadth of it is different according to the several parts, in some 16 or 17 miles, in others not above 5 or 6. On the south it is bounded with the Sheriffdom of Haddington for 13 miles together; on the east with the Baillery of Lauderdale for about four; on the south with the Sheriffdom of Twededale for 13 miles; on the south-west with the Sheriffdom of Lanerick for 6 or 7 miles, and on the west for two miles by

Sir John Sinclair. (From Thomas Thomson, *A Biographical Dictionary of Eminent Scotsmen* (London: Blackie & Sons, 1872))

the said Sheriffdom; on the north-west with the Sheriffdom of Linlithgow for 14 miles; and on the north with the Firth of Forth for the space of 8 miles.[17]

In a later era still, this fertile and varied landscape would become a corner of the far-flung electoral county of Edinburghshire, a constituency of the House of Commons of the Parliament of Great Britain from 1708 to 1801 and of the Parliament of the United Kingdom from 1801 to 1918, consisting of the former county of Midlothian, which elected one Member of Parliament by the first-past-the-post system of election. In 1918 it was divided into new constituencies – Midlothian and Peebles North, and Peebles and Southern.[18]

It was not until the eighteenth century, however, that a satisfactorily comprehensive account of the landscape in which Rosslyn Chapel stands was written. This was compiled by Sir John Sinclair (1754–1835) in his ground-breaking *The Statistical Account of Scotland*. Sinclair, a barrister and MP and first president of the Board of Agriculture under William Pitt the Younger, edited the twenty-one volumes of *The Statistical Account of Scotland* between 1791 and 1799. It was the first attempt to gather statistics for every parish in Scotland and was in many ways a precursor of today's Scottish census. Sinclair, with the agreement of the General Assembly of the Church of Scotland (of which he was a member), edited reports on every parish in Scotland, which he had invited local ministers to collate, so creating a comprehensive description of parochial Scotland as it was in the eighteenth century, written at the local level by those who were in the best position to know their parish, its history and its people.

At that period, Rosslyn Chapel was in the Parish of Lasswade; it was also part of the Church of Scotland's Presbytery of Dalkeith and of the Synod of Lothian and Tweeddale in the County of Edinburgh. The minister, the Revd John Paton (1755–1835), wrote that his parish was very varied in surface, soil and climate. On the north it included the eastern edge of the Pentland Hills, partly covered in heath, and partly with fine green pastures. On the south was a large track of moor and wet moss. About 1,000 acres were covered with natural and planted timber such as oak, ash, elm, Scotch fir, spruce and larch. The rest, by far the largest part of the parish, was arable land. The soil was extremely varied, but, in general, it was of good quality, 'producing excellent crops of all the common grains'.[19] Among the many valuable products that originated in Midlothian is the Hawthorndon variety of Scottish apple, noted in the National Apple Register of 1971.[20]

As for geology, John Paton described Midlothian's main formations as 'coal metals – sandstone, (or freestone), clays of great variety, having different names according to their colour and degree of induration, a very great number of different seams of coal, and three beds of limestone'.[21]

He added that the North Esk had

a most beautiful run for several miles within this parish. On its banks are to be seen many of those favoured spots, which nature and art have combined to adorn to an uncommon degree. The winding course of the river, appearing often to lose

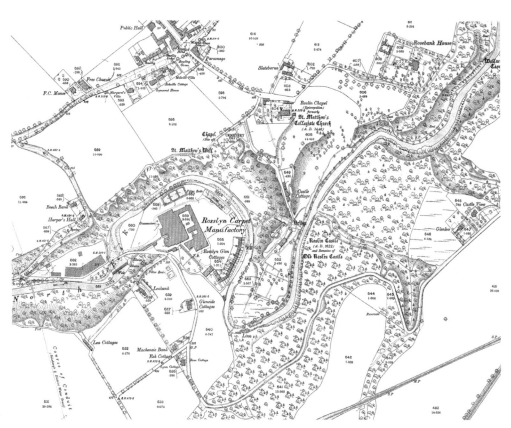

Rosslyn Chapel and Castle: 25-in Ordnance Survey of Edinburghshire (1894). (By permission of the Trustees of the National Library of Scotland)

itself among the rocks; its banks, which are remarkably bold and finely wooded; the huge pieces of rock seen projecting at proper intervals from among the trees, form an assemblage of the most romantic and picturesque scenes that are to be met with in the southern parts of Scotland.[22]

The climate was as varied as the soil, 'in so much, that, from the lower to the higher extremities, the distance of two miles makes a difference of ten to twelve days in ripening the productions of the earth'.[23]

Two generations later, the *Second Statistical Account* was published.[24] This time, the minister of the parish of Roslin was the Revd David Brown (1783–1870). Mr Brown was educated at Glasgow University and, at the time of the 'Disruption' (1843), left the Church of Scotland (mainly over the question of patronage and the appointment of ministers) and joined the new Free Kirk. However, in spite of his change in religious affiliation, his benevolent account of the parish of Roslin was still printed and published.

The river North Esk [noted Mr Brown], which traverses the parish little more than a mile, but which forms its boundary for about five miles, is one of the most remarkable streams in Scotland for magnificent scenery, from its commencement in the Pentland Hills, to its termination in the Firth of Forth, at Musselburgh. It is chiefly, however, in that part of the Vale of the Esk which has been denominated 'Roslin's rocky glen', where there is the principal concentration of beauty and grandeur.

Speaking of the interaction of geology and hydration at Roslin, he added:

Along the precipitous banks of the Esk, there are multitudes of springs of the purest water. One of these, in the neighbourhood of the castle, is named St Matthew's Well, from which the greater number of the inhabitants of Roslin village are supplied with water. The extreme purity of the water of this well is owing to its filtering through a very deep stratum of gravel; and this may be regarded as one cause of the salubrity of the surrounding district.[25]

It was this 'salubrity' that Mr Brown emphasised when discussing Roslin's climate: 'The parish, varying in elevation from 300 to upwards of 800 feet above the level of the sea, possesses an atmosphere considerably lower in temperature than that of the metropolis, from which it is distant about seven miles. The climate has often been remarked to be uncommonly salubrious in its nature . . .'.[26]

The rocky channel of the North Esk River. (The Bryce Collection by permission of Midlothian Library Service)

Beehives: a Roslin beekeeper in summertime. (The Bryce Collection by permission of Midlothian Library Service)

In spite of Roslin's obviously therapeutic qualities and atmosphere, when we come to examine the word 'Roslin' and guess at its origins, a problem arises. No one is entirely sure what the name 'Rosslyn' means. It may derive from a forerunner of Celtic as a combination of *ross* (rocky promontory) and *lynn* (waterfall) or even *Roskelyn* (hill in a glen), but in the eighteenth century it was asserted (more fancifully perhaps) that the word was 'derived from the Gaelic, in which language *Esk*, or *Usk*, means *water*. Hence *Usquebaugh*, the water of life.'[27]

Today, Rosslyn Chapel and Rosslyn Castle lie at the eastern end of the tiny modern village of Roslin – almost a land that time forgot – and there have been periods in Scotland's history when that very inaccessibility was extremely useful. Large caves hollowed out of the steep banks of the North Esk River were used as effective hiding places by William Wallace during the battle of Roslin in 1302, by Sir Alexander Ramsay in 1338 and by Prince Charles Edward Stuart (Bonnie Prince Charlie) in 1746.

Nevertheless, lest anyone imagine that Roslin Glen was entirely unmarked by industry or technology, there were to be three important if massively polluting industrial works hidden in its wilderness.

The Revd John Thompson (1837–1921), for twenty years the Episcopal priest in charge at Rosslyn Chapel and chaplain to the Earl of Rosslyn, noted that, while Roslin was famous for its strawberries, it had also at one time been the site of extensive shale works producing oil and paraffin candles, while in the immediate vicinity of the town were fire-clay, iron and coal pits. He reminds his readers that, a century earlier, Fr Richard Augustine Hay recalled that his own mother had found the 'best burning coal in Scotland' at Roslin, probably at what became known as the

The Henry, Widnell & Stewart carpet factory at Roslin Glen, *c.* 1900. (The Bryce Collection by permission of Midlothian Library Service)

'Moat' pit.[28] In confirmation of Thompson's statement, details of expenses incurred by the Earls of Rosslyn during the 1660s for stonemason work at Roslin colliery are today available for consultation at the National Archives of Scotland in Edinburgh.[29]

There were also other, equally significant industrial activities at Roslin. The first linen-bleaching field in Scotland was established there in 1738 by Robert Neilson, whose father had once been Lord Provost of Edinburgh. Neilson learnt the art of bleaching linen in Holland in a process that used rubbing boards, washing mills and other mechanical devices. He subsequently put what he had learnt in Holland into practice at Roslin.[30] By the 1860s Roslin bleachfield and the premises of Messrs Read & Son saw large quantities of chloride of lime used to whiten linen. As can be imagined, the environmental effects were highly undesirable: the lime was washed clean before flowing into a tank – to be used later by the workforce as whiting for their houses. Likewise, lye (vitriol mixed with water) from the boiler, along with depleted chloride, was allowed to run into the North Esk River, so producing a most noxious concoction.

Not far off, at Lasswade, stood Messrs Widnell & Company's carpet works, where burning furnace ash and oat husks, used in steaming dyed worsted yarn, were also consigned to the river, while dye stuff also regularly escaped from a pipe down into its waters.[31] In 1868 the bleach works at Roslin was acquired by Widnell's, who extended their carpet operation there, exploiting the invention of tapestry carpet by damask and printed furnishings manufacturer Richard Whytock of Edinburgh, a process that he had patented in 1832. Whytock's tapestry was a cheaper version of Brussels carpeting, made by simplifying the weaving and printing processes.

Linen-bleaching and carpet-making were not the only industrial processes to populate Roslin Glen with workers' houses and machinery centuries after Sir William Sinclair had housed his stone workers in the town. Sometime not long after 1790, a number of gunpowder manufacturers (probably from Kent) arrived in Midlothian.[32] After a disagreement, two of them, John Merricks and John Hay, set up a new gunpowder factory at Roslin. Supplying blasting powder and sporting powder for hunting, they prospered, for, during the Napoleonic Wars and later during the Crimean War, they were also invited to supply military grade gunpowder. In the 1840s the Roslin Gunpowder Works were the largest in Scotland, employing some sixty workers, half of them coopers making the gunpowder barrels.

But gunpowder manufacture was dangerous work. Forty barrels blew up in 1805, destroying a building and all its machinery. One observer wrote:

The materials of the roof, the rafters, the immense water wheels, in fine, the thick stone and lime walls of a building forty feet in length, had been broken in pieces, projected into the air, and scattered over the fields to a distance of several hundred yards . . . One man was thrown across the river Esk; the other to the top of a precipice overhanging the water – their mangled appearance was uniform – no remnant of their cloaths covered them – no blood flowed from their lacerated bodies . . .[33]

The Glen Cottages and bleachfields at Roslin, where brown linen was laid out for several months to be bleached in the sun. (The Bryce Collection by permission of Midlothian Library Service)

Andrew Fuller Hargreaves, consulting chemist at Roslin gunpowder mills, later general manager. (The Bryce Collection by permission of Midlothian Library Service)

Gunpowder factory workers. (The Bryce Collection by permission of Midlothian Library Service)

As can be imagined, the threat to both Rosslyn Castle and Rosslyn Chapel was not inconsiderable.

A second-hand steam-powered beam engine was installed in 1863, but working conditions were still very dangerous, and in 1882 it took the threat of legal action from the government to bring them up to an acceptable standard. Nevertheless, safety continued to be a problem: another violent explosion in 1890 killed six men at a time when horse-drawn carts carried the powder along a system of tramways to each mill: 'The sound of the explosion was heard some 15 miles distant, and for miles around it had effects similar to those caused by an earthquake, the shock being felt in many of the houses in Dalkeith by the rumbling of the windows and the rattling of the dishes.'[34]

After 1905 gelignite was manufactured at Roslin and (by the time of the First World War) incendiary bombs in a bomb section where 300 women produced bombs under contract to the Army and Navy. By the 1930s the gunpowder mills had become part of the ICI Nobel Division; they were closed down in 1954.

In the twenty-first century Roslin Glen and its picturesque country park (created on the very land once dominated by the heavy machinery for making linen, carpets and gunpowder) provide shelter and nourishment to hundreds of plants and animals. Visitors can see frogs, green and great spotted woodpeckers, roe deer, badgers and the common blue butterfly, while, high overhead, a kestrel can be glimpsed hunting for prey. At the river's edge dippers search for food, and, at sunset, the Daubenton's bat glides over the surface of the river, 'snatching insects with its feet and eating them while still in flight'.[35]

A young frog sitting in the sun on the path beside the river.

Westwards, near the Pentland Hills, Old Pentland, with its picturesque cemetery and its vanished church, was also once Rosslyn land, as was that part of the Pentland Hills around the Glencorse Reservoir. In the middle of the reservoir, deep under water, are the remains of the church of St Catherine in the Hopes (hollows), also once Rosslyn land, named after the healing Balm Well at Mortonhall on the south of Edinburgh, whose waters were rich in oily coal tar and so excellent for treating diseases of the skin. On the opposite, western side of the reservoir are King's Hill and the Knightfield Rig, names that commemorate a legendary hunting contest in which Sir William Saintclair won a wager (and his head) against King Robert the Bruce.

Today, what has become Pentland Hills Regional Park is not, of course, a large fenced-off area for the monarch and the nobility to indulge in what most people today would view as a 'cruel sport'. Instead, the area makes use of the Land Reform Act to offer access to members of the public by means of an infrastructure of recognised routes, coupled with educational initiatives and the promotion of responsible behaviour in the hills, so that sustainable recreation, land management, conservation and landscape protection can coexist.[36] Walkers, runners, horse-riders and cyclists now enjoy an area that was formerly the domain of a privileged few – the monarch, the nobility and the other powerful men of Scotland – among them the Sainteclaires and one of their adopted sons, Fr Richard Augustine Hay.

Fr Richard Augustine Hay

Apart from the evidence of our own eyes and what professional archaeology tells us, what we know of the origins and development of the St Clair family, the construction of Rosslyn Chapel and its subsequent early history depends almost exclusively on the work of one historian, Fr Richard Augustine Hay (1661–1736/7), a seventeenth-century Scottish Roman Catholic priest and pioneering records scholar, whose *Genealogie of the Sainteclaires of Rosslyn* (written just before 1700 but not published until 1835 – over a hundred years after his death) provides much of the essential foundation to the many guidebooks to the chapel and the story of the St Clairs of Rosslyn published over the following years.[37] As Will Grant admits in his *Rosslyn, The Chapel, Castle and Scenic Lore* (1947), little new information of any importance has been found since Hay produced his manuscript history, carefully transcribed by a continental copyist in 1700 and now available to the general public at the National Library of Scotland. Accordingly, the first critical step in understanding the history of the chapel is to appreciate Hay's role in its compilation, his methods and his motives.

In an autobiographical sketch in his *Genealogie of the Hayes of Tweeddale* we learn that Fr Hay was born in Edinburgh on 16 August 1661 and baptised at the Tron Kirk by the minister, Mr William Annan DD. Richard was the second son of George Hay, the youngest son of Sir John Hay of Barra, Lord Clerk Register of Scotland. His mother was Jean Spottiswood, daughter of Sir Henry Spottiswood, High Sheriff of Dublin.[38]

Shortly after the battle of Rullion Green – fought at Pentland (for centuries part of the Earl of Rosslyn's estates), where General Tam Dalyell crushed the dissenting

Fr Richard Augustine Hay's unofficial heraldic arms. (By permission of the Scottish Catholic Archives)

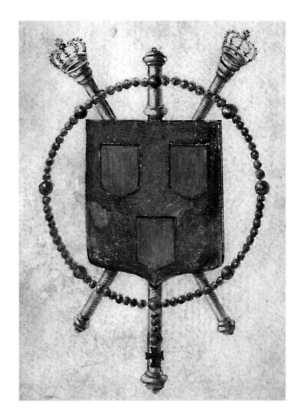

Covenanters on 28 November 1666 – Hay's natural father died. Hay writes with a twinge of Hamlet-like bitterness that his mother was 'married shortly thereafter' to James Sinclair of Roslin (a Roman Catholic – a religious persuasion not widely popular in Scotland at the time). Under his new stepfather's influence, the young Richard also became a Roman Catholic and was brought up with his cousins in a series of Scottish houses, at Innerleithen and Traquair (in the Borders), Dysart (Fife) and Ford (Midlothian), and sent to school in Edinburgh and Dalkeith. His education did not progress as well as it should have, for which Hay later blamed the indifferent skills of his teachers.

As a stepchild Hay was passed from pillar to post and complains that 'he was toss'd up and down', although, after his stepfather had died, he would write kindly of him.[39] Like so many well-to-do stepchildren who are difficult to manage, he grumbles that he was then packed off to boarding school in the summer of 1673, in his case to France, and 'there thrust into the Scots College, Paris', where he lodged until August 1677. At the college he seems to have had a personality clash with David Burnett, Prefect of Studies (1676–80), of whose 'hard and wearisome dealings' he grew tired. He decided to study elsewhere in Paris, choosing to take a course in grammar at the Collège de Navarre (1673–7).[40] In later life, his days at the Scots College still rankled, and he wrote disapprovingly of how he felt the college management had taken advantage of his stepfather's generosity by persuading him to give them more money than they needed.

Hay's education then continued at St James of Pouvins, Saint-Rille (near Fougers in Brittany) and with the Augustinian canons regular at the abbey of Saint-Charon near Chartres. Clearly, Hay was not only developing his formidable array of academic skills but also actively thinking of entering the Roman Catholic priesthood, as this would give him some security and stability as well as the opportunity to continue his researches into Scottish history, in which his fluency in Latin and French would be invaluable. It would also place him in direct conflict with the established Kirk in Scotland and make a public return to his native land, a step that could not be taken without risk.

In 1678 Hay entered the novitiate of the Augustinian canons at Sainte-Geneviève, Paris, appropriately taking the religious name of 'Augustine'. After a year's novitiate he made his solemn vows. Over the next six years he studied for the priesthood at Chartres (while also teaching) and then was ordained there in 1685.

On 6 February 1685 King James II of England and VII of Scotland succeeded to the throne of Great Britain. Since the new king had converted to Roman Catholicism shortly before his accession, the political and religious climate changed, making it more favourable to Roman Catholics. As the Duke of York, James had lived in Edinburgh in 1679 and again in 1680–2, on three occasions acting as his brother Charles II's commissioner at the Scottish Parliament. He also contrived to irritate the Reformed Church authorities by gestures such as the promotion of theatrical performances in the Holyrood tennis court, playing golf and wagering on the outcome. Hitherto James had worshipped in private, within his own household. But now that he was king, he decided he should worship in public and therefore ordered the large Holyrood Council Chamber to be adapted for the Roman Catholic liturgy as a temporary measure, while more permanent changes were carried out at the adjacent abbey. The King's yacht duly arrived at Leith, with, as Lord Fountainhall put it, 'the Popish altar, vestement, images, Priest and other dependers for the Popish Chapell in the Abbey'.[41]

The ruins of Holyrood Abbey.

Interior of the Chapel Royal of Holyrood House, 1687 (after Wyck and P. Mazell). (From James Grant, *Edinburgh Old and New* (London: Cassell, Petter, Galpin, 1880?–1883?))

The following year (1686), as Hay explains in an unguarded personal aside, homesick and 'longing to see the smoke of his own country', he was invited to travel to England and Scotland by the abbot of Sainte-Geneviève with the aim of setting up communities of Augustinian canons regular in those countries, with the blessing of their new Roman Catholic monarch, James VII of Scotland and II of England.[42] Hay 'kiss'd the King's hands at Windsor', stayed some weeks at court and then set off by boat for Leith.

By the time he got to Edinburgh the Catholicism of King James had seen a Jesuit-run Roman Catholic school and a printing press established at Holyrood. More provocatively, the Roman Catholic chapel opened at Holyroodhouse was the first step in setting up a full-blown Catholic Chapel Royal, which would necessitate the removal of the incumbent Reformed parish congregation.[43] Fr Hay was at the heart of the Roman Catholic celebrations: he attended the inaugural mass of blessing at the new Chapel Royal on 30 November 1686 (St Andrew's Day) in a building that had once been part of the Augustinian monastery established by King David I. Subsequently, vested in his white Augustinian habit, with surplice, *amice* (an oblong piece of fine linen resting on the shoulders) and *rochet* (a linen garment with sleeves reaching to the hands), he carried out the ordinary work of a Catholic priest, noting that he 'buried, being in my habit . . . in the abbey Church of Edinburgh, the body of Agnes Irwin, after the rites of the Roman Church'.[44]

The Lord Chancellor, James Drummond, Earl of Perth, had converted to Catholicism in 1685. In May and June 1687 Hay had discussions with the Earl regarding his project of establishing the canons regular at Holyrood. The Earl asked if the Augustinians would be willing to build a church with a ground plan in the shape of a cross and bear the costs of construction. The Earl was a visionary entrepreneur, taking an active interest in a number of other building and scientific projects (and, with William Penn as a partner, would even go on in 1681 to establish a settlement at East New Jersey in America). These endeavours embraced Hay's proselitising work and the activities of Sir Robert Sibbald (himself a recent, if temporary convert to the Roman Catholic faith). Sibbald was not only Geographer Royal but also a botanist and a doctor of medicine who would later collaborate with Captain John Slezer in the production of *Theatrum Scotiae*, a book of Slezer's drawings of, among other subjects, Rosslyn Chapel (executed with the help of a portable camera obscura).

Although Hay was unable to provide the financial support for a new abbey in the Canongate and so had to decline the Earl's proposal, it is possible that, through the Earl (who sponsored them both), Hay may have had some contact with Sibbald. For a short space of time Roman Catholicism seemed to be in the ascendant. Hay maintained an out-of-town study at Rosslyn Chapel, storing his books and papers there (perhaps in the crypt, which could be locked and had a fireplace), until an anti-Catholic mob disrupted his antiquarian activities.

Meanwhile, the Earl of Perth and his brother had set up a Roman Catholic chapel inside their house at the Canongate, but, albeit held privately, the celebration of mass there in 1686 caused violent public outrage and the house was immediately looted by the protesters.

In July 1687, much against their will, the parishioners who had worshipped at Holyrood Abbey as their parish church were removed to Lady Yester's Kirk in what is today Infirmary Street, where they stayed until they were eventually able to transfer to the newly built Canongate Kirk.

Hay, meanwhile, was in constant contact with the official face of the King's Roman Catholic administration. He records that he was with the Earl and the Archbishop of Glasgow when a letter of authorisation arrived from Paris, and also attended mass along with the Earl, the Duke of Gordon and 'several other persons of different religions'.[45] He officiated at the requiem mass for 'Old Father Murray', a Jesuit of whom he rather surprisingly appeared to approve, and was present at his interment in the Abbey Church.

However, on 10 December 1688, Hay notes angrily that 'the monuments of Catholicity were destroyed by the mob'. Public resentment of James VII and his associates had reached boiling point:

> The mob gathered, and, assisted by the city train-band, forced the palace [Holyrood], killed a number of the soldiers who defended it, and soon rifled the shrine which had excited their rage. They carried the images in triumphal procession through the streets and then solemnly burnt them . . . they proceeded to search the houses of the Roman Catholics in the city, and to carry off their books, beads, and crucifixes, that they might commit them to the flames.[46]

Although Roman Catholics were still officially permitted to exercise their religion (as long as it was in private), soon afterwards a proclamation was issued 'against Papists, discharging them the exercise of all offices'. The following evening Rosslyn Chapel was damaged by a mob from Edinburgh, assisted by local inhabitants and tenants of the St Clairs. In the confusion, Hay lost several books of note.

The Revd John Thompson adds that the objective of the mob was not so much to damage the building as to destroy the Roman Catholic liturgical furniture and vestments, which they saw as popish and therefore idolatrous. Although the Earl continued to be sympathetic to Hay's mission, the flight of King James in December 1688 put an end to any plans to expand the Roman Catholic presence.

An autobiography in manuscript, the 'Life of James Currie, Merchant in Pentland' (privately printed and in the possession of the Sainteclaire family), had been lent to Mr Thompson. It supplies more detail of the destructive efforts at the chapel: 'On this same night [11 December 1688] some men went over to Rosslyn Castle, and burnt their images and many of their Popish books, I telling them where they would find their Priests' robes; but I desired some to go after them and hinder them from taking or hurting anything, except what belonged to their idolatry; for at this time the Prince of Orange was come to England.'

Hay avoided immediate expulsion from Scotland because he was neither a Jesuit (Jesuwit, as he sneeringly called them), a Benedictine nor a 'seminary priest' – clerics who, because of their barely concealed attempts to interfere in matters of state, would not be tolerated by the new Protestant regime now determined to assert its authority by sweeping away all vestiges of Roman Catholic belief. In spite of the apparent toleration of Hay, his life in Scotland was uncomfortable enough to persuade him to submit an official petition to be allowed to leave Scotland.

He was able to remain in Edinburgh, however, for some further months until, in May 1689, he was finally given permission to sail for France. There he took up his priestly life again with the canons regular, holding over the following years various administrative posts, bearing the title of sub-prior and, in 1695, was made prior at Saint-Pierremont in northern France.

During this time Hay, who still had access to Scottish historical documents preserved in France, continued to work on half a dozen substantial collections of Scottish historical texts, also corresponding with the leading French scholar Jean

Parliament Hall, Edinburgh, with the Advocates' Library to the right. (From James Grant, *Edinburgh Old and New* (London: Cassell, Petter, Galpin, 1880?–1883?))

Mabillon (1632–1707), a Benedictine monk regarded as the founder of palaeography and 'diplomatics' (the science of establishing the authenticity of official historical documents, such as charters). Once the hostile climate of opinion against Roman Catholics in Scotland had changed, Hay planned to return to Edinburgh to compile a history of the monastic system in Scotland, and to do so using the services of the publishers and printers then active and widely available in the city.

A manuscripts conservator at work in the National Library of Scotland. (By permission of the Trustees of the National Library of Scotland)

The Holyrood silver: monstrance, ciborium, thurible, incense boat, chalice, paten and spoon, bought mainly in London in 1686 by the Earl of Perth. Fr Hay would probably have used this altar service at Holyrood. (By permission of the Roman Catholic Bishops of Scotland)

Hay's own aims as a historian are clearly set out in his *Genealogie of the Hayes of Tweeddale* (published in 1835 in an edition by James Maidment), in which, as part of his 'Proposals for Printing the Scotichronicon' of John of Fordun, he speaks of 'clearing the dark Parts of our History . . . for the greater intelligence of our History'.[47] He was a protector and respecter of books and describes how he rescued a manuscript from the Abbey of Coupar, saying that 'I recovered it from the rabble and carried it beyond the seas'.[48]

Hay did return to Scotland some time before 1719 and, by that date, was preparing to bring out an edited version of John of Fordun's *Scotichronicon*, a project that never came to fruition, partly because another historian published his version first. Meanwhile, he had brought out two well-argued and well-researched papers challenging the assertion that the Stewart dynasty had no claim to the throne.

His final years in Edinburgh, however, were largely years of disappointment, penny-pinching and penury, to the extent that he sold a number of his manuscripts to the Advocates Library, including a large bundle of assorted notes made while preparing a number of projects. These are crowded onto scraps of paper of differing sizes, filled with his frenzied handwriting, so cramped as to be often indecipherable, in order to economise on paper. He lodged for a time in the Southside (at Howison's Land in Potterow) but died in what was at that period the more affluent Cowgate 'in very mean circumstances', possibly at the Earl of Rosslyn's town house at Blackfriars Wynd (now Blackfriars Street).

Hay was a compulsive historian who wrote sometimes in English, sometimes in French, but mainly in Latin. His notes, drafts, letters and even accounts (for tutoring private pupils) that survive are held at the National Library of Scotland in Edinburgh.

Perhaps it was the difficulties that he had faced as a child in dealing with the rejection he must have experienced after his father's death that, paradoxically, made Hay so intensely interested in the history of the complicated branches of his extended family – of his own, the Hays of Tweeddale, and his adopted family, the St Clairs of Rosslyn. Perhaps he looked to find in genealogy the stable roots that his troubled childhood had denied him. And the Roman Catholic Church, for all its failings, also attracted his deep loyalty and interest, as can be seen in the endless and meticulous descriptions of religious houses and their histories. But it was, above all, the history of the land that had twice rejected him that held an overarching fascination for Hay.

As the National Library of Scotland was founded out of the library of the nearby Faculty of Advocates (some of the volumes even for some time being housed in the underground tunnels leading to the High Court), part of Hay's works are classified under the heading 'Advocates' manuscripts'. In this category are his life of Sir William Wallace (early eighteenth century);[49] extracts by Robert Mylne from Hay's transcript of the chartulary of Arbroath Abbey;[50] three volumes comprising Hay's *Diplomatum veterum collectio* (edited copies of various chartularies, 1696);[51] Hay's Antiquities called *Scotia Sacra*: 'Ane account of the most renowned churches, bishoprics, monasteries and other devote places from the first introducing of Christianity into Scotland to . . . the severall reformations of religion' (1700);[52] and

'Memoirs, or a collection of severall things relating to the historicall accounts of the most famed families of Scotland' (1700; two volumes).[53]

In a separate collection of Hay's works, contained in the National Library of Scotland's catalogued manuscripts, is a letter Hay sent to James Drummond, Duke of Perth – Hay's 'Lettre écrite au duc de Perth [Paris], 1712', with extensive manuscript notes and corrections in the hand of the author.[54] These notes, however, are considerably different from those, also in Hay's handwriting, on another copy of this pamphlet.[55] Other Hay material consists of letters to Hay, 1716–28;[56] an inventory of Hay's books, c. 1732;[57] and draft notes on monastic houses in Scotland, possibly compiled by Hay (undated).[58] In the National Library of Scotland's collection of uncatalogued accessions are also papers of Hay, 1679–1718;[59] papers of Hay, early eighteenth century;[60] and a notebook, which Hay apparently intended originally for notes, meditations and extracts of a religious nature, but used almost entirely for transcripts of documents relating to the family of Sinclair of Rosslyn (fols 3–83).[61] These latter show that he not only examined charters but also consulted the standard histories of Scotland, such as those of John of Fordun and George Buchanan.

The Lady Chapel at Rosslyn Chapel, drawn and engraved by J. & J. Johnstone, Edinburgh (1825). Note the guide with pointing stick. (From *Picture of Rosslyn Chapel* (Edinburgh: Oliver & Boyd, 1825)

His compilations of charters associated with the St Clair family, on which he worked for many years, were published only long after his death. However, their influence has been considerable and they are much quoted from.

Although we may suspect that Hay was too close to the St Clair family to treat their historical records with total impartiality and that, judging by his manuscripts, his working habits were not always entirely methodical, there is no doubt that his transcriptions of now-destroyed charters and other documents have saved material that is of historical value. In addition, because he was related (through his stepfather) to the St Clair family, he was able to have privileged access to the charter chest at Rosslyn Castle and was completely trusted to treat its contents with due respect. Hay was, moreover, not merely a scribe or copyist of long-neglected legal documents, but an erudite and conscientious historian who carried out work that he believed to be vital. Many writers of fiction or poetry took inspiration from Hay's historical collections: Sir Walter Scott, for example, who lived nearby at Lasswade, used Hay's works as a source for his 'The Lay of the Last Minstrel'.

The dominant aim of Hay's rather rambling *Genealogie of the Sainteclaires of Rosslyn* is to show that the Sinclair family had long been associated with power but were able to exercise that power only because they were completely loyal subjects of the kings under whom they served. Although Hay made value judgements as to the long-term legal significance of the charters and other documents he recorded, his selection is clearly intended to illustrate the Sainteclaires' undeviating loyalty to the Crown, which, in turn, repeatedly rewarded them with land and high office.

While, on the one hand, we must be grateful to James Maidment (1795–1879), a Scottish advocate and historian who published a large quantity of historical material either anonymously or privately printed, and contributed to collections published by learned societies such as the Spottiswoode, Maitland, Abbotsford, Hunterian and Bannatyne Clubs, it has to be recognised that Maidment did not do full justice to Hay's work as a historian and attempted subtly to undermine its historical value.

In his 'Introductory Notice' to Hay's *Genealogie of the Sainteclaires of Rosslyn* Maidment begins by recommending the text as being of interest not only to historians but to genealogists. However, he sounds a note of caution by describing Hay's original manuscripts as 'curious, but sometimes inaccurate, collections', which nevertheless are preserved in the library of the Faculty of Advocates.[62] Maidment continues: 'It is to be regretted that the reverend gentleman was so careless in making his transcripts, as, in many instances, various evident mistakes have crept in, which the absence of the original documents renders it sometimes difficult to correct.' Having assassinated Hay's academic character, in order to promote his edition of Hay's work Maidment rapidly backtracks, as he wishes to avoid any negative impact on the sales of this edition through loss of confidence in its historical accuracy. 'Fortunately,' he adds, 'these inaccuracies, generally speaking, are of no very great moment.' In any case, he continues, Hay was a creature of his own era, at a time when historians did not set any great store by total historical accuracy – which, by implication, Maidment understands to be the norm in his own day. Maidment concludes that his readers should, in the final analysis, be grateful that such valuable documents were copied by Hay, as by 1835 the originals had all apparently been destroyed.

Fortunately, other and later opinions of Hay's importance have been expressed. The Dominican historian Fr Anthony Ross describes him as an 'outstanding scholar' but of 'troubled life and character'.[63] He points out that Hay was personally acquainted with Mabillon and Ruinart and other French scholars and that his 'industry and learning were immense'. But he concludes that Hay was 'essentially . . . a record scholar, whose projected publications were more ambitious than contemporary interest could accept'.

In fact, Maidment seems to have deliberately made Hay's text appear more old-fashioned than it actually was. Where Hay's manuscript clearly has the carefully scripted title 'Genealogy', Maidment changes the final 'y' to an 'ie' to give an impression of antiquated erudition; at the beginning of the manuscript Hay's neatly written 'Table directing to the Principal Matters' (which lists every charter in the work and the pages on which they occur) is omitted by Maidment, so making the location of the contents much more problematic.[64]

Hay himself, however, had no time for false history. Even James Maidment grudgingly comments that 'he appears to have been no believer in the fables with which it was the fashion of those days to obscure Scottish History, and he gives a remarkable instance of this in his contraverting the then generally received romance of the descent of his own family from the imaginary hero of Luncarty'.[65]

THE GENEALOGY OF THE SAINTECLAIRES

The name 'Sainte Claire' or 'St Clair' is French but is clearly derived from that of the Italian nun St Clare (Santa Chiara) (1194–1253), the associate in religion of St Francis of Assisi. When we come to analyse the structure of Hay's manuscript, 'Genealogy of the Sainteclaires of Rosslyn', it is difficult to determine whether Hay's unquenchable enthusiasm for his adopted family's roots compromises his impartiality as a historian. The two are inextricably intertwined, partly because the St Clair dynasty held some of the most important offices in Scotland, excelled in service to their country in both peace and at war, and had diverse international interests; something of that breadth of vision seems to have been absorbed by the much-travelled and much-educated Fr Richard Augustine Hay. However, Hay did not invent his history – he consulted the most reliable historical documents available and extracted from them his own synthesis. Because of his trusted status as a priest and his erudition, Hay gained access to private archives and was able to compare primary source material with the secondary texts written by those who drew up the family trees or published historical works. He wrote disapprovingly that not everything that had been recorded by the genealogists matched the evidence, or the histories, registers and other private memoirs he had personally examined. This gives us an idea of how meticulously Hay researched and prepared his own conclusions.

Although he certainly did Hay and Scottish history a service by publishing Hay's work, James Maidment failed to edit Hay's text robustly enough. The *Genealogie of the*

Rosslyn Chapel from the north, drawn and engraved by J. & J. Johnstone, Edinburgh (1825). (From *Picture of Rosslyn Chapel* (Edinburgh: Oliver & Boyd, 1825))

Sainteclaires of Rosslyn is in places rambling and hard to follow because Maidment as editor has failed clearly to identify its constituent parts and arrange them in a coherent form. Hay's manuscript is in two sections. It begins with the story of the Sainteclaire family and its role in Scottish history taken from an unidentified (and presumably lost) manuscript dedicated to the Earl of Caithness. There then follows Hay's transcriptions of sixty-four documents (mainly charters, most in English, but some in Latin) taken from the archives at Rosslyn Castle and elsewhere, interspersed with Hay's commentaries. The relationship of the charters to the initial Sainteclaire history is not always entirely clear.

In his printed edition of Hay's elegantly transcribed manuscript, Maidment begins by telling us that the male line of the Rosslyn family ended with the death of the nineteenth baron, Sir William Saintclair on 4 January 1778. This final Rosslyn is understood to have sold the remaining family estates to General Saintclair, the second son of Henry, Lord Sinclair, heir of William Earl of Orkney by his first marriage. By 1835 the male representative of the Sinclair family was the Earl of Caithness. Sir Walter Scott – a proud member of the Six-Foot Club – knew him well and, using all the powers of description that his legal training had given him and his native gift for storytelling, wrote wistfully of the last male representative of the family:

The last Rosslyn (for so he was uniformly known by his patrimonial designation, and would probably have deemed it an insult in any who might have termed him Mr. Sinclair), was a man considerably above six feet, with dark grey locks, a form

Rosslyn Castle from the west, engraved by John Gellatly after Fr Richard Augustine Hay's manuscript 'Genealogy of the Sainteclaires of Rosslyn' published by James Maidment (1835).

upright, but gracefully so, thin-flanked and broad shouldered, built, it would seem, for the business of the war or chase, a noble eye of chastened pride and undoubted authority, and features handsome and striking in their general effect, though somewhat harsh and exaggerated when considered in detail. His complexion was dark and grizzled, and as we schoolboys, who crowded to see him perform feats of strength and skill in the old Scottish games of golf and archery, used to think and say among ourselves, the whole figure resembled the famous founder of the Douglas race, pointed out, it is pretended, to the Scottish monarch on a conquered field of battle, as the man whose arm had achieved the victory, by the expressive words, *Sholto Dhuglas*, – 'behold the dark grey man'. In all the manly sports which require strength and dexterity, Roslin was unrivalled; but his particular delight was archery.[66]

After Hay's book had been published by Maidment, the next publication on Rosslyn Chapel is a fifteen-page article in the *Edinburgh Magazine* (January 1761) written by Dr Robert Forbes, Bishop of Caithness, under the nom de plume Philo-Roskelynsis (lover of Rosslyn), headed with a dramatic sectional elevation of the choir of Rosslyn Chapel engraved by Andrew Bell. Subsequently, Forbes (again using his pseudonym) published *An Account of the Chapel of Roslin* (1774), this time illustrated with a south view of the chapel engraved by J. Johnston. This second work by Forbes formed the basis of a number of other descriptive studies of the chapel, a direct line of popular historical writing that culminated in the Revd John Thompson's authoritative *The Illustrated Guide to Rosslyn Chapel and Castle, Hawthornden, &c.*

(1892), a sound foundation on which, in turn, every good guidebook written about Rosslyn Chapel has been constructed.

THE SAINTECLAIRES AND SCOTLAND

In the introductory pages of his manuscript, Hay explains that the historical account of the family that follows has been taken from a manuscript dedicated by its (evidently anonymous) author to the Earl of Caithness and to his cousin, Sir William Sainteclaire. It is not clear whether Hay has summarised the details in his own words or quoted them verbatim. What we do not get is Fr Hay's opinion as to the accuracy of this account, only that it is authentic. We may infer from the tone and structure of this historical account that it is a summary that focuses almost exclusively on the heroic role of the Sainteclaires, that it is a laudatory piece of literature, intended to flatter and perhaps written to celebrate a particular event. In that Hay does not specifically dismiss this summarised and rather simplified account of Scottish history, it would appear that it is broadly accurate. However, he does not provide his readers with any critical apparatus in the form of footnotes or contrary opinions.

Hay begins by telling his readers that Roslin itself did not come into Sainteclaire hands until the reign of William the Lion (1143–1214). He then prefaces his own 'Genealogy' with a lengthy and detailed history of the Sainteclaire family from the coronation of Malcolm Canmore (1061) to the death of Sir William Sainteclaire's first wife in 1447. He records that, according to a manuscript entitled 'The History of Sutherland', the Sainteclaires originally came from Woldonius (Walderin) in France. Hay's approach matches his own statement – that he was given access to a number of charter chests, for he writes with all the excitement of a man who has just raided his grandfather's attic and discovered long-neglected treasures.

Essentially, his own overarching aim is to prove that the titles held by the Sainteclaires are legitimate and that their award by the monarch is in return for loyalty, courage and robust decision-taking in periods of crisis. His account is also intended to identify the dates when specific territories were assigned to the Sainteclaires and to show that their gift was a matter of public knowledge, as it generally took place in the context of a successful battle in which a number of other commanders were similarly rewarded. Lastly, Hay is at pains to trace the shifting patterns of the Sainteclaire family tree in order to demonstrate the unassailable legitimacy of the family's titles and their possession of land. His history, therefore, is essentially a summary of the contents of legal documents and the circumstances in which they came to be written. This leaves little room for entertaining asides or much in the way of character description in the style of Sir Walter Scott's pen picture of 'the Last Rosslyn'. What we glean from Hay's narrative of the fortunes of the kingdom of Scotland is tantalisingly brief and compressed (if not simplified in some cases), as the complexities of national

The seal of William Sinclair.

history are deliberately avoided unless they relate to his main purpose of identifying legal entitlements.

At this point it may be worth noting that, although the spelling of the family name has changed over the centuries – Sainteclaire, Saintclair, Sinclair, St Clair – the name denotes the same family.

In summary, Hay's story of the development of the family tree, taken from an anonymous manuscript, begins with a clear statement of the importance of legitimacy – with King Malcolm Canmore and his repossession of his kingdom to reinforce the stability of his kingship. Canmore's coronation is described as taking place on 5 April 1061 at Scone near Perth, and is then followed by a Parliament at Forfar, Angus, at which the King creates a number of earls, lords, barons and other titles as a reward for loyalty and service. Shortly after the Norman Conquest, Hay tells us, many gentlemen preferred to move to Scotland as they did not recognise William the Conqueror's right to the English throne.

Towards these gentlemen the monarchy behaved relatively cynically, playing with admirable realism on their greed and self-seeking with the tried and tested carrot-and-stick approach provided by the feudal system. Thus, the kings consciously made use of feudal obligations to ensure that their aristocracy were completely loyal in time of war and then gave them titles named for the territories they had been given, so tying title to land tenure and loyalty. One of those who came to Scotland in

Rosslyn Castle from the south, engraved by John Gellatly after Fr Richard Augustine Hay's manuscript 'Genealogy of the Sainteclaires of Rosslyn' published by James Maidment (1835).

Rosslyn Castle form the west, showing the garden with strawberry beds and the ancient yew tree. (From George Aikman, *The Mid-Lothian Esks and their Associations* (Edinburgh: David Douglas, 1895))

search of preferment was a Frenchman, Sir William Sainteclaire, who was made cupbearer to Queen Margaret. Some time later Sir William returned to his home in France and then came back again to Scotland, bringing gifts for King Malcolm III (*c.* 1031–93).

Such generosity pleased the King: Sir William was given the Earl of Marche's daughter in marriage and was duly made Baron of Roslin. His son Henry then received Roslin in free heritage and also the nearby barony of Pentland; he served the King well in battle, for which he was knighted. In turn, his son would later act as ambassador for King William I (1143–1214), being sent to King Henry of England to ask that Northumberland be handed over to Scotland. King David I (*c.* 1084–1153) later rewarded Sir Henry with the some of the territory of Carden in north-east Scotland, made him commander of 8,000 foot soldiers and knighted him.

Shortly after King Malcolm was killed by Henry Percy at the siege of Alnwick (1093), Sainteclaire married the daughter of the Earl of Strathearn. They had a son, Henry Sainteclaire, to whom his father resigned all his lands, asking the King to have fresh charters drawn up as the originals had been lost (a regular occurrence, it would appear).

King David then knighted Henry Saintclair and made him a privy counsellor, and the new Sir Henry took up residence at Roslin, a settlement said to have been founded by the Pict Asterius, whose daughter had married King Donald I. During the reign of King David, Hay informs us, Roslin was part of a great forest, along with the Pentland Hills and much of the countryside round about, and was filled with great numbers of deer and other wild animals.

NORSE WAR-GALLEY OF THE VIKING AGE.

A Viking long ship. (From Roland Williams Saint-Clair, *The Saint-Clairs of the Isles* (Auckland: H. Brett, 1898))

Then, because King David had refused to pay him homage for Northumberland, King Stephen of England (*c.* 1097–1154) sent the Duke of Gloucester to that part of the country to lay it waste with fire and sword. When he heard of this expedition, King David put Sir Henry Sainteclaire in command of 8,000 foot soldiers assembled from the northern parts of Scotland. At the battle of Allerton (1138) Sir Henry forced the English to retreat; many English were killed and many taken prisoner, among them the Duke himself. King David then returned home, where he rewarded his nobles generously, giving to Sir Henry all that part of Scotland known as Carden.

King David I died in 1153 and was succeeded by his 13-year-old grandson, Malcolm the Maiden (1141–65), so called because he never married. After a reign of twelve years, Malcolm died and was succeeded by his brother William the Lion, who sent Sir Henry Sainteclaire as ambassador to King Henry II of England, demanding the return of Northumberland. The English king appeared to agree, so Sir Henry returned to Scotland, dying some time later. He was in turn succeeded by his son Sir William, who was the 6th Baron of Roslin, Pentland, Baron of Cousland and held the offices of Sherriff of Lothian and Great Master Hunter of Scotland.

On King William's death, after a reign of twenty-nine years, his son became King Alexander II (1198–1249). The new king trusted Sir William Sainteclaire and bestowed on him gifts and titles. Some time later the people of England, in the person of the Commons, appealed to Alexander to help them end the tyranny of King John (1167–1216). King Alexander gathered a force of 30,000 fighting men and met Louis the Dauphin in London and then King Philip II in France to renew the long-standing relationship between Scotland and France known as the 'Auld Alliance'. While in France he left his army behind under the command of Sir Henry.

Not long after King John died, removing the main cause of the conflict, and Alexander was able to return to Scotland, where he rewarded his nobles, making the Barony of Cousland heritable by Sir Henry and his heirs and recording this act in a charter (which Hay notes as still extant in the seventeenth century). The King also had new charters drawn up showing that Sir Henry had legitimate title to his lands of Roslin, as his own charters had either been accidentally burnt or deliberately destroyed during the reign of William the Lion, one of the periods when Scotland was torn by conflict. The King later gave Sir William the Baxter lands of Innerleithen. In 1249, shortly after this business had been completed, the King died.

The new king, Alexander III (1241–86), soon faced a challenge to his authority and had to raise an army of 40,000 men to confront King Acho of Norway, who had invaded the Isles and taken control of them. Alexander divided his forces into three units, one of which, composed of men from the Merse (the eastern part of the Scottish Border, or March, between the Lammermoors and the Tweed), Teviotdale, Lothian, Berwick, Fife and Stirling, was under the command of the Earl of Marche and Sir William Sainteclaire of Roslin.

The Scottish king attacked Acho with his forces and defeated the Scandinavians, who lost 24,000 men. Acho was driven back and fled to Orkney, where he died. This day of victory was marked by the birth of a son to the King, also christened Alexander.

When some of the English nobility rebelled against King Henry III, they asked the Scots to assist them. John Comyn (d. 1306) and Sir Henry Sainteclaire were sent with an army of 5,000. They quickly brought a resolution to the dispute, and peace was restored.

Then a tragic accident robbed Scotland of its king. In 1286, Alexander, on horseback, returning from Edinburgh in the dark to visit his wife, Queen Yolande, at Dunfermline near Kinghorn, was thrown from a cliff into the sea and broke his neck.

The absence of a legitimate successor to Alexander (Queen Yolande was still pregnant with his child) meant that temporary guardians had to be appointed to govern Scotland. This led to a conflict between Robert Bruce, Earl of Carrick, and John Balliol (c. 1250–1313), Earl of Galloway, as to who should be king. It was decided that King Edward I of England should adjudicate in the dispute, and, although by right of descent Robert Bruce should have been chosen, Edward awarded the kingship to John Balliol, on condition that he acknowledge Edward's sovereignty over him – a condition that Balliol accepted.

However, when King Edward asked Balliol to support him against the French, Balliol did not do so. Edward responded by assembling a fleet, which he sent to attack the Scots at their stronghold of Berwick. The Scots managed to cripple eighteen English ships, whereupon Edward sent more vessels, but was still unable to take the town. He then turned to deceit, pretending to retreat and having flags made that were similar in appearance to those of the Scots. He then sent the English forces back to Berwick, where, as intended, they were mistaken for Scots, and so gained entry to the town. Their ruse successful, the English slaughtered the inhabitants, sparing neither men, women nor children, and capturing several knights (among them Sir William Sainteclaire), who were forced to yield themselves up as they had run out of supplies. John Balliol was also handed over to the English. He resigned his title as king and was then subjected to the cruelty of his captors.

That would have been the end of the Kingdom of Scotland but for an act of God that produced Sir William Wallace (c. 1270–1305), a young man, son of Sir Edward Wallace of Craigie, who, by his heroic and victorious action, released his country from oppression and as a reward was handed the guardianship of Scotland. However, not long afterwards the Scots turned against him and made John Comyn, Earl of Buchan, the guardian of Scotland. Along with Simon Fraser of Biggar and Sir William Sainteclaire of Roslin, Comyn had defeated a large English force at the battle of Roslin on 24 February 1303.

On that occasion, King Edward had sent 30,000 hand-picked men to Scotland and divided them into three equal but separate armies, ordering them to assemble at Roslin Moor and then march through the rest of Scotland, slaughtering and burning. Although the Scots had only 10,000 men under John Comyn, Simon Fraser and Sir William, they engaged the first English army at the Bilston Burn on Roslin Moor, where they defeated the English and killed their general. As the Scots, who were completely unaware of any impending danger, were collecting booty after the battle, they suddenly saw another army of 10,000 men coming towards them. They were

A stern and defiant Sir William Wallace (right), and King Robert I (Robert the Bruce) (left), either side of the entrance to the Scottish National Portrait Gallery, Edinburgh, by William Birnie Rhind (1895).

astonished and immediately killed all their prisoners so as not to be encumbered with them in the ensuing battle and to avoid them escaping to fight again against the Scots.

Sir William Sainteclaire, who knew the countryside intimately, showed the Scots where to cross the Draidon (Straiton) Burn, in an area where there was plenty of forest into which they could escape if they had to.

The English, looking to avenge the deaths of their comrades, engaged with the Scots but met the very same fate. This second victory was scarcely accomplished when the Scots saw yet another army of 10,000 men making ready to attack them. At first the Scots were dismayed, but through the exhortations of their leaders they regained their courage. The three Scots commanders again went through all the companies where the English wounded and dead were held and executed all those still living. They ordered the English weapons to be gathered together and handed to every Scottish soldier. Then the Scots were called to prayer, asking God to forgive them their sins and to take into account the justice of their cause.

The English, thinking that the Scots were surrendering because they had knelt down and uncovered their heads, unsuspectingly crossed the Straiton Burn; expecting to find allies, they found enemies instead. After a short, hard-fought engagement the English were put to flight.

When the battle was finally over, the three commanders met to discuss the spoils. To Sir William Sainteclaire, because his home was in that part of the country, was given the ground on which the battle had been fought – the ground at Bilston Burn near Straiton (known as Shin Bones, as bones and weapons were found there well into the seventeenth century) and the place called 'The Graves' between Straiton and Hawthornden.

Sir William returned home with a single English prisoner, a man of some importance, whom he entertained so well that the Englishman often offered Sir William the benefit of his informed military advice. The most important observation he made was that he could see that Rosslyn Castle (where it stood on what is today College Hill and the present site of Rosslyn Chapel) was not strongly enough defended. He urged Sir William to rebuild it on the high and craggy rock on which it now stands. Sir William took his advice, although his ancestors were already buried on top of the hill under his first castle. Then he constructed the Wall Tower and the other buildings and moved his residence down from College Hill to the more inaccessible new fortification high above the North Esk River.

In the years that followed Scotland was continually harassed by King Edward Longshanks until Robert the Bruce came to the throne (1306). After much striving to be free of English domination, Bruce established his own government in Scotland and rewarded those who had struggled so hard with him against the English. Sir James Douglas and Sir William Sainteclaire were respected above all others because of their faithfulness, which they demonstrated at the Battle of Bannockburn (1314). Sir William's two sons, Henry and William, were promoted, the first into the king's service and the second chosen to be Bishop of Dunkeld.

The Saintclairs again helped King Robert I when he crossed over to Ireland to assist his brother, leaving the Scottish borders relatively unguarded. Hearing that the king was abroad, the English gathered a fleet of ships and sailed up the Firth of Forth, devastating each place where they landed with fire and the sword. The Earl of Fife learnt of this and with some 500 men came to confront the English forces, but, seeing their large number, he hesitated. However, William Sainteclaire, the second son of Sir William and Bishop of Dunkeld, came to his aid with sixty well-armed knights. He saw that, although much greater in numbers, the English were poorly organised and ill-disciplined, so he attacked them, killing some 500 of his enemies. Those who remained retreated to their ships, but, unable to contain the large numbers on board, one of the vessels sank with the loss of all lives.

In gratitude, King Robert named William 'his Bishop'. When he had returned to Scotland, the King arranged for a great celebratory hunt on the Pentland Hills (then known as the King's Forest). Having assembled his nobles and enjoyed three days of entertainment, King Robert announced that he had often hunted a distinctive white deer, but none of his hounds could catch up with it. He asked the nobles if any of them had hounds capable of matching the deer for speed, but the nobles replied that none of them had any hound capable of catching and killing the white deer.

Sir William Sainteclaire, however, had two dogs from the same litter named Help and Hold. Without thinking, he said that he wagered his head that his two hounds could kill the deer before they reached the March Burn. Word of this boast was brought to the King, who grew angry and wagered all the Pentland Hills and the whole of Pentland Moor with the forest against Sir William's head.

The King immediately issued a proclamation ordering everyone to tie up their dogs and then keep quiet to avoid frightening the deer, except for a few horsemen with ratches (slow hounds), who would try to flush out the animal.

The Rosslyn Hunt: Help and Hold. (From George Aikman, *The Mid-Lothian Esks and their Associations* (Edinburgh: David Douglas, 1895))

Sir William was very ashamed of his reckless boast, but nevertheless went with his hounds to the best hunting ground he could find and, according to the custom of the time, prayed to Christ, the Blessed Virgin Mary and St Catherine to save him from death. No sooner had he finished his prayers than the white deer, hearing the loud noises and sudden shouts of the onlookers, came off the back hills to where Sir William was galloping after his two hounds, having called first for Hold and then Help. Seeing the hind go past into the middle of a stream, Sir William dismounted and prostrated himself on the ground, pleading with Christ to have mercy on him. His hound Hold quickly reached the deer and held her at bay in the water, and then Help arrived and forced her onto the bank where Sir William waited. There the hounds killed the deer.

When the King saw this, he came and embraced Sir William and gave him the lands he had promised 'in free forestry'. Some time later, in remembrance of the place where he had prayed to God and the saints, Sir William built the church of St Catherine in the Hopes (today submerged under Glencorse Reservoir). This was named after St Catherine of Egypt, whose holy 'oily' well was not far off at Mortonhall. The hill where the King watched the deer being chased and killed was ever afterwards called the King's Hill and the open ground where Sir William hunted The Knight's Field.

This episode has parallels with the foundation legend of the Abbey of Holyrood, in which King David I, a keen hunter, rejects the advice of his confessor not to hunt on a holy day and is attacked by a stag, between whose antlers he sees a cross. From that event derives the heraldic symbol of the Canongate (a cross set between a stag's antlers) and the former crest of Edinburgh, which originally featured St Giles standing beside a deer. Hunting was a life or death activity for both man and beast and provided fertile soil for the medieval preacher to highlight the role of religion in everyday life.

To the east, the King's Hill is still indicated on the 1913 Ordnance Survey map of Edinburghshire (from a survey of 1892), as is the Knightfield Rig (to the west), while the site of St Catherine's Chapel is marked in the middle of the Edinburgh and District Water Trust's Glencorse Reservoir.

The piety of Sir William Sainteclaire is further illustrated by Fr Hay in the story of St Catherine's Balm Well at Howdenhall near Liberton. It tells how Sir William sends a priest to the Holy Land to the grave of St Catherine, where her bones were said to produce a restorative holy oil. The priest duly returned with the oil and was in the process of carrying it to the newly constructed chapel of St Catherine in the Hopes. However, out of exhaustion, the priest was forced to stop and rest a mile south of Liberton Church (today part of Edinburgh). The priest fell asleep in a thicket of rushes and the precious oil spilt onto the ground. When Sir William heard of this, he ordered his workmen to dig at the spot. Soon a fountain of water gushed out, with a black oily substance floating on the surface that cured diseases of the skin. Today, it is known that the well and the

The tomb of Sir James Douglas, St Bride's Church, Douglas, South Lanarkshire. (From Herbert Maxwell, *A History of the House of Douglas*, vol. 2 (London: Freemantle & Co., 1902))

oil came from seams of coal deep in the earth and that they did indeed have therapeutic value.

The St Clair story then continues and we see Sir William once more serving his king, this time after the death of King Robert the Bruce. To grant the King's long-held wish, together with the Earl of Douglas and Sir Robert Logan, he sets out to carry the King's heart, enclosed in a small casket of gold and kept sweet-smelling with spices, to Jerusalem, where they intended to bury it with full royal honours at the tomb of Jesus and then join other Christians fighting to free the holy places from Saracen control. On the voyage out their ship was blown off course onto the coast of Spain, where they joined the King of Aragon's war against the Saracens. However, they grew overconfident of their martial skill, and on 25 August 1330 were killed in battle at Teba, in the Malaga province of Andalucia, but not before the King's heart had been hurled into the fray. Although Sir James Douglas was killed, so impressed were the Saracens by the Scots' bravery that they returned the heart in its casket to Sir William Keith and allowed him to bring it back to Scotland, where it was buried at Melrose Abbey.

Sir William Saintclaire's eldest son, Henry Prince of Orkney (a title he had gained by marriage to the daughter of Malesius Spar), was more powerful than any of his ancestors, as he had power to issue his own coinage, make laws and forgive crimes during the reigns of David II and Robert II. Wherever he went, he had his sword carried before him; he sported a crown in his heraldic crest, wore a crown on his head when making laws and was answerable to no one but the King of Denmark, Sweden and Norway. He built the castle of Kirkwall in Orkney and for his courage and fidelity in time of war was made Lord Sainteclaire, Lord Chief Justice of Scotland.

After his death in 1400 he was succeeded by his eldest son, Henry, also Prince of Orkney and Admiral of the Seas, as well as Lord Chief Justice of Scotland. 'He was a valiant Prince,' comments Hay, 'well proportioned, of middle stature, broad bodied, fair in face, yellow haired, hasty and stern.' He adds that in his household Sir Henry always had 300 gentlemen able to ride a horse, fifty-five gentlewomen, thirty-five of whom were ladies. He had his food tasted before he ate it, and, when he travelled to Orkney, he would be met by 300 men dressed in scarlet gowns with coats of black velvet.

It was he who built the great dungeon at Rosslyn and other walled defences, as well as preparing enclosed parks for fallow and red deer. King Robert III (1337–1406) trusted him completely and made him the guardian of his son, Prince James. Prince Henry, meanwhile, was told by the king to take his son by sea to England to escape any possible treachery by his nobles. After sailing for some time the young Prince grew afraid of the waves and asked to be taken back to the shore. So they landed in England, where both were immediately taken prisoner.

Hearing of their capture, the King of Scotland sent one of Prince Henry's tenants to the rescue, a man from Pentland, who pretended to be a half-wit and so was not prevented from getting close to the Prince's prison cell. Afterwards, when it was dark, he helped them to escape dressed as poor working men and then to find horses. They managed to reach a forest where they stayed till night fell again, when they travelled north, finally reaching the Scottish border.

Map of Orkney. (From Roland Williams Saint-Clair, *The Saint-Clairs of the Isles*
(Auckland: H. Brett, 1898))

There two Englishmen attempted to detain them, but Prince Henry killed them
both. When at last they reached Rosslyn, they were welcomed by two great nobles,
Archibald Douglas and George Dunbar. However, when he learned of Prince Henry's
escape, Robert Duke of Albany (1339–1420), Governor of Scotland and a malicious
tyrant, was consumed with anger and nursed hatred deep in his heart because his
protection of James, the Prince of Scotland, had been circumvented. Therefore he
issued a summons for the forfeiture of Prince Henry's lands, titles and possessions for

treasonably allowing Prince James to fall into the hands of the English, and called Prince Henry to Edinburgh to answer the charges immediately.

Burning at the injustice of this false charge, Prince Henry called upon his friends to assist him and sent for a large force of men from Shetland and the Orkneys. To the Governor he replied that Edinburgh was not big enough or well furnished enough to accommodate him and his followers and demanded that the Governor provide him with suitable lodgings and stables for his horses.

This antagonised the Duke, who arrived in Edinburgh on the day of the trial accompanied by 10,000 men. Receiving word of this, Prince Henry prepared to enter Edinburgh with 40,000 men, but the Duke, now intimidated, fled to Falkland. Then Prince Henry and the other two great princes of Scotland, Douglas and Dunbar, called a Parliament in which they arranged for the Duke of Albany to be stripped of his rank and possessions because of his treason and the tyranny he had exercised in his treatment of David, eldest son of King Robert, whom Albany had imprisoned and starved (ostensibly because of his wild lifestyle). At this the Duke became fearful and repented his actions, promising to change his life in the future and asking to be forgiven for his harshness, which, he said, was due to bad advice. His explanation was accepted by the three nobles, and the Duke was restored to office.

Not long afterwards a dispute arose between Prince Henry and Archibald, 3rd Earl of Douglas, over the post of Sheriff of Nithsdale, the Barony of Roxburgh and Cavers and the wardenry of the three Marches between Whithorn and Berwick. So acrimonious were their relations that the Prince would not allow the Earl to travel to Edinburgh through his land. Yet, for all the animosity, there was no bloodshed.

In those days Prince Henry had all his provisions brought in by sea from the north in great quantities. He kept open house, so that none of his friends wanted for anything in the way of food or clothing; none of his tenants was harshly treated, but all had enough for their maintenance – in the eyes of posterity the Prince was a model of piety. So great was his zeal that before all things he preferred the service of God, richly endowing the Abbey of Holyrood with land and the church of St Catherine in the Hopes, territory that was estimated to be able to sustain 7,000 sheep. He also bestowed upon the Abbey of Holyrood rich vestments for the celebration of the liturgy, made of gold and silver threads and silk.

At this point, Hay breaks into his historical narrative, switching to his role of Roman Catholic priest. He cautions his readers: 'Here you are to be warned, that the affectionate zeal and love for God's glory and service (which was tenderly cherished in the hearts of these our worthy ancestors), should be a spur to encourage us in devotion and virtue to imitate their pious example – otherwise God will make their zeal grounds for accusation at the Last Day.' He then tells us that not long afterwards Prince Henry died, leaving behind his son William and a daughter married to the Earl of Marche.

Aside from his many other titles, William Sainteclaire was Prince of Orkney, a knight of the French Order of the Cockle, the English Order of the Garter, Great Chancellor, Chamberlain and Lieutenant of Scotland. He lived during the reign of the Stewart king James I of Scotland (1394–1437). The Prince was very good looking,

The remaining buttresses of the old St Matthew's church in what is now Roslin Cemetery.

fair haired, very tall, broad-bodied, straight, well proportioned but also a humble, courteous and practical man, interested in land management, including the construction of castles, palaces and churches, the fencing of forests, the laying-out of enclosed parks and the protection of trees by hedging, as the results of his endeavours still testified even in the seventeenth century.

The King thought highly of him, assigning him to protect his sister Lady Margaret (1425–45) when she travelled to France at the request of the Dauphin (later Louis XI), who wished to marry her. Prince William executed this assignment with great success, accompanied by one hundred fine gentlemen: twenty were dressed in cloth of gold and wore golden chains and black velvet foot-mantles; twenty wore red velvet, again with golden chains and black velvet; twenty were attired in white and black velvet in imitation of the Prince's heraldic crest (a ragged engrailed cross on a silver ground); a further twenty were clad in gold and blue velvet (showing the heraldic crest of Orkney – a golden ship with a double tressure decorated with fleurs-de-lis on a blue ground; and twenty more were dressed in different and contrasting colours, displaying the crests of the many different titles held by the Prince.

When they arrived in France, the Prince was honoured by all. The King of France made him a Knight of the French Order of the Cockle. Once the wedding celebrations were over the Prince returned to Scotland, but his departure saddened the French King and nobility. On his arrival in Scotland, Prince William was welcomed by the King and his friends, to all of whom he showed his great happiness at being home again.

Shortly afterwards, in the old St Matthew's Church (close to St Matthew's Well, which supplied the people of Roslin with pure water), he married Elizabeth Douglas, Countess of Buchan, widow of John Stewart, the Earl of Buchan who had been killed at the battle of Verneuil (1424), a conflict fought by the French and Scots against the English. But the marriage did not last long, as, under the canon law of the Roman Catholic Church and, indeed, according to both Jewish and Roman law, it was considered invalid, because of their blood relationship in the direct line (consanguinity) and their relationship through marriage (affinity), as the mother of Prince William was godmother to Elizabeth.

Coincidentally, Aegidia (widow of Sir Henry Sinclair) had also received a dispensation to marry Alexander Stewart, even though they were related within the second and third degrees of affinity. They had petitioned the Pope to allow their union, as only marriage, they said, would bring peace between their relatives and friends. On 29 April 1422, Pope Martin V granted the dispensation.[67]

In 1432 Prince William, unhappy at his enforced separation from Elizabeth, wrote to Pope Eugenius IV, asking him to grant a dispensation.[68] This the Pope did, taking into account the two petitioners' desire to have their offspring declared legitimate. So Prince William married Dame Elizabeth for a second time, again in the old St Matthew's Church, where they had been forcibly separated and their marriage declared invalid.[69] The ruined west buttresses of the old church can still be seen today, standing stubbornly in Roslin's historic parish cemetery, 200 yards below Rosslyn Chapel.

Once again, Dame Elizabeth was shown great respect by all, both for her own high birth and for the position she held through marriage. She had a retinue of seventy-five gentlewomen to serve her (of whom fifty-three were the daughters of noblemen), all of them dressed in silk and velvet, wearing golden chains and other ornaments and 200 gentlemen on horseback who accompanied her throughout her journey. If it was dark when she was going to Edinburgh, she had eighty lighted torches carried before her to her lodgings at the foot of Blackfriars Wynd. No one matched her for magnificence in the whole of Scotland except the Queen.

Her husband, Sir William, the eleventh baron, had his halls and chambers richly decorated with embroidered hangings; he fitted his domestic chapel to the north with high external wedge-shaped defences to protect it and his other fine rooms and galleries. He also put in place the forward battlements, which faced north-east, the bridge under the castle and various administrative quarters. On the south-east side, opposite the wall of his chapel, he exposed the bedrock so as to strengthen the castle, and then planted a fine fruit orchard. To the west of the castle was an ancient yew tree and enough ground to grow root vegetables and herbs.

Such were the happy personal circumstances of Sir William. He had the horn of plenty within his grasp, but something still eluded him, and the elegant solution he chose forms the subject of our next chapter.

CHAPTER 2

The History of Rosslyn Chapel

BUILDING THE CHAPEL

Now that we have examined both the physical and the political landscape of Roslin and the family tree of its earls – encompassing geology, geography, flora and fauna, industrial topography, the growth of the St Clair family and the development of their lands and properties – it is time to turn our attention to the construction of the tantalisingly magnificent Rosslyn Chapel.[1]

We are told by Fr Hay that, as old age was creeping up on him, Sir William began to reflect upon his earlier life and to ponder how he should live out the rest of his days. Since he did not want to seem ungrateful to his creator for the many benefits he had given him, he devised a plan to show his deep and unequivocal devotion to God.

Looking back at his ancestors and then facing forwards towards his descendants, Sir William fixed upon an elegant solution: he would commission a church that would be highly distinctive in design and decorative style. As he wanted his project to be magnificent and overwhelmingly impressive – and therefore attract people to worship there – he arranged for artisans to be hired both from Scotland and from south of the Border.

As was the practice when dealing with the powerful stonemason guilds, Sir William commissioned a principal mason-architect and, with his advice, indicated his preferences in the overall plan and some of the more detailed features. After the mason-architect had submitted his proposals on paper based on his discussions with Sir William and the drawings had been approved, the patterns for each section of the stonework (handed down in the craft and often the property of each masons' lodge) were measured from existing master patterns and then cut from the flat and close-grained spruce boarding Sir William had had shipped over from Norway.

Next the wooden patterns for each individual block of stone were given to the stonemasons to guide them in their cutting and carving. These boards would consist not only of exact sectional templates but also of negative 'moulds' against which the accuracy of each carved stone component could be precisely checked.

Architectural drawings on boards of this kind were found in the early part of the twentieth century during repairs at Glasgow Cathedral: there, one board carried a 'draught' to guide the stonemason in the carving of one of the bosses in Archbishop Blackadder's Crypt (the board in question was, in 1915, part of the collection of the Art Gallery, Glasgow).[2] Such numbered templates for accurately and consistently

Apprentice stonemason working the stone with tools similar to those used by his medieval predecessors. (By permission of St Mary's Episcopal Cathedral, Edinburgh)

cutting the profiles of pillars and other architectural forms were jealously guarded by the master masons.[3]

The sketchbooks of the French mason-architect, Villard de Honnecourt (*c.* 1175–1240), show wooden templates for profiled boards, with masons' marks being drawn on the different profiles on the basis of their experience and their ability to carry out each specific type of carving.[4] De Honnecourt, typically well educated and well travelled and an outstanding principal architect-mason, shows by his drawings and notes in copious sketchbooks how well he had absorbed the instruction he had received at school in arithmetic, geometry, grammar, rhetoric and dialectic. It is certain, therefore, that the more experienced senior architect-masons working on the design and construction of Rosslyn Chapel would have been educated to what we today understand as university standard and that, on the other hand, the use of the cryptic 'masons' marks' were not necessarily an indication of illiteracy but rather a record of the ownership of the work put into each specific stone section in a building.

Nor is the use of templates for carving the stone merely a medieval tool. Today, stonemasons permanently engaged in the running repair and restoration of churches, such as the workshop of St Mary's Episcopal Cathedral in Edinburgh, still use

Incised stonemason's identification mark at the south door. (By permission of Rosslyn Chapel Trust)

Stonemasons' marks on the Prince's Pillar. (By permission of Rosslyn Chapel Trust)

patterns and reverse templates to check that the proportions of each carved section of stone are correct – just as their medieval counterparts did; but in 2007, instead of wood, the patterns are made of light and flexible plastic!

Norwegian wood was used at Rosslyn Chapel because Scotland could not supply wood of the required consistency, having lost its native spruce during the last Ice Age, with only oak and Scots pine available locally. Because of the exposure of the trees to Scotland's strong winds and cold weather, the trees did not grow upright, but curved and twisted, full of knots. Norway, on the other hand, grew natural stands of spruce, a very straight and uniform wood. Spruce is also soft, and so would be ideal both for marking out architectural plans and for cutting the templates to guide the stonemasons; it was, moreover, a material that could be relied upon not to twist or buckle when used as scaffolding.

There is no doubt that, while Sir William Sainteclaire may have indicated in a general way the style of church he wanted, the detailed design was carried out by highly trained master masons who functioned as principal designers and subsequently monitored the work in progress in much the same way as modern architects do today. By 1350 every member of a craft guild had completed a basic apprenticeship of at least seven years' duration; normally begun at the age of 13 or 14, it was a very thorough process of practical and business training.[5]

The preparations for this prestigious project started with the laying of the foundations in 1446. Every day there would have been large numbers of workmen busy on the site – stonemasons, carpenters, blacksmiths, barrowmen and quarrymen. This was a relatively simple matter for Sir William to organise, as over the previous thirty-four years he had already given employment to many such skilled craftsmen for the repair and construction of parts of his castle and other properties and therefore had a good knowledge of how contractors worked and how to find them and deal with them.

Sir William not only made sure he procured the best-quality materials but took care to treat his workmen correctly – although the strength of the medieval guild structure would have ensured that he would find it hard to employ them on adverse terms and conditions. According to Fr Hay, who not only used documentary evidence but also drew on Sainteclaire oral tradition, as the nearest existing town was a mile or so away at Bilston Burn, Sir William established what would later become the town of Roslin by giving each of his craftsmen a piece of land on which to build a house – an early example of enlightened self-interest. He paid them fair wages graduated according to the work they did and their level of responsibility: an annual sum of £10 to the ordinary stonemasons, £40 to the master stonemason, with similarly differentiated sums to the blacksmiths and carpenters. Here, however, we may suspect that Hay may have somewhat exaggerated Sir William's generosity and benevolence.

Sir William had deep personal motives for wanting to create a magnificent religious centre on his doorstep to replace the small, cramped one inside Rosslyn Castle and the later but increasingly dilapidated Church of St Matthew halfway down the neighbouring slope. He must have had mixed memories of the latter (having married his wife, been cruelly separated from her and then remarried her, all in the very same building). He also badly wanted to establish a local church that would, by the efficacy of its prayer life, turn the wrath of the Almighty away from him and his family, his ancestors and his descendants, as well as from the Christian community at large.

Innocently enough, Sir William longed to see a church set upon a hill high above him, a beacon to all men, a status symbol but also a powerhouse of prayer, satisfying the Christian Gospel's call for every believer to proclaim the Good News and not hide the light of the Gospel. Sir William wanted a Burning Bush set on his hill, and the structure that gradually rose before his eyes would satisfy that longing in every way. Carved out of the local stone from Roslin Glen, its surface would, if the atmospheric conditions were right, seem to catch fire in the rays of the setting sun!

Of course, the irony is that even in the fifteenth century a Christian needed to take responsibility for his actions and serve out his own punishment. Forgiveness could not be earned by others; it required true repentance on the part of the sinner. Hiring others to pray for the repose of one's soul would not satisfy a God who could see into men's hearts, and masses said on behalf of a wealthy founder (whether alive or dead) could not be limited in their spiritual benefits to exclude other Christians in what was traditionally understood as an interconnected community of believers – the Body of Christ. Hence, every mass that was celebrated played its part in the saving self-sacrifice of Christ, offered for the whole human race. A mass was understood to be the supreme form of prayer for the whole Christian community, and could never be offered exclusively for the benefit of a single named person.

Fr Hay paints a picture of Sir William as a generous and fair-minded employer and landowner. As a successful former soldier and statesman, he would also have known how to motivate those under him. Not only did he look after his craftsmen and labourers, but, because so many people came to him for help and advice, what at first would have been a little shantytown of workers at Roslin grew bigger and better, stocked with food and supplies, so that in time it became an important centre in the Lothians. Moreover, in his piety Sir William also supported any of his tenants who became impoverished and set aside victuals for any poor person who came to beg at his gates.

The type of church through which Sir William chose to show his devotion was one that was becoming increasingly fashionable in Scotland and England at that time. Fifteen collegiate churches were to be erected in Edinburgh and the Lothians between 1342 and 1540, including Dirleton (1444), Crichton (1446), Dunglass (1448), Markle (1450), Restalrig (1487), Corstorphine (c. 1429) and Seton (1488); St Giles, the parish church of Edinburgh (which dated from the twelfth century), became a collegiate church in 1466.

With some notable exceptions, most collegiate churches were founded by wealthy noblemen, one of the advantages to the founder being that a collegiate church was built on his own land, often right beside his home and often considerably closer than the existing parish church. Collegiate churches were also cheaper to endow than monasteries, as they usually supported less than ten clergy and other staff, while the

St Giles High Kirk, Edinburgh, a former collegiate church.

The crypt, Newbattle Abbey. (From Cecil Kerr, *Cecil, Marchioness of Lothian* (London: Sands and Company, 1922))

larger monastic foundations might have between fifteen and thirty mouths to feed.[6] In the case of Newbattle Abbey, a few miles from Rosslyn Chapel, the monastic community at one time numbered well over 100. Newbattle was patronised by the Sainteclaires, one of whom (Sir Henry) had endowed it with flocks of sheep, a fine silver cross and a number of books, in return for which the monks prayed annually for the repose of his soul and marked the date of his death with an allocation of funds to be used for celebratory food and drink.

By the fifteenth century, however, there was growing economic pressure on the monasteries, mainly through the decline of the formerly lucrative wool trade; in the sixteenth century this would lead to the 'feuing' of monastic lands and the deliberate secularistion of monastic property, contrived by the monasteries themselves as a way of continuing to keep their heads above water.[7] (*Feuing* is the feudal tenure of land, its rental paid in money or grain rather than military service.) At the same time, new styles of piety, such as the institution of votive masses said in perpetuity (a devotional vehicle that could be seen as mechanising religion to the extent of becoming a serious misunderstanding of grace, salvation and the nature of forgiveness), encouraged especially those living in towns to invest large sums in drawing up legal contracts (charters) for burgh collegiate churches.

Founding a collegiate church was something of a private–public partnership initiative between the founder and the Church in an age that found it increasingly difficult to support what were in effect multinational corporations – such as the twelfth-century monastic houses that had been at the forefront of David I's plan to revitalise his kingdom. Although the less expensive collegiate option had the danger that it might also cheapen religion, it could be seen by some as a revolution in piety where holiness might perhaps be achieved vicariously and sanctity acquired in return for financial investment.

The lantern and tower of St Giles, Edinburgh. (From James Grant, *Edinburgh Old and New* (London: Cassell, Petter, Galpin, 1880?–1883?))

One of the larger burgh collegiate foundations was at St Giles in Edinburgh. On the ridge of the High Street, St Giles (named after the patron of huntsmen, but also a symbol of compassion for animals and nature conservancy) eventually had more than forty altars, while Trinity College (endowed nearby by Queen Mary of Gueldres) had more than thirty. Many of the altars in the former were founded by local trade guilds as a form of spiritual insurance, while the latter was also connected with the hospital at Soutra.

There were also churches founded by trade guilds for the almost exclusive use of their brethren and these can be seen as an even more cost-efficient version of the collegiate church, since they combined social action with prayer – the indigent were housed and fed but also obligated to pray. The Magdalen Chapel in the Cowgate, close to the east end of the Grassmarket, was founded by Michael Macqueen, a local burgess, in the early years of the sixteenth century. The chapel supported a chaplain and seven poor men (living in an attached hospital), who in return bound themselves to pray for the repose of the soul of Mary Queen of Scots, for the founder and his wife Janet and their descendants, and for the patrons of the chapel (the Deacon and Masters of the craft of the Hammermen of the City of Edinburgh, whose responsibility the endowment was to be in future years).

Trinity Collegiate Church, Edinburgh, on the site of the present Waverley station. (From James Grant, *Edinburgh Old and New* (London: Cassell, Petter, Galpin, 1880?–1883?))

The Magdalen Chapel, Edinburgh, in the Cowgate. (From James Grant, *Edinburgh Old and New* (London: Cassell, Petter, Galpin, 1880?–1883?))

Collegiate churches were so called because they were endowed as a 'college', a community of religious men who were bound together by vows of poverty, chastity and obedience and who followed a rule, a set of regulations that laid down the aims of the college and its way of life, its discipline and other matters such as the resolution of conflicts. It would, however, be a caricature to describe a collegiate church as a mere prayer factory, as the way of life to which its members dedicated themselves was to be open to God, so allowing the clergy (known as canons) to pray for the salvation of all humanity, both living and dead; in any case, a single prayer uttered in devotion and sincerity could be just as effective as a multiplicity mouthed or mumbled in rapid succession.

Sir William's endowment at his new Collegiate Chapel of St Matthew evidently provided for a provost, six prebendaries (priests who lived on a share of the chapel's financial endowment) and two young boy choristers (who would probably also have received an education in what was known as a 'sang scule'). It is not clear when St Matthew's College was first established as a community, but it is possible that the canons may initially have been provided with accommodation at Rosslyn Castle and then, perhaps, in a row of small adjacent houses on the road between the chapel and the castle, known in the nineteenth century as the Midway Cottages. No record of

The south door of the chapel, presumably intended to complement the north (bachelors') door, and therefore at one time where the women of the congregation made their entrance. The south door is continually bathed in sunshine, while the north door struggles to find the light! (By permission of Rosslyn Chapel Trust)

any agreement between the Earl and the canons has survived before 1523, when Sir William Sainteclaire drew up a charter for this purpose, making land available for the canons' houses and gardens.

Hay makes two references to the testament (will) of Alexander Southerland, father of Sir William's second wife, Marjory, signed at Roslin on 15 November 1456 by which he left the church at Rosslyn (where he had chosen to be buried) the sum of £10 a year rent to pay a priest to sing masses for his soul in the collegiate church in perpetuity. He also left £100 for the building and repair of the church and for the purchase of a stone slab to lay on his grave.[8] In another volume Hay gives the full text of the testament in which Southerland reveals that he is 'syke in body but hayle in mind'.[9] These documents show that Rosslyn Chapel was known as a collegiate church by 1456. The official 'erection' of the foundation under a presiding prebendary dates from 12 February 1477, while the provostry itself dates from the early 1520s.[10] Over the succeeding years the provosts included John Dickson (1524), David Hutchesoun (1540), John Sinclair (1542–c. 1556), John Robeson (1563–83) and Henry Sinclair (1601–6).

However, it is possible that there never was a charter of foundation before 1523. In East Lothian, in what had been a parish church since 1242, George Lord Seton founded a college of priests to offer prayers in perpetuity for himself and his family. With a tall and stately choir he began upgrading the original structure in 1470, when Pope Paul II granted permission for a college. Yet the rector (the spiritual and managerial head of a diocesan church) was still being described as such – and not as provost, the superior of a regular church – in 1482, four years after Lord Seton's death. It was not until 1492 that the bull of foundation was granted by Pope Alexander VI to his successor, the 3rd Lord Seton.[11] Perhaps something similar happened at Rosslyn, since Hay would surely have mentioned any such document drawn up before 1523, had it existed. However, no papal foundation bull for Rosslyn Chapel has survived.

In the case of St Giles in Edinburgh, the provost, bailies, councillors and the community of Edinburgh had first ratified the details of their proposed Collegiate

The Seal of Holyrood Abbey. (From James Grant, *Edinburgh Old and New* (London: Cassell, Petter, Galpin, 1880?–1883?))

Church of St Giles and its financial support (in the form of annual rents to be given to the provost and his chapter) with the Bishop of St Andrews, but were also prudent enough doubly to safeguard the legal status of the college by asking the Pope to ratify the institution so that its status under canon law would have greater force.[12]

We may assume that the cutting of the first turf and the laying of the foundation stone at Rosslyn was carried out as part of an elaborate religious ceremony at which Sir William and his family would have been present, as well as representatives of the Bishop of St Andrews and senior clergy from Edinburgh (probably from St Giles), and other members of the royal administration of Scotland.

The progress of the chapel's construction was at the mercy not only of the weather and economic conditions (and, perhaps, illness), but also of accidents not directly connected with the building work. Not long after the start of construction (begun, as the tradition of the stonemasons dictated, at the east end), a great calamity was narrowly avoided. Down below in Rosslyn Castle, Sir William's wife, who loved small dogs, asked one of her ladies-in-waiting to take a lighted candle and look under a bed to bring out one of her dogs, as it had just produced some puppies. In the process of doing so, the lady-in-waiting accidentally set fire to the bed. The flames leapt up, burnt through the bed and then reached up to the ceiling of the great dungeon chamber where Sir William's wife was. She and everyone in the room had to run in fear of their lives.

Fortunately, Sir William's chaplain saw what was happening and, remembering that all his master's private papers were in that chamber, moved quickly to the top end of the room and immediately threw out of a window four large archive trunks stored there. Sir William heard the pitiful screams of his wife and her ladies and was informed of what had happened; he saw the confusion for himself from where he was standing on the College Hill, but he feared for nothing except the loss of his family charters and other writings.

The chaplain (who had saved himself with some very unclerical panache by sliding down the bell-rope that he had managed to tie onto a wooden beam) told Sir William that his precious charters and other important papers were safe. Sir William became cheerful again and went down to his wife and her ladies to comfort them, telling them to forget their sorrows and asking them to go swiftly to reward the chaplain handsomely for his quick thinking and bravery.

This near disaster did not divert Sir William from overseeing the construction of the Chapel, nor prevent his continued and signal generosity to the poor – indeed, he appears to have grown even more generous. But he no longer worried about the survival of his charters, consigning their care to God's providence. His wife, Lady Margaret Douglas, unhappily died not long after. Following her death, Sir William married Lady Marjory Southerland, a direct descendant of Robert the Bruce, in old St Matthew's Church, just down the hill from the new chapel.

Hay records that Sir William laid the foundation stone of the chapel on St Matthew's Day, 21 September 1446. The work of laying the foundations was very extensive and seems to have taken around four years to complete, judging by the date (1450) on the carvings in the outside corbels on top of the north clerestory

The slopes below Rosslyn Castle, drawn by W. Westall ARA.

windows.[13] In 1880, the architect Andrew Kerr exposed the foundations of the chapel beyond the existing west transept. Digging with a 5-foot crowbar to a depth of 2 feet, Kerr discovered four parallel aisles.[14] He traced them as far as the western boundary wall, which surrounded the garden of Collegehill House, but did not disturb the turf of the garden beyond; later investigators have found them to extend for a total distance of 91 feet from the west transept.

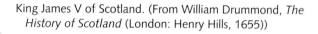

King James V of Scotland. (From William Drummond, *The History of Scotland* (London: Henry Hills, 1655))

Although the original foundation charter has not survived, it was confirmed retro-spectively by King James V in 1523.[15] Since no original charter to that effect survives, it is not entirely clear that Sir William's intention was immediately to set up a collegiate church: perhaps he intended to establish it first with a small nucleus of one or two priests and then gradually expand their number. However, he undoubtedly did endow the canons with property that would bring in an annual revenue – the church lands of Pentland, 4 acres of meadow near Roslin and other grasslands (also at Pentland). What is also undis-putable is that at least since the mid-fifteenth century Rosslyn Chapel was publicly assumed to be a collegiate establishment – certainly, the will of Alexander Southerland of Dunbeath, dated 15 November 1456, describes it as such.[16]

For the forty years during which the chapel was under construction, worshippers would still have used the old St Matthew's Church, situated in what is today the village cemetery, beside St Matthew's Well.

Upon what became known as College Hill stonemasons were encamped in their wooden lodges, carving the separate and highly intricate pieces for the roof of the Lady Chapel, making up a complex jigsaw of stone. As the walls were constructed they would have been covered by a light wooden roof to protect the craftsmen from the elements.

One can imagine the village where the extended family of labourers, stonemasons and other skilled workers lived, and also the yard with its construction booths close to the building itself, where the laborious work of cutting the blocks of freestone and then carving the finer detail would have taken place. For many years Rosslyn Chapel was a living construction site, with ongoing development proceeding at varying rates, according to the interest of the St Clair family, the availability of funds and the condition of Scotland, whether at peace or at war.

COLLEGIATE WORSHIP

Not from until over seventy years later, on 5 February 1523 (in the reign of King James V), does a legal charter survive with a description of the entire foundation already in existence as a collegiate church. There appears to be no other documentary evidence that establishes the precise date of the erection of the chapel into a collegiate foundation. In 1523 one of Sir William's successors (also Sir William) named the Revd John Dickson as the provost (head) of the college along with three assistant priests (prebendaries), James Maxwell, James Mossman and John Davidson (a graduate of St Andrews University). By 1531, when a charter was drawn up by Sir William for his son Alexander, the canons consisted of Robert Dickson, James Whitehead, Alexander Scott, John Ker (the chaplain) and John Maxwell (probably also a graduate of St Andrews).[17]

Each priest had his own altar. They were set in a line of four along the east wall between the windows and probably separated by wooden screens. It is also possible that a separate mass might have been celebrated by each of them at intervals staggered throughout the day so as to leave the other canons free to work at other tasks, such as teaching the boys in the small *schola* (the *sang schule*, or choral school), cleaning and preparing the vestments or the sacred vessels and parish visitation. The altars would have been screened off from one another, just as the choir itself would have been screened and provided with wooden stalls for the canons to sit in while reciting the Divine Office (the canonical hours – chiefly the singing of Psalms). Indeed, early photographs show the sockets in the choir pillars into which the wood was once fixed.

The canons' parochial duties were of various kinds and might include such relatively unpleasant tasks as debt collecting, as well as the care of souls. As a severe warning in July 1546, for example, the curates of Dalkeith, Lasswade and Roslin were required to proclaim the names of those tenants who had not yet paid their

A religious community at prayer: the Cistercian monks of Sancta Maria Abbey, Nunraw, East Lothian. (By permission of Sancta Maria Abbey, Nunraw)

teinds (equivalent to the English tithes – the tenth part of their produce, which had to be donated by parishioners for the upkeep of their local priest and church).[18]

The specific duty of the provost was to take responsibility for administering the college and to celebrate mass at the altar of the founding patron saint, St Matthew; the first prebendary canon was to celebrate mass at the altar of the Blessed Virgin Mary and also to act as sacristan (taking care of vestments, candles, incense and the gold or silver vessels used in the services, such as chalices). The second prebendary was to celebrate mass at St Andrew's altar and the third was obliged to do the same at the altar of St Peter. On important feast days all four priests would take part in a mass under the great east window, in the centre of the choir, along with the choristers.

Day in, day out, the college gathered together in the chapel, sitting in the wooden choir stalls, with their misericords on the reverse of every hinged wooden seat, which allowed each canon a small resting place (akin to the support of a shooting stick), even when standing up in the early hours of the morning in their enveloping habits, their cowls pulled down over their heads.

However, it is important to underline that, according to the charter of 1523, the clergy were first and foremost to celebrate more than masses. Their primary remit was to celebrate the Divine Office – namely, the liturgy of the hours, sung together by the clergy in the body of the church. This is a quite separate function from the celebration of mass (which each priest would also do separately once a day), daily mass being a part of their duties but by no means the most time-consuming. The community of canons would spend around six hours a day together, reciting and singing the Divine Office but less than an hour celebrating mass.

The fact that there were two choristers in the establishment at Rosslyn points to the use of polyphony in the chapel's celebrations, as well as plainsong (much of which was derived from Jewish and Roman religious chant). One can make an educated guess at the possible range of polyphonic music that might have been available to the clergy at Rosslyn.

Scottish polyphonic music written prior to its systematic destruction at the Reformation survives in four main sources. As the late Arthur Oldham (1926–2003), composer and choirmaster at St Mary's Roman Catholic Cathedral, Edinburgh, and founder of the Edinburgh Festival Chorus and Scottish Opera Chorus, points out, there are still some vestiges of Scottish pre-Reformation church music in the Scone Antiphonary (now in the National Library of Scotland), the Dunkeld Music Book (in Edinburgh University Library), the three 'St Andrews Music Books' and the works of the composer Robert Johnson from Duns, who, having been branded a heretic, managed to escape to England, taking a number of his compositions with him.[19] By a quirk of fate, the 'St Andrews Music Book' also survived destruction at the Reformation simply because it was stolen to order by an agent of a German collector of manuscripts. In 1553 Marcus Wagner, a Protestant agent of the German music collector Falcius Illyricus, gained entry to the Augustinian priory at St Andrews posing as a pilgrim calling on his way to Jerusalem. With great subterfuge Wagner managed to steal and make off with a number of rare volumes, which are today still

Teaching Gregorian plainchant in the *schola* at St Benedict's Abbey, Fort Augustus (*c.* 1880). (By permission of the Scottish Catholic Archives)

preserved in the Herzog August Bibliothek at Wolfenbüttel, Germany, having escaped the fate of the rest of the priory's collection. The stolen manuscript was compiled in the thirteenth century and contains a substantial proportion of music written specifically for the church at St Andrews.[20]

The college at Rosslyn was not large: its choir of four priests and two singing boys compared unfavourably with Aberdeen's twenty vicars-choral and six choirboys who sang there after 1437, the twelve prebendaries and ten choirboys at the parish church in Peebles, the nine prebendaries at Restalrig (in 1487), or the eight prebendaries and three choirboys at St Mary's and St Anne's in Glasgow.[21]

As in every collegiate church, the prebendaries at Restalrig had to have mastered not only the antiphons, responses and versicles of Gregorian chant but also the art of singing in parts (discanthus) for masses – referred to later by the Reformers as 'curious' (meaning 'antiquated' and 'complicated'), an adjective perhaps also explaining the design of Rosslyn Chapel itself – as well as how to teach in the *sang schule* and even how to play the organ.[22] The collegiate church of the Holy Trinity in Edinburgh had, as well as a provost, eight prebendaries and two choirboys, and an organ with three rows of pipes, the front row of which held eighteen pipes. This can be seen in the *Trinity Altarpiece*, a magnificent religious painting now in the Queen's Collection but permanently displayed at the National Gallery of Scotland at the Mound in Princes Street.

Royal patronage for church music was often vigorous. Scottish church music was strongly supported by King James I, who had spent eighteen years as a prisoner in England, where he was educated and taught the rudiments of music by followers of the English composer John Dunstable (d. 1453). Indeed, James I is credited with having introduced the organ into Scotland.[23] The king's organ at the Chapel Royal in Stirling Castle was constructed by Gilleam, the maker of the king's organs, out of goatskin, parchment (for the bellows), nails, iron springs, glue and paper; a small portable organ (known as a regal) even followed James I wherever he went.[24] By 1505 the Chapel Royal had three pairs of organs. King James III (1460–88), who planned to develop the Chapel Royal as a music conservatory, took musicians with him when

King James III of Scotland. (From William Drummond, *The History of Scotland* (London: Henry Hills, 1655))

King James IV of Scotland. (From Oliphant Smeaton, *The Story of Edinburgh* (London: G.M. Dent, 1905))

he travelled, but it was his son, James IV, who had the Chapel Royal established as a collegiate church.

In his poem 'Palice of Honour' (*c.* 1501) the poet and priest Gavin Douglas (at that time provost of the Collegiate Church of St Giles and later Bishop of Dunkeld) described with relish the magnificence of music in the church liturgies, with a nervy excitement (both intellectual and sensual) at the music's complex geometry, using onomatopoeic words from Latin, French and Scots, which also revealed the rich cultural melting pot out of which the compositions were created:

> Proportionis fine with sound celestiall,
> Duplet, triplet, diatesserial,
> *Sequi altera*, and decuple resortis
> Diapason of mony sindrie sortis . . .
> In modulation hard I play and sing
> Faburdon, priksang, discant, countering,
> Cant organe, figuration, and gemmell.[25]

The stonemasons who decorated the 'curious' Chapel at Rosslyn clearly enjoyed music, for they portrayed a bagpipe player (see the chapel ground plan between

Pillars 4 and 5), the macabre Dance of Death (in the Lady Chapel) and an angel musician (at the window to the left of the north door). Among the other musical instruments visible in the carvings that run round the top of the pillars at the Lady Chapel are: a trumpet, a lute, a hurdy-gurdy, a dulcimer, a drum, a shawm (wind instrument), a vielle (stringed instrument played with a bow) and the portative (an early form of portable organ, whose bellows lies flat on the player's knees). Completing Rosslyn's medieval orchestra is a musician (perhaps the conductor), who holds the music book open on his knees.

Masses would be divided into sections that had different but related functions. There were two main parts to the mass – the Liturgy of the Word and the Eucharist. The first was divided into general prayers for forgiveness (the *Kyrie*, recited in Greek), the *Gloria* (praising God), readings from the Old and New Testament and then from the Gospels. This would be followed by a sermon (if there was a congregation), the solemn *Credo* (I believe), the Offertory, the *Sanctus*, the Consecration, the *Agnus Dei* and the breaking of bread. Each part had an interrelated function in the service, in which prayers and petitions were raised to God on behalf of the whole human race, and not just for the donor. The music for important services would be provided by a small organ and the voices of the priest and the boys in the haunting and hypnotically clear vocal lines of Gregorian chant or in more florid, intertwined polyphonic pieces, which would have echoed and re-echoed through the nooks and crannies of Rosslyn Chapel's intricate decoration. It is possible that vocal music such as that preserved in the St Andrews Music Book at Wolfenbüttel was available to the choristers at Rosslyn.

The liturgical practice followed in Scottish churches tended to be modelled on that of Salisbury Cathedral.[26] This was known as the Sarum Rite or Sarum Use, a variant of the Roman Rite that allowed greater scope for hymns and music and more elaboration of the ceremonial that surrounded the mass and the singing of the Divine Office – including the French style of swinging the incense thuribles (censers) or reserving the consecrated host in a sacrament house instead of having it placed in a pyx (gold or silver container) suspended over the altar.[27]

The bagpiper hidden high above the back of the Prince's Pillar. (By permission of Rosslyn Chapel Trust)

Some records of medieval Scottish libraries and their liturgical books survived destruction at the Reformation – a number of these being saved by the Earl of Rosslyn. These catalogues list the 102 books that belonged to Henry Sinclair, Bishop of Ross (d. 1565) and the 31 from the personal library of John Sinclair. Bishop of Brechin in 1565 and formerly Dean of the collegiate church at Restalrig, he succeeded his brother as President of the Court of Session.[28]

One of the finest collections of Scottish liturgical books in existence today is the Arbuthnot Manuscripts – a missal, prayer book and psalter. The missal (mass book) contains 246 vellum leaves and what is believed to be a portrait of Cheves, the second Archbishop of St Andrews at the time when Rosslyn Chapel had just been constructed. The prayer book is the 'Office of the Blessed Virgin', written on eighty vellum leaves, with six full-page painted miniatures, one of which is 'The Holy Eucharist', depicting priests elevating the sacred host at the consecration. The artist is undoubtedly Scottish. The psalter (142 pages) contains the Latin inscription: 'May this book remain here until an ant shall drink all the waters of the ocean and a tortoise perambulate the globe.' The scribe responsible for all three manuscripts (but not the illustrations) was James Sibbald, vicar of St Ternan's Church, Arbuthnot. The prayer book was written in 1482–3, the missal in 1491 and the psalter in 1482. Sibbald himself died in 1507. All three volumes are today held at Paisley Museum.

Providing support for the singing of the collegiate clergy were libraries of liturgical books specially written for each type of service. These varied in quantity, depending on the character of the establishment: in 1505 the Chapel Royal at Stirling Castle had four large antiphonaries inscribed on parchment with large gilt capital letters; Glasgow Cathedral in 1432 had seven. While the Chapel Royal had four antiphonaries, Glasgow had only five processionals to the Chapel Royal's ten. Other books in daily use included missals and breviaries.[29] Parts of the liturgy of Holy Week, settings for the Palm Sunday procession and fragments from a Latin grammar that was part of a song school's teaching programme were also discovered reused in the binding and the cover of a later volume preserved until the end of the twentieth century in the Library of St Benedict's Abbey, Fort Augustus.

One missal (named the 'Rosslyn Missal' by Bishop Alexander Penrose Forbes) written between the twelfth and thirteen centuries in England (but copied from an Irish model), which was in the possession of the Earls of Rosslyn from around 1560, is in the National Library of Scotland, although scholars question whether, with the spelling mistakes it contains, it could ever have been fit for daily use in services.[30] Another, now in the Bodleian Library, Oxford, consists mainly of a New Testament in English dating from the early fifteenth century, with a Gospel of St Matthew that differs from the other Gospels in having a written chart that allows the reader to locate the lessons, epistles and Gospels to be read in church according to the Sarum Rite.[31] Those volumes for use in Rosslyn Chapel would have been stored in a secure, lockable location, probably down in the crypt or, earlier still, at Rosslyn Castle.

Some idea of the rituals associated with collegiate endowments can be glimpsed in the instructions that Queen Mary of Gueldres left after her death for the canons at

Trinity College Church, Edinburgh, which she had founded to pray for the souls of the royal family. She directed, that after he had celebrated his daily mass, each canon should process (still in his vestments) to her tomb, sprinkle it with holy water, while at the same time reciting the 'De Profundis' ('Out of the depths have I cried to you, O Lord').[32]

Like any collegiate church, however, the establishment at Rosslyn also ran the risk of degenerating into *simony*. Essentially, what the Roman Catholic Church defined as 'simony' was based on the story of the popular magician Simon Magus (Acts 8: 9–24), who tried to offer St Peter money in exchange for the power to confer the gifts of the Holy Spirit – not so much *glossolalia* (speaking in tongues), but rather wisdom and understanding, right judgement and courage, knowledge and reverence, wonder and awe in God's presence.

If Sir William believed that he could automatically double or triple his chances of salvation after death (or the chances of his relatives), he was sadly mistaken. Nor could he avoid responsibility for his own actions (nor his own penance) by paying a college of canons to pray vicariously for him. Sir William would probably be well aware of such spiritual pitfalls and knew that, ultimately, theology taught that he could not force God's hand with money. Such a mechanistic concept, nevertheless, was one of the scandalous abuses that Martin Luther and the Reformation would later seek to abolish.

In a very real sense, private acts of worship were a contradiction in terms: the church was the whole community of worshippers participating in the mystery of Christ's Passion (suffering), death and Resurrection, which culminated in the magnificent and deliberately therapeutic ceremonials of the forty days of Lent, followed by the climax of the Church's year at Holy Week and Easter.[33]

Establishing a collegiate church could not be done solely on the whim or individual initiative of a rich lay person or persons. A college needed to have an approved domestic rule, a vision statement that governed its daily life and established norms for such matters as the adjudication of disputes. Hence, the college would (under canon law) be to some degree independent of the diocesan regulatory power of the local bishop. However, to operate in this way a collegiate church also needed to defer in some matters to the authority of the local bishop, to Rome and to the monarch of the day. Writing a charter and having it publicly witnessed by high officers of Church and State were therefore essential.

Nevertheless, by the time Rosslyn Chapel came to be constructed, a new separation had emerged between priests and people – active participation at mass tended to be reduced merely to catching a glimpse of the sacred host after the consecration. The private mass, which was the form most frequently celebrated at Rosslyn Chapel, would often be said with only an altar boy reciting the responses, responses that in earlier times would have been vigorously voiced by the whole assembled community.

The life of such a priest (whose main role was to pray for the salvation of named individuals or members of a family, living or deceased) was not necessarily a life of luxury. In his *History of the Holy Eucharist in Great Britain* T.E. Bridgett writes:

Occasionally we find an appropriate house and garden provided for the accommodation of the chantry priest; but for the most part he had one or two small rooms in a half-timbered hut, with little light, no fire-place, and an open chimney, with turf burning on the hearth . . . A bench or a stool, a wooden bedstead and a mattress of straw, would comprise the furniture and household comforts of these ecclesiastics. It is hardly to be supposed that the priest had a servant to stock his larder or minister to his culinary wants, and he probably prepared his own frugal fare. This would consist of salted meat twice a week. On the day of his patron saint, or on some great anniversary, he would have fresh meat and fish, and on high festivals a double mess. Beans to boil, and oatmeal for porridge, with ling fish, red herrings, cheese, oat cake and apples, would be ordinary food, while eggs, coarse barley-bread and fresh fish would be among the luxuries of the table.[34]

Although the spirit of the lost foundation charter at Rosslyn would no doubt have given greater security to the canons at the Collegiate Church of St Matthew than the chantry priests of Lancashire enjoyed, life for the priests of Rosslyn would have been a simple one with only the most basic comforts. Everything we know of the living arrangements of the canons comes from a much later document, a charter of 1523, when (presumably because the houses for the clergy that had existed up to that point had deteriorated) the Earl decided that new accommodation for his canons was urgently needed. He gave them the use of the land near his west barn, which stood on the north side of the cemetery (that is, just below the west end of the chapel), and other pieces of land. Each priest would have a house 168 feet by 105 feet, with all the houses built adjoining each other.

This later endowment was intended to ensure that the Earl's wishes were put into effect: that the Divine Office would continue to be celebrated in perpetuity at the Collegiate Church of St Matthew the Apostle and Evangelist, not only for the salvation of his soul and those of his ancestors and descendants, but also (as the customary formula he was very careful to insert in his charter emphasised) for the salvation of *all* the faithful departed, for those whose property he or his ancestors had wrongly taken without making full restitution and for all the benefactors of the college.[35]

That central eastern part of the planned church known as the choir was also intended to be the heart of the chapel where the community of priests, clerks and choristers came together several times a day for worship, to celebrate holy mass at the central high altar or at the side altars, and to sing the Divine Office of the Roman Catholic Church daily beginning with nocturns (at midnight), followed by lauds (3 a.m.), prime (6 a.m.), terce (9 a.m.), sext (midday), nones (3 p.m.), vespers (6 p.m.), and compline (9 p.m.).[36] These short daily services were composed of prayer, psalm singing and accompanying actions such as kneeling, bowing and perhaps the use of a small bell or the lighting of candles.

Nocturns were chanted in memory of the birth of Christ; lauds were sung in remembrance of Christ's betrayal and the Resurrection; prime recalled the mockery of Christ in front of Pontius Pilate; terce was in commemoration of Christ's sentence to death and the subsequent descent of the Holy Spirit upon the Apostles; sext remembered the Crucifixion; nones recalled Christ's death; vespers remembered the taking down of Jesus' body from the Cross; and compline, at the end of the day, focused on the respose of Jesus' body in the tomb. Another type of prayer was also available to worshippers in the form of the rosary, beads fixed on a string to count the number of prayers recited. This was a prayer structure brought back from Palestine by the Crusaders and first developed by monks in Tibet. Recent medical research has also discovered that praying the rosary reduces myocardial ischaemia and encourages calmness and well-being.[37]

In 1484 Sir William St Clair died and was buried in the chapel he had founded, although it was then still unfinished. He was succeeded by his second son, Sir Oliver, who, by roofing the choir, completed the Chapel as far as the west wall. His fourth son, Sir John, was parish priest at Pentland, and afterwards Dean of Restalrig in Edinburgh, then Bishop of Brechin (1540) and finally Lord President of the Court of Session. Sir Oliver officiated at the marriage of Mary Queen of Scots and Lord Henry Darnley in Holyrood on 29 July 1565 but died in the following year.[38]

It is not clear when Rosslyn Chapel was officially consecrated, but it was very likely by the Bishop of St Andrews – either James Kennedy (in 1440), Patrick Graham (in 1466) or James Stewart (in 1497). Normally, consecration would not take place until the whole structure was complete. This would suggest that the date of consecration followed the decision to abandon the original plan of constructing the north and south transepts and the 91-foot nave. At any rate, the consecration crosses are still visible, carved deep into the stone, and were once carefully anointed with holy oils.

Consecration cross on the south side of the ruined west transept. (By permission of Rosslyn Chapel Trust)

There is, however, some evidence that during the following years at least one of the canons at Rosslyn was sympathetic to the aims of those who tried to reform the Roman Catholic Church from within. Although the Scottish Parliament had offered a reward in 1541 for information regarding secret associations of Christians meeting in conventicles who were described as 'disputing in Sacred Scripture and dishonouring the Virgin Mary', David Hutchesoun, provost of Rosslyn, appears to have condoned and supported such movements.[39]

As the Reformers gained greater strength in Scotland, the provosts and prebendaries had their endowments seized by the adherents of Reform who used 'force and violence' to do so. Typically, church libraries were destroyed: volumes of the Early Church Fathers, of councils, other books of civilised learning along with the church baptismal, marriage and death registers, were all thrown into the streets, collected into heaps and afterwards set on fire and reduced to ashes in an attempt to erase the documentary underpinning of Roman Catholicism.[40]

Essentially, the new Reformed Church enjoyed no formal statutory recognition until 1567, after Mary Queen of Scots had been deposed and James VI had come to the throne; indeed, the pre-Reformation church administrative systems remained in place both financially and legally.[41] However, the pressure on those who persisted in the observation of the Roman Catholic faith was intense: no one, high or low, was exempt from the enquiries instigated by the new Reformed Assembly.

In 1571 matters came to a head for the Collegiate Church of St Matthew and its canons. Intimidated by widespread changes in land tenure that would require that the properties that had formerly been theirs by right would now have to be held in leasehold, John Robeson, Provost of Rosslyn, fixed upon a device to keep the chapel in Sainteclaire hands. He handed the properties of the college over to Edward Sinclair, heir to the family title. This decision had been taken by all the canons meeting together in chapter, following many years in which the income due to them from the college lands had been withheld. Signing the document with Robeson was a pensioner vicar of Pentland, the Revd John How, and a prebendary, the Revd Henry Sinclair. They feared that the properties would otherwise be taken from them, either by violence or by trickery. Robeson appears to have been succeeded in his post by the elderly John Dickson as Provost.

Robeson was right to be wary of what the immediate future might bring. He had merely bowed to the inevitable. In 1572 the General Assembly decided to convert the wealth of the collegiate foundations and their elderly canons from religious purposes to educational ones for the benefit of the younger generation: 'All provestries and prebendaries in college kirks founded on temporal lands or annuals, and all chaplainries of the same foundation, now vacant, or that shall hereafter be vacant, shall be given and bestowed by the King's Majesty or other lawful patrons, to bursaries or students in Grammar, Art, Theologie, the Laws, Medicine.'[42]

The pressure on the clergy to relinquish the old religion continued. In 1589, for example, the former Roman Catholic cleric William Knox (a local minister and a close relative of the founding father of the Scottish Reformation, John Knox) was censured for reverting to Roman Catholic ritual in baptising 'the Laird of Rosling's

John Knox, leader of the Scottish Reformation. (From James Grant, *Edinburgh Old and New* (London: Cassell, Petter, Galpin, 1880?–1883?))

bairns' at Rosslyn Chapel. A year later, the Presbytery of Dalkeith forbade the Revd George Ramsay, minister of Lasswade, from burying the wife of Sir Oliver Sinclair in the chapel. Sir William Sinclair himself was repeatedly warned and ordered to destroy the altars inside Rosslyn Chapel. He was summoned before the General Assembly of the Church of Scotland and threatened with excommunication. Later that year, on 24 September 1590, it was reported that 'The last Wednesday, Mr George Ramsay said he had gone to Rosling, enterit ye Kirk and y^r [there] fand [found] sax alteris standing haill undemolishit, and some broken images'.[43]

Ramsay's description of the altars is significant: there were six and, therefore, the four that are to be found today against the east wall of the chapel interior (in the Lady Chapel) are only two-thirds of those that remained 'haill' (whole) in 1590. This tends to support the argument that, even if we subtract an additional altar in the crypt, there was almost certainly a larger principal altar in the centre of the chapel where the provost and prebendaries could celebrate mass together as one community.

Answering a complaint lodged by the Reformed minister Mr George Lundie, the Assembly of the new Reformed Church, meeting early in May 1590 at the former Trinity Collegiate Church in Edinburgh, ordered the Presbytery of Dalkeith to call Sir William of Rosslyn and Sir Oliver Sinclair before them. Lundie had complained that they had prevented him from getting to the kirk at Pentland so as to discharge his office.[44] By October of that year the Assembly were again questioning Sir William, this time about his retaining religious images in his chapel and for giving house room to the excommunicated Mr David King (no doubt a former Roman Catholic priest who had refused to change to the new Reformed religion).[45]

Sir William, the fourteenth baron, strongly denied both accusations, but the Assembly persisted, ordering the Presbytery of Dalkeith to enforce the ban against images and other 'monuments of idolatry' by making him demolish them.[46] The Assembly also ordered Sir William to be accompanied by members of the Presbytery to ensure that George Lundie was able to establish residence at Pentland Kirk.

By April 1592 the Assembly were losing patience and, that October, tried a different tack to put pressure on Sir William. They issued a summons against him to appear in answer to a charge of fornication. Sir William duly appeared and admitted the 'misbehaviour' of which he had been accused, confessing that the experience of appearing before a religious court of the new Church had led him to repent.[47] One can almost feel him wriggling like a worm at the end of a hook. The Assembly pulled short of calling him a papist (an accusation routinely used against others), still deferring to his title and position in the community, but appointed two members of the Church to interview him and deal personally with his continued intransigence.

Eventually, Sir William agreed to confess his misbehaviour publicly before the Assembly and then before the Presbytery, and did so. But there were other, more radical changes afoot, as arrangements were put in place to accommodate the Reformed faith. At this time the Presbytery of Dalkeith was in the process of carrying out the Assembly's instruction to design manses to house the new church ministers and establish appropriate land (a glebe) for every church within their boundary.[48]

The pressure the Assembly brought to bear on Sir William did not extend to seizing Rosslyn Chapel and turning it into a parish church: Sir William was protected by his charters as far as that was concerned, and it probably suited the Assembly and Presbytery to establish a new church elsewhere. However, in general, churches that had previously been Roman Catholic had their statues, vestments and church plate sold off, their altars ripped out and their mural-covered walls whitewashed. Otherwise, the leaders of the new faith were careful to recycle the fundamental structure of church buildings and adapt them appropriately for the much less ritualised worship of the Reformed Kirk.

The pressure on those who did not conform was nevertheless systematic and many-layered. In April 1593 the Presbytery of Dalkeith summoned the parishioners of Lasswade to appear in front of the Provincial Assembly of Lothian and Tweeddale because they had refused to accept the Bible teaching and pastoral authority of the new Protestant ministers. Sir William was one of those called, but he replied that he was a parishioner not of Lasswade but of St Catherine in the Hopes because of his residence at the Logan House tower and because there was no minister at that time appointed to that church.[49] However, by 1592 the Revd George Ramsay reported with some satisfaction that the altars at Rosslyn had all been demolished. The chapel then ceased to be a house of prayer and fell into disuse.

Such hostile experiences for Rosslyn Chapel (and what was left of its congregation) began at the Scottish Reformation and ended with the departure in 1650 of General George Monck (1608–70). Monck brought destruction and chaos to many church and other buildings in Scotland by stabling his troopers' horses in them (as he did at Rosslyn) and violently destroying the interiors – which he did not do at Rosslyn Chapel, apparently being content with bombarding Rosslyn Castle. Monck, however, also experienced personal tragedy in Midlothian: his infant son lies buried in the ruins of what was once the Collegiate Chapel of St Nicholas in Dalkeith.

For Rosslyn Chapel there would come greater violence than the clashing of the hooves of troopers' horses or the ordure they left behind: on 11 December 1688, as William of Orange was sailing for England, a group of zealots from Edinburgh (along with some local villagers) entered the chapel and vandalised it in their search for Roman Catholic church furniture and vestments. Fr Richard Hay wrote that during that night he lost several books of importance when the mob attacked the chapel, causing damage both to the interior and to his place of study – probably the crypt, which normally could be locked with a stout door and had a number of cupboards available for storage, as well as a fireplace.

Some time afterwards, Hay records a petition from Lady Rosslyn to Queen Mary (1662–94) asking to be granted a pension to enable her to provide for her large family, to pay off her debts, to educate her children, to repair her castle, which was almost ruined in the service of the Crown, and to restore a chapel 'ever devoted to the true service of God Almighty' but now 'very much out of repair'.[50] It is not recorded what the Queen's reply was, but it seems to have been in the negative – or perhaps her death in 1694 put an end to the matter. The chapel was finally abandoned and the windows sealed with wooden shutters. It is not certain if during these years it was ever used for worship again.

The generally accepted view is that Rosslyn Chapel received little care from the Reformers for nearly 100 years. However, a parish session minute dated 3 July 1696 states: 'The Session understanding that many people come from Edinburgh and other places upon Sabbath and Fast days to see the College of Roselin, therefore they appoint two elders in Roselin to go to John Dobbie (?) who keeps the keys of the said College and discharge him to open the door to any upon the foresaid days.' This is evidence that the Reformed Church assumed the responsibility of managing access to the chapel during this period and, hence, also saw to it that there was no damage done to the building. It is also proof that, even in the late seventeenth century, visitors flocked regularly to see Rosslyn Chapel and its astonishing interior.

However, a proactive programme of conservation did not materialise until 1736, when Colonel Sir James St Clair Erskine engaged a stonemason, Mackenzie Buchan, and a wright (carpenter), William Irvine, to repair the chapel, having also completed necessary repairs to the roof of Rosslyn Castle.[51] The following year more repairs were undertaken – the west end of the castle wall was pinned and harled (with pebble-dash), slates were replaced, the castle kitchen windows glazed, the kitchen door and the stairs replaced; at the chapel, meanwhile, fifteen panes of glass were installed, along with a new pair of shutter hinges, and the shutters themselves were painted.[52]

In these repairs the polymath Sir John Clerk of Penicuik (1676–1755) played a leading role. A visiting enthusiast reported of the chapel:

It has laid open to the weather ever since the Reformation, but has withstood all its effects, by the goodness of the materials, and the excellency of its work is a miracle; however, the rain now penetrating through the roof which is vaulted with stone, would in a few years have dissolved it entirely, had not that true lover of antiquities and all the liberal arts, Sir John Clerk, persuaded the present Lord Sinclair to put it into compleat repair. The workmen have been upon it all this summer, and as Sir John has the whole direction of it, in a year more it will not only be secured from ruin, but be made as beautiful and stately as most of that sort of edifices in the kingdom, though it is like to be used as only a burying-place for that noble family of whom there is only one tomb in it now, and that in the same wretched condition as the rest of the fabric . . .[53]

The choir at Rosslyn Chapel, drawn and engraved by J. & J. Johnstone, Edinburgh (1825). Note the guide holding a long pointing stick. (From *Picture of Rosslyn Chapel* (Edinburgh: Oliver & Boyd, 1825))

Some of the correspondence between Colonel James Erskine St Clair and Sir John Clerk has survived, as well as a copy made by Sir John of the frieze on the north side of the chapel.[54] These repairs would enable the chapel to survive into the nineteenth century. Writing in his introduction to the *Memoirs of the Life of Sir John Clerk* (1892), John M. Gray stated emphatically that Sir John Clerk was 'the preserver – one is glad to say, not the *restorer* – of Roslin Chapel'.[55]

A charming description of the stone in the interior of the chapel in 1820 emerges from a letter from the Earl of Rosslyn to his wife: 'all the Chapel stone is a rosy fawn', he wrote affectionately. However, not all was well with the underlying structure of the building. In 1836 the architect William Burn (1789–1870) was called in by the Earl of Rosslyn: 'Mr Burns [sic] is requested to cause an immediate examination of the state of the Chapel at Roslin and to send a Report . . . [to] examine Foundation of the Chapel and the projecting Crypt . . . [the] state of Roof especially the sloping side covered with slates.'[56]

Over the next five years, however, the number of tourists coming to Roslin did not diminish. On 28 July 1840, according to the chapel visitors' book, 'Victoria Regina London, Queen of Great Britain and Ireland', visited the Chapel. The Earl was now proposing to remove the two side roofs and to cover up the side aisles with a new roof, so uncovering the parts of the windows previously hidden by the existing roof.

Images taken of Rosslyn Chapel by the photographic pioneers David Octavius Hill (1802–70) and Robert Adamson (1821–48) in the mid-1840s show quite clearly the extent of the window glazing, which covered only the lower, rectangular lights of the chapel ground-floor windows; the great east window retained its muscular stonework but no glass.

Visitors and repairs were the responsibility of the Earl's factor (steward). Beginning in 1851, from his residence at College Hill House John Thomson doubled as factor for the Earl's estate at Roslin and also as custodian of the chapel and castle.[57]

However, by the late 1850s James Alexander St Clair-Erskine, 3rd Earl of Rosslyn, had decided that something drastic had to be done quickly to conserve and improve the chapel's condition. Accordingly he engaged the celebrated architect David Bryce (1803–76), the man who would later be credited with the invention of the Scottish Baronial style.

Paradoxically, a certain distaste and aversion towards what were seen as the crudities of fifteenth-century church architecture had become fashionable during this Gothic Revival, itself partly a product of the Oxford Movement that led John Newman to convert to Rome. The Gothic Revival was, too, partly influenced by bodies such as the Cambridge Camden Society, which appeared in 1839 with the aim of reforming church architecture and reviving ritual arrangements.[58]

The launch of the society was followed by that of a monthly magazine, *The Ecclesiologist*, published by the Camden Society (and, later, the Ecclesiological Society, into which it developed in 1879). One of the principles of the Camden Society was 'the restoration of mutilated remains', and this would seem to fit particularly well with the task at hand at Rosslyn Chapel, which had suffered two centuries of substantial structural neglect.

But the temptations to 'improve' the original building inappropriately were always present in the plans of architects such as David Bryce. The art historian Sir Kenneth Clark commented provocatively that 'it would be interesting to know if the Camden Society destroyed as much medieval architecture as Cromwell'.[59] In his groundbreaking *History of the Gothic Revival* (1872), a luminary and President of the Royal Academy, the painter Charles Eastlake (1793–1865), was not impressed by Rosslyn Chapel, which he described as full of 'coarse and vitiated detail'.[60]

In response to the Earl's urgent request, Bryce quickly produced a series of drawings for the proposed repairs to the stonework.[61] Bryce had already modified his ideas for the coping stones of the altars after showing them to the Earl. Bryce wanted to make one a plain moulding and another a splay, leaving one as originally intended. He promised to attend to the Earl's wish to have ornamental bosses added and memorial brasses set into the floor. The architect had also noticed that there had been a small ('high') altar at the window above the stairs leading down to the sacristy (crypt). He planned to rebuild this altar and set a platform over the stairs, wide enough to allow a priest to stand at the altar. He was certain that this could be effective and was convinced that there had originally been such a platform.

The Earl had also asked Bryce to carry out some adjustments to the burial vault. Bryce intended to cover over the grave in the centre compartment to about 5 feet 3 inches below the level of the pavement, which would allow him to form a catacomb on each side of the space. This would provide room for three additional burials in that compartment. Bryce was sure that the graves in the centre were dug deep enough not to be disturbed by this work. He had also been thinking about where to locate the brass handrails. His idea was to make them portable, extending between the pillars but not touching them. They would be inserted into iron or brass sockets sunk into the stonework.

As the work progressed, another, older architect would be called in to collaborate with Bryce: William Burn returned to Rosslyn and put forward some suggestions for new seating, including plain deal benches stained with asphalte.[62]

In a lengthy letter Bryce excitedly explained to the Earl what he had in mind: he planned to heat the chapel by piping hot air into the burial vaults below and directing it up into the chapel by means of a grating in the floor.[63] The smoke flue would be taken out of the Chapel by cutting a hole through the south wall, sloping the flue up the bank on the outside like a drain and then continuing it to the trees on the east side, quite clear of the chapel wall.

Bryce's ingenious plans, however, did not meet with universal approval, especially since he had replaced nearly all the angels below the niches of the east wall and 'renewed' most of those on the south.[64] The Architectural Institute of Scotland wrote to the Earl of Rosslyn urging him to retain as much as possible of the chapel's original integrity and not to do anything to falsify any part of it. The institute was deeply unhappy at the removal of some parts of the original building and warned against any use of chemicals to clean the structure. They deplored the cutting-away of the brackets under the niches in the piers of the east wall, along with others in the jambs of the adjoining windows, the substitution of copies of the carvings (even on

Left: An angel at the west end of the Chapel, intricate, naive and somewhat playful in style, that escaped the controversial 1861 restorations of David Bryce. (By permission of Rosslyn Chapel Trust) *Right:* One of the more clean-cut, self-consciously forceful and quasi-Masonic replacement angels inserted by David Bryce. (By permission of Rosslyn Chapel Trust)

the Prince's Pillar), the renewal of the aumbries (small cupboards for holy vessels) in the east wall and the rebuilding and refinishing of the altars and the scraping, cleaning and recarving in the east range of pillars. All these actions that the Earl and David Bryce had undertaken were condemned by the institute as 'not only unnecessary but highly mischievous in principle, tending to throw doubts on the authenticity of the whole of that portion of the Chapel and thereby entirely destroying its value architecturally and pictorially'.[65]

Lord Rosslyn refused to accept the institute's criticisms. He replied confidently that no alterations were being made to the original structure and that no sculptured stones would be removed without being replaced with an exact copy, using stone taken from what he believed to be the original quarry. He could not see the harm in removing the grime of centuries nor 'incrustations which conceal the sculpture or obliterate the beauty of the original workmanship'.[66] With resignation, the institute accepted that the responsibility for the care of the building was the Earl's, and there was little it could do to persuade him to turn back from the course of action he had chosen.

Nevertheless, the following month, a devastating critique of the restoration was published in the *Building News* (5 July 1861). The writer began by observing that the main purpose of the restoration was to enclose the family graves and carry out some necessary repairs at the east end or Lady Chapel. The article complained:

Brackets and canopies have been, since that time, ruthlessly cut away; the picturesque old stair leading to the Crypt has been modernised; 'facsimiles' of the old sculpture have been substituted; acids have been used for cleaning a portion of the stone, which will surely disintegrate the particles; other parts have been re-chiselled – flayed – destroying the original proportions of the mouldings, and altering the character of the ornament; one third of the cusped points of the arches are executed with *cement*, in place of stone. As if this was not enough, the alterations have been made with the worst quality of stone – the yellow-coloured variety – which is so soft and friable in its nature as to render it unsuitable for the purpose and ill calculated for endurance.

The irate correspondent for the *Building News* disputed the major assumption made by the restorers – namely, that the building was going to ruin because of exposure to the damp and other effects of the weather. This was a mistake, he argued, as the windows and doors had been in place for nearly twenty years, at which time both interior and exterior had undergone a thorough repair under the architect William Burn, who had fixed new windows in the north clerestory and other parts of the chapel. Unfortunately, continued the correspondent, these were made fixtures, which prevented the proper airing of the building, and so, a great deal of the dampness then existing had been caused by the stagnant air inside, not by external causes, and could easily be remedied merely by opening some of the windows.

The periodical's correspondent finished by saying that it was almost certain that most of the decay had taken place during the first century of the chapel's existence

The chapel decorated at Christmas (1862), shortly after David Bryce's restoration. Note the floral ropes that seem to suggest the technique used by the medieval stonemasons in designing the Prince's Pillar. (By permission of the Royal Commission on the Ancient and Historical Monuments of Scotland)

and that the coating of green moss that had formed on the stone gave complete protection from changes in the atmosphere. The stone had given way only when it was not covered by moss.

In spite of all the criticisms, regular Sunday services were eventually started in 1861 by James Alexander, 3rd Earl of Rosslyn, and the chapel was officially rededicated as an Episcopal church on Easter Tuesday, 22 April 1862. The new wooden pews that had been installed, along with the other fittings, were paid for by public subscription. Preaching from Psalm 26: 8, 'Lord I have loved the habitation of Thy house, and the place where Thine honour dwelleth', the Rt Revd Alexander Penrose Forbes (1817–75), Bishop of Brechin, delivered a sermon whose principal theme was a vindication of the use of the decorative arts in buildings dedicated to religious worship:

> The highest manifestations of the beautiful have been evolved in the sublime adoration of God. This thought is very apposite on a day when, after the lapse of nearly two hundred years, the voice of prayer and praise are heard within these sacred walls. The church itself, its situation, the foreign character of its architecture, the era of its erection, the very superstitions that lingered around its walls – all supplies us with special subjects of meditation. And first, as to its situation. Could the least impressible nature fail to recognise a moral fitness and proportion between this rich and gorgeous sanctuary and the matchless situation which the spring, bursting forth in its power, would soon transform into a Paradise of life and verdure? Surely when they thought of the gracefulness of form exhibited in the undulation of the ground, the inimitable effects of colour produced by the tints of foliage, the old red sandstone, and the gushing stream, and knew that these, in their grace and loveliness, were the works of the God and Creator of eternal beauty, it was in strict analogy with the constitution of the truth, that in those structures which men had raised for religious motives, the same external beauty should be aimed at?[67]

But, in Roslin at that time, sweetness and light were soured by a degree of conflict. As John Sang's map of 1862 testifies, there was a difference of opinion between the Earl of Rosslyn and the local community, as the Earl had decided to feu (rent out as under the feudal system) 56 acres of the Roslin lands.[68] Consequently, a dispute developed over the public right of way that ran along the west side of Collegehill House and then down round the south side of the castle into the glen.

There was a similar dispute seven years later (1869) when Lord Rosslyn (still the feu superior) attempted to close up the right of way leading over the hill from the chapel to the castle. 'He at the same time sought to enclose part of the Common ground,' wrote the *Dalkeith Advertiser* (24 August 1893). The villagers hotly resented their pathway being blocked off. 'They determined that it would not be closed, and joining together they tore up the fences. This excited the wrath of Lord Rosslyn, at whose instance two of the villagers, Messrs Davidson and Sanderson, were placed under arrest [in the middle of the night] and taken to Edinburgh.'

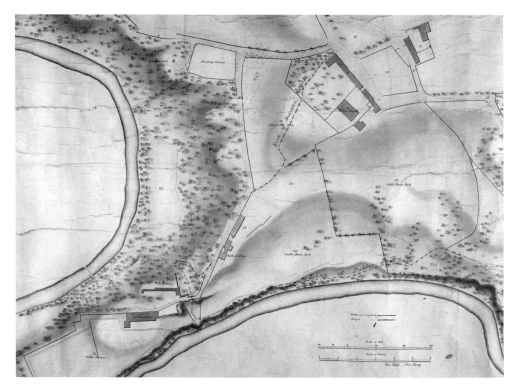

Map drawn by John Sang (dated November 1862) for use in the legal dispute between the Earl of Rosslyn and the villagers of Roslin over a public footpath running down the west side of College Hill House, showing the contours and features of the site as well as the Midway Cottages on the road to Rosslyn Castle. (By permission of the Trustees of the National Library of Scotland)

However, the arrests only made the conflict more intense. The villagers appointed one of their number, who went up to Edinburgh to put their case to the authorities and quickly secured the release of the imprisoned men. No further attempt was made to block the right of way or to enclose the Common. Nevertheless, this uncertainty over the ownership of the Common was to resurface again in the 1890s, when the presence of showmen on the Common caused a nuisance to the villagers because of the vehicles that the show people parked there.

The question of the ownership of public land flared up yet again in June 1905, when Mr Law, a local joiner then engaged in building operations, erected a temporary shed to accommodate his masons on a part of the Common opposite his house that he considered was his ground as it had been in the possession of his family for over seventy years.[69] Following a meeting with a county councillor and three parish councillors, a 'large and representative committee' was formed to enquire into the matter. Within a week 'a large section of the community was up in arms' and the shed was forcibly taken down, only to be re-erected by Mr Law, with this combative result: 'A few nights later a crowd of about 100 men and women headed by the leader of the previous week, armed with hammer and other articles, set to work and erected a substantial barricade around the offending structure, thus preventing its use.'[70]

German gypsies on the village Common in 1906. (The Bryce Collection by permission of Midlothian Library Service)

Episcopalian worship at Rosslyn Chapel in the 1870s. (By permission of the Royal Commission on the Ancient and Historical Monuments of Scotland)

This had the desired effect: Mr Law did not want to begin litigation and, rather than do so, was prepared to remove the cause of the quarrel. However, it took almost two years (and many delays) for the parish council to establish a definitive set of rules to govern the use of the Common.

In Rosslyn Chapel itself, meanwhile, more restoration had taken place in 1869. Inscribed on the east window is the information that it 'was entirely restored and filled with stained glass, November, 1869, by Francis Robert, fourth Earl of Rosslyn'. In the following year, the Earl held 'a Grand Masonic *Fette* [i.e. Fête] at Rosslyn for over a thousand freemasons and was elected Grand Master Mason of Scotland in 1871'.[71]

A comparison of photographs taken in the 1840s by Hill and Adamson with the east window today shows quite clearly that the introduction of the stained glass into the east window involved considerable structural design changes: what had been the very muscular and solid medieval stone tracery in the east window thirty years before was replaced from the top of the supporting side and central pillars upwards with a more delicate and complex design incorporating an elaboration of the Sainteclaire engrailed cross and a new central circle of stone above the two glass lights. This 'restoration' (whether undertaken for practical or aesthetic reasons is not entirely clear, as the medieval stone tracery seems robust enough in the Hill and Adamson images) also introduced a tiny triangle of red glass at the now-redundant apex of the window where previously there had been none.[72]

Whether there was any stained or even plain glass in the original pre-Reformation building may be surmised as a reasonable possibility but has not been definitively established. The Revd John Thompson stated categorically in 1892: 'These [stained glass windows] are all modern. Whatever stained glass there was formerly in the Chapel was destroyed at the Reformation, and subsequently; indeed, for many years there was no glass in the windows, the only protection from the weather being from outside shutters.'[73]

Yet more attempts at restoration followed in the autumn of 1879, when the Edinburgh-based architect Andrew Kerr was engaged by the 4th Earl to survey the chapel and its surroundings and report on the feasibility of carrying out further improvements at its west end. In hindsight, Kerr's thorough survey, along with his perceptive archaeological and historical comments, are invaluable today. At the request of the Earl, Kerr carried out an initial assessment of the state of the chapel, principally the interior. He found 'green mossy surfaces . . . chiefly in the north aisle towards the east end' and added that 'they appear to arise from moist air condensing on the surfaces of the stone . . . [and are] not caused by damp rising from the ground nor coming through the walls'. Once the ground had been surveyed, Kerr submitted plans to the Earl for a new baptistry at the west end as a way of finishing off the uncompleted chapel, disguising the fact that it was only half-finished and also giving some extra space below for a baptismal font and an organ loft above.

After attending to the preliminaries (such as the choice of stone), Kerr completed the plans and specifications for the baptistry in May 1879. By the following July he was arranging to meet tradesmen at Rosslyn to start the preliminary work of marking

The east façade of Rosslyn Chapel, captured in the paper negative of David O. Hill and Robert Adamson in the 1840s, showing the muscular medieval tracery removed in 1867. (By permission of Glasgow University Archives)

The choir of Rosslyn Chapel, looking east – a drawing (probably based on a photograph) made after David Bryce's renovations of 1861 and before the Victorian stained glass was installed (1867). Postcard, by James Valentine, Dundee.

The west transepts of Rosslyn Chapel, with Andrew Kerr's 1881 baptistry in the centre (1969). (Crown Copyright by permission of the Royal Commission on the Ancient and Historical Monuments of Scotland)

off the site and arranging for fencing and the delivery of materials.[74] By the middle of October the baptistry was roofed, the plumbers were on site to install the zinc roofing and estimates for alterations to the organ had been received.[75] Most of the work was completed by January 1881.

The architect's cautious pastiche in designing the baptistry was achieved through careful consultation with the 4th Earl. Kerr took great care to submit his proposals stage by stage, but, although the finished product with its carved screens inside the chapel and its organ in the loft above evidently pleased the Earl, the architect and the congregation, it did not meet with universal critical approval. The *Ordnance Gazeteer of Scotland* (1885) commented that 'the western wall of the Chapel is disfigured by a recently erected Baptistry and organ gallery'; in *The Buildings of Scotland: Lothian* (1978), Colin McWilliam, the doyen of Scottish architectural historians, was equally scathing, describing Kerr's statues on the exterior as 'stodgy'.[76] However, the baptistry and organ loft were functional and relatively inoffensive (Kerr even had the new stone painted to match the old).

Around the beginning of the First World War the fragile structure of Rosslyn Chapel once more became the target of politically motivated violence. At that period suffragettes were active in southern Scotland: one of their methods of public protest was to target places of worship. Alarmingly, an unexploded bomb was found in May 1913 at St Mary's Episcopal Church, Dalkeith – a spherical iron box filled with gunpowder with a fuse 12–15 yards long.[77]

There was also a 'bomb outrage' in the Observatory at Blackford Hill, Edinburgh, and on 26 February 1914 Whitekirk parish church in East Lothian was, tragically, set on fire. Then the protesters evidently turned their attention to Rosslyn Chapel:

An alarming attempt was made late on Saturday evening to injure the historic chapel of which Roslin is so proud. For months past the building has been zealously guarded, because of numerous hints which had been given as to the

Rosslyn Chapel from the north-west, showing the west transepts and Andrew Kerr's 1881 baptistry. (Crown Copyright by permission of the Royal Commission on the Ancient and Historical Monuments of Scotland)

St Mary's Episcopal Church, Dalkeith – photograph by Philip Cockburn (*c.* 1830– *c.* 1925), a local draper and keen amateur photographer. (By permission of Midlothian Library Service)

probability of the chapel being a structure which might tempt the apparently insatiable mind of the Suffragette to wreck. About a quarter to eleven o'clock a low heavy sound like the boom of a cannon startled a number of persons who were passing in the vicinity of the chapel. An examination of the building did not reveal that any damage had been done, but at what is known as the Lower Chapel [the crypt] it was observed that a small bomb had been placed in a niche on the outside of one of the windows. A piece of metal similar in size and shape to a saucer was discovered not far off. Some Suffragette literature was also found in proximity to the chapel, but outwith the grounds, and naturally enough Suffragettes were suspected.[78]

Happily, the chapel survived. But there were to be major changes of personnel. In March 1913, Thomas Thomson, a long-time servant of Rosslyn Chapel, retired, having been custodian there for thirty-one years.[79] One of Mr Thomson's duties had been to conduct many distinguished visitors over the building, and his characteristic lecture tour was always much appreciated. While working at Roslin he became involved in many aspects of village life, principally problems of lighting, water and drainage. He was for twenty years chairman of the Rosslyn Bowling Club, secretary of the Curling Club for nine years and, as a Freemason, a former Master of Lodge Rosslyn St Clair No. 606.[80]

Further repairs took place in 1915, when the roof of the chapel was covered in a protective layer of asphalt. As for nearby Rosslyn Castle, its condition was becoming more precarious. During the summer of 1928 it was confirmed that some of the walls were in a dangerous condition.[81] Over the following years the Earl's family tried to secure central government grants for the necessary repairs. One problem was the status of the building: as a scheduled monument, the castle was given 'guardianship' status in 1936, and after the Second World War this was being actively reviewed.[82]

Rosslyn Castle at that time had an important complementary role to the operation of Rosslyn Chapel as a tourist attraction: the castle dining room operated as a public

The parish church of St Mary, Whitekirk, East Lothian, to which Aeneas Silvius Piccolomini walked barefoot in thanksgiving for his survival from a storm at sea, in the winter of 1435.

restaurant in 1951 and urgently needed upgrading by the installation of new toilet facilities.[83] But the architect Peter Herd reported to the Ministry of Works that there was slight subsidence in the castle courtyard.[84] What gave greater concern, however, was part of the structure of the castle near the old drawbridge: between 40 and 50 tons of masonry were found to be resting on a single stone corbel, which was already showing alarming signs of fracture.[85] These urgent repairs were immediately effected.

As for the chapel, although no major reconstruction work was undertaken there in the inter-war years, the roof was again recovered in the 1930s. By the 1950s, however, it became increasingly clear that the time had also come to consider making significant invasive repairs to the chapel.

A structural report on Rosslyn Chapel for the Ancient Monuments Branch of the Ministry of Works was completed in 1954, with suggestions as to how the problems could be solved. The condition of the internal choir roof was of great concern as it was covered with green algae, while many parts had turned black with dampness, dirt, decay and cobwebs. The conclusions of the report were accepted and acted upon: using a solution of ammonia and water, the surfaces covered with algae were scrubbed with stiff bristle brushes. Gaps in the carved stone decoration were grouted where necessary. When all surfaces had been thoroughly dried, the stone was strengthened with silica fluoride of magnesium applied to the interior of the chapel.

The north door, seen through the anchored galvanised steel supports of the temporary roofing. (By permission of Rosslyn Chapel Trust)

Struts and finials: looking eastwards from the walkway round Rosslyn Chapel and under the protective canopy. This facility allows the visitor to see in close-up arresting features of the chapel building that would otherwise be inaccessible. (By permission of Rosslyn Chapel Trust)

This was (and still is) a well-tried, standard industry procedure for dealing with crumbling sandstone: it formed a chemical bond with the stone itself, so effectively hardening it. However, the final stage of the chosen treatment – the application of shellac and a coat of creamy white cementitious paint to produce an impermeable surface – was more questionable, as, by destroying its characteristic porosity, it made it impossible for the stone to breathe.[86] Over time this would lead to the chapel becoming saturated with water and soluble pollutants, which had entered via the roof above, while there were also significant aesthetic drawbacks to the process – the painted coating replaced the original (and widely admired) variegated yellow, pink and grey stone colouring of the interior of the chapel with a plain and uniform off-white, yoghurt-like surface, which obscured and coarsened the intricacies of the stone carvings.

The final process in this restoration was the construction of a new asphalt roof over both the chapel and the crypt (which had been leaking badly) and the installation of new oil-fired central heating.

The cleaning of the chapel's stone carvings produced some unexpected discoveries: edging his way along a plank in the scaffolding of the interior, the custodian, John Taylor, realised that under the cobwebs and the dust were exquisite images quite

One-eyed head beside the south door. The head is normally upside-down but has been reversed here to make it easier to recognise. (By permission of Rosslyn Chapel Trust)

invisible from the ground. Among Mr Taylor's surprise discoveries were the St Clair coat-of-arms with two hands (even the finger nails were crisply carved) gripping a shield, the figure of Christ wearing a crown of thorns, with the mark of the nails visible in his hands, and Noah's Ark with a dove flying out of it.[87]

Meanwhile, it was with some relief that in April 1983 news came that the Secretary of State for Scotland, George Younger, had decided to sanction a grant of £60,000 towards the cost of restoring the habitable parts of Rosslyn Castle and of carrying out essential repairs to the ruins. However, some damage to the chapel (thankfully only minor) was caused in late September 1987 when earth tremors (recorded as between 1.0 and 1.6 on the Richter scale), affecting Roslin, Rosewell, Auchendinny and Loanhead, cracked the plaster in a number of homes and damaged some of the medieval carvings in the chapel.[88]

By 1995, however, greater structural deterioration was reported, including increasing humidity. After much consultation, a decision was taken to dry the masonry, allowing the paint and shellac coatings to be removed and so reinstating the original permeability of the stone.

Also in 1995 the Rosslyn Chapel Trust was set up to oversee the conservation and care of the chapel. To achieve this, a robust, free-standing steel structure was erected in March 1997 under the management of the Rosslyn Chapel trustees to let the building dry from the top down and from the inside out. This was accomplished with the help of the Heritage Lottery Fund, Historic Scotland, Midlothian Council, Leader Tyne Esk and as a project part-financed by the European Union.

The restoration of Rosslyn Chapel caught the imagination of an increasing number of members of the general public, celebrities and conservationists. In April 1998, for example, Prince Charles came to Roslin for the first time. He expressed his great interest in the chapel carvings and the restoration programme to architect James Simpson and was shown over the chapel by the chairman of the board of trustees, Peter St Clair-Erskine, 7th Earl of Rosslyn.[89]

Simpson and Brown's conservation plan for Rosslyn Chapel (May 2001) again had the 1953–7 restoration work analysed. They found that a largely impermeable limewash (calcium carbonate) coating had been applied to the internal walls, along with a shellac/methylated spirits solution; chronic water ingress had caused the coating to form gypsum, resulting in encrustations, blistering and detachments from the stone surface.[90]

Meanwhile, curiosity as to what secrets the chapel might hold continued unabated. In 1991 the Friends of Rosslyn, who at that time had a curatorial responsibility for the chapel, undertook a number of investigations of the fabric.[91] Between 17 and 18 June 1991, for example, surveys were carried out by Ground-Scan Ltd for Niven Sinclair and Andrew Sinclair (both members of the Friends of Rosslyn) working with Timon Films Ltd.[92] This survey covered the forecourt and vaults of the castle and the chapel, where ground-sensing was carried out to the west of the west wall and the garden behind College Hill. The scans found that, as Andrew Kerr had previously discovered, there were continuous footings defining the transepts and nave walls, but also no sign of any metal chalice inside the Prince's Pillar. Exploratory bores were drilled immediately below the chapel's east wall, but, after a week of drilling into the lower vaults and attempts to insert an endoscope to look into the vaults below, the engulfing rubble and sand finally made it impossible to proceed any further. Nevertheless, speculation did not diminish as to the mysteries that the chapel might contain – ranging from the Ark of the Covenant, to the mummified head of Jesus Christ, to a lost Christian Gospel, a second Stone of Destiny or even to its alternative incarnation as an intergalactic mothership.[93]

Happily, impervious to all such cargo-cult pseudo-scientific theories (which misinterpret Rosslyn Chapel's Christian function and symbolism), Rosslyn Chapel has retained its character and its magnetic glamour despite the relative indignity of the protective roof that still remains in place.[94] The umbrella-like covering has the additional benefit of allowing visitors on the elevated walkway (which runs round three sides of the chapel) to examine the beautifully carved and detailed upper sections of the chapel exterior in close-up; they can also enjoy the stunning panorama of Roslin Glen stretching to the east far below and the imposing silhouette of the rolling Pentland Hills further to the west, so enhancing the tourist experience (which is the subject of our next chapter).

Perhaps visitors can hear the canons of Rosslyn softly chanting their triple mantra of praise 'Holy, holy, holy' (Rev. 4: 8). They proclaimed the victory of Christ and his angels over Death and Chaos – 'Michael with his angels attacked the dragon . . . The great dragon, the primeval serpent' (Rev. 12: 7), and the canons then finished with the hymn of thanksgiving 'Worthy is the Lamb that was sacrificed' (Rev. 5: 12). It is language and imagery such as this that pulsate through the chapel and its carvings, making manifest the very contemporary struggle between Good and Evil.

CHAPTER 3

Visiting Rosslyn Chapel

THE MODERN TOURIST EXPERIENCE

Today, the visitor travels by car or bus south from Edinburgh, or speeds north from the Scottish Borders, or takes the city by-pass from West Lothian or East Lothian, or simply approaches from within Midlothian. Some may cycle but few today will walk. And yet, from the time the chapel began to be constructed in the 1440s, it would have been reached mainly by foot, sometimes on horseback, in a more leisurely pilgrimage, often over rough tracks or rutted roads and, in spite of the king's rule of law, often in danger of ambush from thieves or predatory wild animals. In the eighteenth century, of course, the well-to-do would have travelled to Rosslyn by carriage.

Born out of Sir William Sainteclaire's passion for the service of God and his fear of eternal damnation, Rosslyn Chapel was very precious to its founder: the enormous investment he made in time and money reflected the importance he placed on loyalty to his God and king and on his responsibility to bring Gospel values down to earth by making 'God's Kingdom come'.

The venerable building we see today, wrapped in a cat's cradle of steel, seems to struggle out of the shadows cast by the canopy that enmeshes it, like some giant but ancient crab emerging out of the primordial slime. As you approach the chapel through the visitor centre you come face to face with the north door. The chapel sits, tethered like a ship in

The chapel stands preserved but enmeshed in a 'cat's cradle', much as it is also entangled in a web of extravagant speculation. (By permission of Rosslyn Chapel Trust)

Looking up at the soaring chapel roof past the elegant brass Victorian candelabra. (By permission of Rosslyn Chapel Trust)

port, but a ship with only half a keel – unfulfilled, the nave still waiting to rise, it exists today only as a wished-for vision. Rosslyn Chapel, for all its extravagant beauty, is only half a church, an unfinished dream, a miniature medieval foreshadowing of Gaudí's long-unfinished Barcelona masterpiece, the Sagrada Familia.

Construction at Rosslyn Chapel seems to have stopped abruptly when the builders reached the west end of the choir; they did not complete its great central tower as other nearby collegiate churches did – Seton Collegiate Church, East Lothian (1488), or Crichton Collegiate Church, Midlothian (1446), finished theirs, although, like Rosslyn, their naves were never built. In Rosslyn's case, construction ground to a halt probably because too much time and energy had been expended on the decoration of the choir, the inner sanctum of the church, the power-house where masses were offered daily for the Sainteclaire family.[1]

The modern visitor sees that, like all Christian churches, Rosslyn Chapel faces to the east, to the sunrise, to Jerusalem – an elderly space rocket, with half its payload

Heavily eroded stone carvings at the base of one of the statue niches. (By permission of Rosslyn Chapel Trust)

The belly-shaped bowl of a piscina (wash-hand basin) at the west transept. (By permission of Rosslyn Chapel Trust)

missing, and no fuel. The skin of the chapel, rough as if from ancient eczema, is grizzled and stained by the weather, its grey, yellow and warm pink stone a many-coloured coat. Strangely, it does not wince when we peer at it or point our digital cameras into its pockmarks and blemishes, its intimate orifices or the scars that time and angry men have left behind, or when we stare with fascination at the blood-red iron oxide tears oozing silently down the stone.

Suddenly, conger eels with iron jaws erupt out of the gable, dripping horrors, straight out of Ridley Scott's *Alien*. Your eye is caught by a stunted, quivering subhuman creature, its limbs lashed together as if for roasting, frozen in the stone beside the door. This is one of Rosslyn's gargoyles with the look of a frenzied animal crazed by hunger.

Walking to the west exterior end of the chapel, up to the decayed north and south transepts, you see the ragged rubble filling of the uncompleted wall exposed like fractured bone. The once-pristine carvings (intended as little pedestals for long-broken saints or for use as washbasins at masses celebrated for the repose of the founder's soul) are leprous, deformed and eroded by the wind.

At this stage, it is important to recognise that the fifteenth-century building we see in front of us today is, first of all, not as it was intended (because it is unfinished); second, that it has been stripped of much of its decoration and ornament, losing (unbelievable as it may appear) much of the complex and well-loved symbolism with which it was originally provided; and, third, that additions and alterations have been made over the centuries that were never envisaged by Sir William Sainteclaire nor anticipated by his architects. The truncated Rosslyn Chapel we see today comprises only that highly personal part of the church built over the final resting place of members of the Sainteclaire family.

Who can guide us in understanding the chapel today, in its brokenness, weighed down as it is with the many changes that have been forced upon it? Outstanding among the historians of Rosslyn Chapel is the informed and dignified voice of the Revd John Thompson (1839–1917), who has been much quoted (and will continue to be so). Thompson speaks from a specially intimate knowledge of the chapel, after his many productive years as the Episcopal priest in charge and as chaplain (1886–1913) to the Earl of Rosslyn.

Something of Thompson's importance as a historian and priest can be gathered from how he was remembered. At his funeral in the chapel, his son and daughter joined the mourners (his wife had died in 1906) in listening to his successor as chaplain, the Revd Dr E.F. Morrison, comment that Mr Thompson's 'life of strenuous devotion to the Chapel, to his congregation and to the Church at large' might well be summed up in the words 'Lord, I have loved the habitation of Thy house and the place where Thine honour dwelleth'.[2]

Thompson's great achievement is to have written a small but highly accessible guidebook that proved so popular with the Victorian public that it was republished time and again. Thompson's unassuming *The Illustrated Guide to Rosslyn Chapel and Castle, Hawthornden, &c.* (Edinburgh, 1892) has ever since been the sturdy foundation for every good guide to Rosslyn Chapel. The present author will not presume to differ, only enlarging on John Thompson's succinct account and updating (where necessary) his

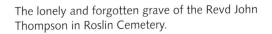

The lonely and forgotten grave of the Revd John Thompson in Roslin Cemetery.

The north door showing a lion gargoyle above and a monkey clutching his knees below. (By permission of Rosslyn Chapel Trust)

text with the help of photographs; Thompson himself used illustrations only sparingly, in the form of line-drawings of the plans of the chapel and castle.

At the beginning of his slim publication of 126 pages, Thompson (a Fellow of the Society of Antiquaries of Scotland) hints at his personal assessment of the decorative scheme of the chapel. Taking a lead from the prurient and somewhat hidebound philosophy of the Gothic Revival, he does not entirely approve of what he sees as the often crude and exaggerated medieval carvings at Rosslyn Chapel. Even to his modestly tasteful nineteenth-century eye, some aspects were inelegantly devised and difficult to take seriously (particularly on the exterior); yet there were other features (mainly within the chapel) that took his breath away.

Thompson tried hard to be balanced.

There are, doubtless, many things which the critical eye cannot but condemn, but there is undoubtedly very much to admire, and not a few things to puzzle the antiquarian. There is a great deal to be seen outside to excite wonder and admiration: much that is grotesque and amusing. For example, on the north side, besides the strange gargoyles over the porch, there is to the right a man with pointed ears, bound round with ropes; a man with a stick between his arms and legs; a warrior on horseback. On the left of the door is a representation of the ancient nursery rhyme, viz., a fox running away with a goose, with a farmer (or perhaps his wife) in pursuit: and many others too numerous to mention; while heads, and hands holding foliage, appear in all imaginable and unimaginable places.[3]

What we have to appreciate is that, since Thompson first wrote these words in 1892, many details of the carvings have been erased by weathering or other damage – and that is an additional reason for using his invaluable guide as a starting-point, for he is able to describe features that are no longer wholly decipherable.

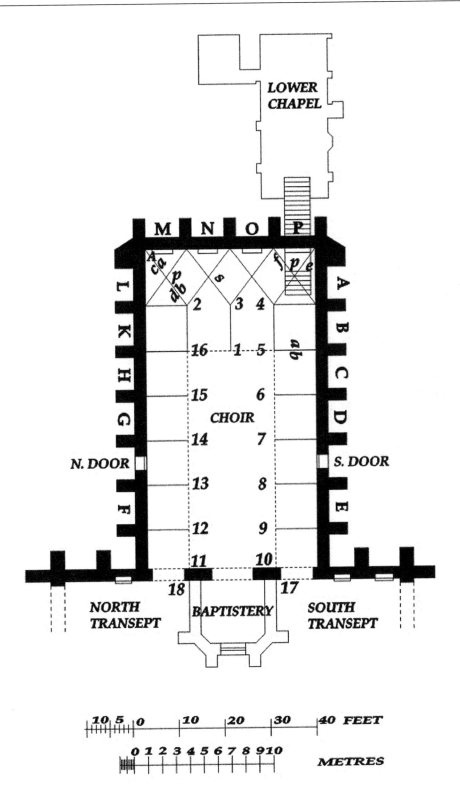

A ground plan of Rosslyn Chapel. (By permission of Adrian Bloore)

THE EXTERIOR

As we begin our visit to the chapel, it is best to part company with Mr Thompson and his guide for a little while and try to explore those aspects of the chapel that he found unappetising. In spite of the greater attraction that the interior of the chapel has for him, the exterior (particularly with today's functional walkway high above the ground) offers the visitor a revealing glimpse into the iconography (and perhaps also the psychology) of our medieval past. We can examine, for example, the strange and rather barbarous stone pinnacles and their carvings from just a few feet away, instead of staring from ground level a considerable distance upwards.

The outside of a building, of course, is what the visitor sees first and so it probably makes a more immediate and lasting impression than the interior. Rosslyn Chapel's exterior, for all its sadly truncated and weathered shape, is in its own way as powerful as the interior is dazzling. In the external and unfinished north and south transepts it is even possible to glimpse the construction methods of the stonemasons with the rubble infilling between the outer and inner courses of the dressed stone, much patched by later hands. Furthermore, the weathered texture of the external masonry has an excitement all its own and shows the true face of Rosslyn Chapel – the exterior walls fortunately escaped being coated in the deadening, cream-coloured and all-enveloping coating of silica fluoride of magnesium applied in the mid-1950s. In the weathered exterior of the chapel it is as if it were possible to read this ancient building's character from the lines and furrows and blotches on its skin and through the deformations of its body.

Here it is worth making two more points about the appearance of the chapel. First, it is generally accepted that images, signs and symbols were used in churches during the Middle Ages because most of the congregation would have been unable to read or write – such also was partly the purpose of the geometric stonemasons' marks that were used to determine qualification for payment. Images, signs and symbols were designed as visual aids during weekly services such as the masses, much as we use colour-coding in traffic lights or football shirts today. Second, symbols, naturally, have to communicate immediately, or they fail in their purpose. Introducing some comic figure or a well-known nursery rhyme (of the kind that every mother might tell her children) would reinforce the Christian story for illiterate worshippers in the pews and would be as popular as cartoons are today. Hence there would be no sense in making the symbols and signs in the church comprehensible only to an esoteric clique – as some modern Freemasons or Templars claim – nor could such symbols be reasonably supposed to operate at two levels of meaning: one for the illiterate and one for the cognoscenti.

Part of the distaste experienced and the reservations voiced by the Revd John Thompson and his generation at Rosslyn Chapel was due to the fact that the rude and crude realities of medieval life were frozen for ever in stone in a building whose primary purpose was to provide solemnity in worship. The exuberance of the stonemasons who carved the racy scenes from medieval folklore on top of a pillar, or introduced onto a lintel a smirking human face with vegetation oozing out of its

The menacing face of a grinning half-human Green Man on the chapel wall. (By permission of Rosslyn Chapel Trust)

skin, was rooted in a down-to-earth view of life that understood that solemn rituals were only part of religion – that, as Fr Roland Walls, priest in charge at Rosslyn Chapel (1962–8) observed, nonsense, nothingness and insignificance are powerful ways to open people up to God.[4] But such subtleties did not endear themselves to the po-faced and bowdlerising devotees of the Gothic Revival.

As you walk round the outside walls and go inside the chapel, you have to remember that from the time of the Scottish Reformation (1560) up to c. 1736 there was no glass whatsoever in the chapel windows. In 1736 plain glass was installed and the windows were further protected by external wooden shutters and heavy interlaced iron bars. However, according to the evidence of the Hill and Adamson photographic images taken in the 1840s, the glazing extended only to the two upright lights, while the asymmetrical tear-drop tracery above was left open and unglazed. None of the coloured stained glass to be seen today at Rosslyn Castle is medieval: it was all placed there in a series of installations, beginning in the 1860s. Neither the great east window nor the west window contains any pre-nineteenth-century glass.

One of the biggest changes in the chapel between the medieval era and modern times is that, as you walk around the exterior and the interior, you will be able to count around 200 now-empty plinths and niches (beginning at ground level on the buttresses, then on the pointed finials and finally around the windows); they were

Variation of flower-pot-shaped statue niche supports. (By permission of Rosslyn Chapel Trust)

originally intended to support large, medium and small stone figures on the exterior and, probably, a similar range of statues in the interior, many of these being relatively fragile ones made of wood or plaster to reduce their weight. They would have been painted with bright colours and probably also decorated with silver and gold leaf to catch the flickering lights of the many candles or the bright rays of the sun. Similarly, we can expect many of the carvings to have been painted, with key parts of the design highlighted to add to their impact.

Not all those who visited the chapel were able to resist the opportunity to exaggerate (so often a temptation of travel writers): John Macky, who came to Roslin in the early eighteenth century (perhaps uncritically accepting the descriptions of an impressionable assistant), inflates the scale of the carvings at Rosslyn: 'It's a Gothick Building on the Outside each Buttress being adorned with Statues as big as the life in the Niches; and of each Side of the Windows, which are very spacious.'[5] But, setting aside the over-enthusiasm of those who have gone before us, it is now time to start our tour proper by walking towards the external south-east corner of the building to the first bay with its window (which, after John Thompson's arrangement, is labelled **A** on the ground plan).

Roslin Glen seen from the east end of the chapel. (By permission of Rosslyn Chapel Trust)

We will find ourselves at a location that offers an impressive panorama of the wooded expanse of Roslin Glen far below – which may well explain the broad stone seats fitted below the windows of the east wall. As with most churches built in the Christian tradition, Rosslyn Chapel is designed to be a public landmark, calling men and women to worship in a place where they can be enabled to bring heaven down to earth.

THE SOUTH WALL

We begin by moving westwards along the usually sun-warmed exterior south wall of the chapel. Inside the left side of the hood (a partly decorative protective moulding) of the first window (see **A** on the ground plan) is what looks like a lamb, with another similar image on the right, but the weathering of the stone is so advanced that it is difficult to be sure. Whatever figures were once around the second window (**B**) there have also been eroded beyond recognition. The next window (**C**) is more promising, as it features a Green Man at the base of the right inside part of the window hood, and a horn player at the base of the one on the left.

At the fourth window (**D**), the base of the left side of the hood has what seems to be a lamb, the left plinth below evidently shows a camel and the base of the right half of the window is carved with a monkey, while from the right plinth a griffin with bat wings leers provocatively.

Next is the South Door. Here we see an angel holding a musical instrument on the base of the left window hood with two Green Men under the left plinth, an angel holding a scroll at the base of the right window hood, with two more Green Men beside it. Finally, two gargoyles can be seen below the right plinth. The south side of the chapel ends with a window (**E**), the base of whose left inside section of the hood is decorated with figures of two men playing musical instruments, one strumming a harp (on the base of the right inside part of the hood) and a monkey clutching its knees on the right buttress. This collection of figures and animals has all the grotesque fascination of a circus.

THE TRANSEPTS

At the south transept is another dog-like gargoyle. Note the fine carving of the small, angular canopies surmounting the empty niches. At the south-facing wall end of the transept the consecration cross can still be seen. As we turn the corner at the end of the southern extremity of the west wall, the intimate inside wall of the central sacred space comes into view: high above the south wall of the Victorian baptistry is a heavily carved but well-weathered plinth; below, at around head height, are three evenly spaced and robustly carved plinths for statues. We see the evidence of the place's religious functions – a hand basin with a funnel-shaped drain known as a *piscina* (pool of water). This would have been a very practical fitting for making sure the hands of

the priest, his assistants and the two little choir boys were clean of grime or dirt, ready (much as a surgeon preparing for an operation) to perform the sacred mysteries. Beside it is a sacrament house, a carved recess for keeping the consecrated bread (known as hosts today). In the corner of the join between the transept and the baptistry, thin multiple pillars rise to a carved figure, while, high above the baptistry roof is a carved plinth (17) depicting St Christopher with the infant Jesus in his arms.

Pass round the outside of the baptistry, with its statues of the

Piscina at the west transept. (By permission of Rosslyn Chapel Trust)

Andrew Kerr's the four Evangelists, Anna and St Anne around the baptistery. (By permission of Rosslyn Chapel Trust)

four Evangelists (Matthew, Mark, Luke and John), Anna the prophetess and St Anne. Go to the north side of the transept, where there is an almost identical layout, except that there is no sacrament house this time and the statue at the corner of the wall and the baptistry is different – what appears to be the figure of a very confident man, posing proudly with legs apart. High above the baptistry is the base of a plinth (18) depicting St Sebastian tied to a tree by two men, his martyrdom indicated by the arrows sticking out of his left side.

At the north-facing end of the north transept is a carving of a devil with a rope running round his back and behind his knees. Perhaps he is tied up for punishment, or perhaps he is merely enjoying himself swaying on a tree swing?

THE NORTH WALL

Progressing round to the left of the first window (F) on the north side of the chapel, we find carvings of a man's face, with a ram and a bush under the left plinth, another face on the right inside and a man on horseback on the outside.

Now we arrive at the North Door (also known as the Bachelors' Door, reflecting the fact that at one time male and female worshippers were segregated in the chapel).

Heavily weathered monkey-shaped figure clutching an object to its chest. (By permission of Rosslyn Chapel Trust)

To the left of the door is an angel and to the right a head with a plaque; to his right again is what appears to be a monkey – in medieval iconography a symbol of wilfulness and indiscriminate destruction.

Going on to the next window (**G**) we are confronted by yet another Green Man at the bottom of the left hood moulding, with a man beside him, apparently engaged in eating and another with a bird under the left plinth. Visitors can make up their minds whether these figures provide a coherent underlying message or are simply a wilfully playful and whimsical collection of carvings intended to entertain and surprise worshipper and visitor alike.

A human face with grinning teeth sits at the left of the following window (**H**) and below it is a snake, part of a series of images that would have communicated as powerfully as a comic strip does today.

To the right a man holds a book (perhaps a cue for the illiterate congregation or the choirboys that it is worth going to school). To the left of window (**K**) is a much-damaged angel counterbalanced by a devil on the right, while window (**L**) – the last one on the north side – displays a face on the left, monkeys on the right and a hand carved onto the right buttress.

THE EAST WALL

Turn the corner to your right to the east side of the chapel. The first window (**M**) has a human head and shoulders on the left, a Green Man on the right and a sinister squatting figure under the right plinth. The next window (**N**) has a Green Man on the left, while the following window (**O**) has a devil at the end of the left side of the hood and a man below the left plinth. Finally, window (**P**) has two sets of what appear to be animals – one at the end of the left inside moulding, and one at the end of the left side of the hood.

THE INTERIOR

Much of this weathered or deliberately damaged extravagance of ornamentation is dismissed by John Thompson with the words 'heads, and hands holding foliage, appear in all imaginable and unimaginable places', which seems to imply less a disapproval of Green Men than that he considered the apparent lack of overall control of the details of the decorative design as evidence of degeneracy and confusion. However, Thompson reveals his instinctive passion for antiquarianism in a subsequent comment: 'The most interesting figures . . . are to be found in the interior. Many of these are not easily seen, and may easily be passed over, unless you know where to look for them. Indeed, they are a separate study, and need frequent visits and careful examination, and a good light to see them properly.'[6] The last is a piece of advice we can all take to heart.

According to Thompson, the measurements of the choir are 48 feet 4 inches by 17 feet 10½ inches, with a height of 33½ feet to the springing arched roof (including aisles and Lady Chapel), the total length being 69 feet 8 inches, the breadth 35 feet, the height (to the apex of the roof) reaching 41 feet 9 inches.

The first point to remember when entering the chapel is that most of the interior structure we see does not have the original fifteenth-century warm pink, yellow and grey stone, nor the bright colours that once probably highlighted the carvings. Today, the walls and carvings of the interior of the chapel look seamlessly blanched, giving the effect (in the words of the eminent architectural historian Colin McWilliam) of icing on a wedding-cake.[7]

However, even in the days of John Thompson, much of the finer detail of the carvings seems already to have been lost, either through the effects of deliberate destruction at the Reformation or when General George Monck stabled his horses in the chapel in 1650 while laying siege to Rosslyn Castle, or in December 1688 when an angry mob attacked the building, having heard that William of Orange was heading for England. Thompson warns us sadly: 'Unfortunately, a good many of the carvings have been so defaced as to make it rather difficult to decipher them.'

Naive and unassuming, an angel carrying a scroll. (By permission of Rosslyn Chapel Trust)

Chunky stone blooms at the door from the baptistry into the choir. (By permission of Rosslyn Chapel Trust)

In spite of such painful misgivings, John Thompson ushers us reverently into the ancient building, not (as so often today) by the North Door, but from what would have been the nave of the chapel, through the fragmented west transepts, via the Victorian baptistry, moving forward towards the east.

THE BAPTISTRY

In the relative darkness of the baptistry, the two stained-glass windows (right and left) shine out: to the left is Carrick Whalen's vision of St Francis of Assisi surrounded by animals and birds (most appropriate in the rich environment of Roslin Glen), dedicated to Princess Dimitri, grandmother of the present 7th Earl and a well-known lover of animals. The window was put in place in 1970.

To the right is William Wilson's figure of an airman on the White Cliffs of Dover, celebrating the life of the present Earl's uncle, the Hon. Peter St Clair Erskine, who died while on active service in 1939, and of his stepfather, Wing Commander Sir John Milbanke, who died in 1947 from the injuries he suffered during the war. Both windows were commissioned by the 6th Earl of Rosslyn, the second completed in 1950.

Down to the left of the west door into the chapel, set into the wall, is an aumbry (a small stone cupboard used to hold precious vessels for mass). Round each side of the west door chunky stone blooms welcome you with enthusiastic ripeness. You step into the choir, not knowing quite what to expect.

THE CHOIR

In an instant, the roof is high overhead. It soars away like an enormous hang-glider, as if you were upside down in an aeroplane and saw, far below, a field richly planted with symbols – reminiscent of clusters of five-pointed stars (like those on the shoulders of a Russian general), of wild roses, daisies, lilies and other flowers.

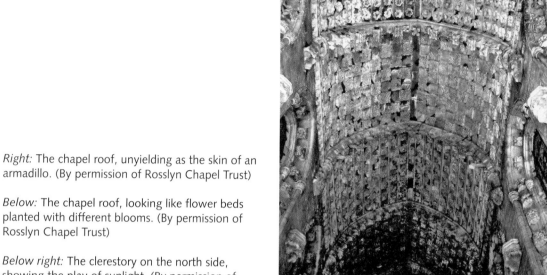

Right: The chapel roof, unyielding as the skin of an armadillo. (By permission of Rosslyn Chapel Trust)

Below: The chapel roof, looking like flower beds planted with different blooms. (By permission of Rosslyn Chapel Trust)

Below right: The clerestory on the north side, showing the play of sunlight. (By permission of Rosslyn Chapel Trust)

The choir, which comprises the main part of the existing building, is supported by thirteen shafted or beaded pillars with carved capitals (each 8 feet in height), which form an arcade of twelve pointed arches, five on each side, and two under the east gable, while three other pillars divide the east aisle from the Lady Chapel. Over the arcade is an ornamental string course, above which are clerestory windows of single lights, without tracery, five on each side. The east window, which is of two lights, is on the same level as the clerestory windows, but much larger and much higher.

Between the clerestory windows is a double row of brackets for statues, the canopy of the lower forming the base of that above. Here perhaps once stood a figure of the Virgin and Child. Figures of the Apostles and other saints would have occupied all the other brackets up to the Reformation, when they were either removed or destroyed.

As noted above, there were four altars in the Lady Chapel, dedicated (from the north side) to St Matthew, the Virgin Mary, St Andrew and St Peter, the last referred to in Victorian times as the high altar. It stood on an elevated platform in order to give headroom to the stair leading down to the crypt. The high altar proper would have been in the centre of the choir, where it is today.

On your right hand, at the west door into the choir, directly overhead, guarding the entrance to the sanctuary of God, one of the stone blocks is carved with an angel; on a second block is another angel (but this time with a sword); while near the rib is a group of two figures; on the block above is yet another angel, both hands uplifted.

The word 'angel' is derived from the Greek *angelos* meaning a messenger and describes what in the Middle Ages were believed to be spiritual intelligences who could move from place to place and communicate instantly but unobstrusively with one another.[8] Angels were divided into three hierarchies, each with three subordinate orders: seraphim, cherubim, thrones; dominations, principalities, powers; virtues, archangels, angels. Each kind of angel had different responsibilities and functions. They were one of the ways in which God was believed to protect and advise human beings. The fact that they were usually shown with wings is an Assyrian characteristic also still retained in the modern symbolic use of the Greek goddess Nike to represent speed and effectiveness.

You may have observed that the left-hand part of the roof has an astronomical dimension, for it contains a crescent moon and a small star at the lowest corner of its first compartment, perhaps references to the birth of Christ and the journey of the Magi. Above is a fluttering dove with outspread wings, symbol of the Holy Ghost, the Comforter (Paraclete), the third person of the Blessed Trinity, who, in absolute unity, was understood to proceed from the Father and the Son.

This was the great mystery of the Christian faith but also a paradigm for the human family. The Holy Ghost (or Holy Spirit) is expressed by fire and wind, the breath of the Word of God, and God breathing over the waters in the process of Creation, and this was the principal function of the chapel: to communicate the Gospel and help the Word become Flesh by uniting God and Man.

On the third block of stone above is a sun, carved like a gas burner with beams of fiery light jetting from its sides. The sun signifies warmth and fruitfulness in

Angel with pudding-basin haircut, clutching the Holy Scriptures. (By permission of Rosslyn Chapel Trust)

personal relationships and in the bountifulness of harvest. The sun was also the Roman emperor Constantine's way of making sense of his swithering allegiance to Sol (the pagan God of the Sun) and the new Sun, Jesus Christ, Son of God, whose Greek *Chi Rho* saltire cross Constantine saw burning in the red beams of the setting sun on the eve of the battle of the Milvian Bridge (AD 312), which was fought against the rival emperor Maxentius across the River Tiber in Rome.

Below the sun is a carving of an open hand, a symbol of trust, generosity and friendship. It is also the sign of peace, of the absence of threat – the hand of beggar and sinner, asking for alms or for forgiveness.

Now, surrounded as you probably are by curious fellow-visitors, you need to turn quickly back towards the west, to look high above the level of the north door, where the roof curves steeply down to meet the north and south walls. Here is said to be evidence of the tragic fate of the young apprentice who is understood to have been executed by the furious master mason for exceeding his remit by carving the elaborate Prince's Pillar while the master mason was away in Italy.

In the north-west corner, at the very apex of the roof, you may see a face with what appears to be a deep gash on its right temple – believed by some to be that of the unfortunate apprentice. On the south side (under the pedestal of the niche with a statue of St Paul), about halfway up the west wall of the choir, is yet another head of the apprentice, also with a deep wound to the right temple; in the opposite corner is, some believe, that of the jealous master who killed him.

Panorama of the chapel and the east window with its elaborately reconstructed Victorian tracery. (By permission of Rosslyn Chapel Trust)

To the east of the apprentice's head the tale of blood and revenge is completed. There, under the next niche, is yet another head – said to show the sorrowful widowed mother of the apprentice (the legend of the apprentice will be dealt with later in Chapter 4).

When the chapel walls had reached their full height, all these sad and angry heads (telling this cautionary tale of workplace bullying and intimidation) are said to have been carved by the apprentice's fellow-masons as a lesson to posterity and placed in the roof as a way of commemorating the tragic fate of their companion, the talented but unfortunate apprentice.

THE CENTRAL PILLAR

Above the central pillar (1) is a niche of a different design from the rest. It contains a modern figure of the Virgin and Child – the original 200-odd figures here, as elsewhere in the chapel, having been destroyed or perhaps hidden at the Reformation. It is doubtless under this niche that the main altar stood, where mass would have been celebrated on special feast days, which required the participation of every member of the congregation. As it stands today, the chapel can still accommodate a congregation of up to around 140 persons.

Here, at the centre of the Choir the canonical hours would be celebrated, sung together by the canons sitting as a college (*collegiater* in Latin). They would have sat in carved wooden choir stalls, the morning matins and vespers in the evening being sung in common. In such collegiate churches the liturgy was celebrated with great care and ceremonial.

At the back of this central pillar begins a series of tableaux from the Bible, starting with the Fall of Man and the expulsion from Eden. This is a scene that would have been familiar to all adult Christians and would also be an extremely powerful story for children. We can see the Tree of Good and Evil, with two happy figures (Adam and Eve) approaching it and then two tormented ones walking sadly away from it.

On the north side is a huge beast, held back by a chain round its neck, biting a rope, and a man lying flat on his back – an image illustrating the power and strength of sin after the fall from grace. On the opposite, south side, waving palm leaves are depicted, symbolising the victory that Christ achieved over sin.

THE LADY CHAPEL

Moving on from this pillar you come to the Lady Chapel (also known as the Retro-choir). Filling the east end of the building from north to south, the Lady Chapel is 9 feet 6 inches wide and 15 feet high and runs the whole width of Rosslyn Chapel; it is distinguished by the richness of the carvings, especially in the groined roof (formed from two barrel vaults intersecting at right angles) and on the capitals of the pillars.[9]

At the east end in the Lady Chapel (beginning at the north corner), were the four altars dedicated respectively to St Matthew, the Virgin Mary, St Andrew and St Peter.

As mentioned, the last was sometimes also called the high altar, as it stood on a platform to allow headroom for the stairs leading down to the crypt.

The Lady Chapel was set aside for devotion to the Virgin Mary, Our Lady. In medieval Catholicism, it was where the intentions (requests through prayer to God) of the mass were channelled through the intercession of the Mother of God, whose joyous *Magnificat* ('My soul glorifies the Lord') was Man's demonstration of her total submission to the Almighty.[10] The belief was that, imitating the close relationship between a mother and child, the Virgin Mary would have unique access to the Risen Christ and that He would take a special interest in her pleas for help and mercy.

The Lady Chapel would also have been decorated with fresh flowers such as lilies or roses when they were available, and the colour blue (with its evocation of the purity of a cloudless blue sky) would have been used to accentuate the connection with Mary. Here, women and children would have a special place, while the priests and deacons would also have regarded the Virgin Mary as a valuable source of strength to help them persevere with their vocation as men devoted totally to God.

The unique position that devotion to Mary held in the medieval Christian Church is perhaps one of the reasons why the stonemasons lavished such a wealth of ornamentation on this part of the chapel. Yet the relatively small proportion of carvings with biblical themes causes the Revd John Thompson some regret. He makes the comment: 'Yet, even here, the carving seems to be confined to certain sections, probably the result of the death of the founder preventing the original design being carried out in all its planned fullness and profusion: where we might expect to see more human or animal figures there is only greenery and foliage.'

Some of the scenes carved here are not biblical at all, but reflect the stresses and strains of fifteenth-century life. A careful look at the stone ribs of the groined roof in the first (north) compartment of the Lady Chapel, for example, reveals a series of small figures (only about 8 inches long), making up what has been interpreted as a Dance of Death. The Dance of Death was a kind of frightening medieval lambada or conga in which the skeletal figure of Death danced in black all over the countryside (reminiscent of an Ingmar Bergman film) and through the cities, collecting men and women behind him from all walks of life, an obscene Pied Piper. Rich and poor, once unwittingly sucked into the hypnotic rhythm of the dance, could not break free – they could be seen, hands locked together, their journey to the charnel house already begun! The Dance of Death reflects a keen awareness of sin and the fragility of human life at that period and the certainty of punishment; it is an image that also arises from the all too familiar effects of the Black Death.

There are several other moral teaching techniques that the anonymous stonemasons at the chapel employ. We can see the influence of the rumbustious morality and mystery plays, which were so popular in all medieval communities, allowing the expression of feelings and ideas normally discouraged and giving the common people an opportunity to cut the authorities down to size.

We know that, only a year before the Scottish Reformation (1560), morality plays were still being performed at Rosslyn by travelling players. In 1559 William Sainteclaire, Lord Justice General under Mary Queen of Scots, saved a gipsy from a

The Dance of Death, a human chain tugged off to damnation. (By permission of Rosslyn Chapel Trust)

hanging on the green expanses of the Boroughmuir near Edinburgh. The Sainteclaire family had a long-standing relationship with the gypsies, as, every May and June, these came to Rosslyn to present morality, mystery and other traditional plays. The gypsies were provided with accommodation in two of the castle towers, appropriately named Robin Hood and Little John, nicknames taken from one of the gypsies' most popular offerings, the story of Robin Hood.[11]

Perhaps at Rosslyn also, during December, the Abbot of Unreason presided at the chapel and the castle (as he did at Holyroodhouse) or on New Year's Day the King of the Bean ruled. But such frivolities, along with the ever-popular Robin Hood plays, were suppressed in Edinburgh, at least, by order of the provost and bailies in 1579; eight years later, the town council expelled all minstrels, pipers, fiddlers and singers of what were then regarded as profane songs.

The theme of morality is continued in a series of figures that represent all sections of Scottish life. The underlying message is that, no matter what one's station, God knows the human heart and His millstones grind exceeding fine. Springing from a carved human or animal figure designed to support a vault known as a corbel at **A** (see the ground plan), on side *a*, towards the pendant (hanging stone feature) **P**, there are nine figures: (1) an abbot (a senior monk elected as head of a monastic community, living under vows of poverty, chastity and obedience and the rule of the particular religious order to which he belonged); (2) an abbess (elected as leader of a community of nuns, with vows similar to those of a monk); (3) a figure of indeterminate identity, now headless and considerably damaged – perhaps a soldier or even a stonemason; (4) a fine and elegant lady admiring herself in a mirror, rich and unhappy, detached from ordinary human life; (5) a carving completely defaced (perhaps at the time of the Reformation); (6) a bishop (a priest who is the leader of a diocese, normally chosen by Rome and distinguished by the colour purple); (7) a cardinal priest, one of the supreme leaders of the Roman Catholic Church (from among whose number the Pope was normally chosen, distinguished by the colour crimson); (8) a beautifully dressed but obsequious and slippery courtier; finally (9), a magnificent king with power but also responsibility. Looking at these carvings would

Rosslyn Chapel, looking east – a photograph by George Washington Wilson, showing the renovations of 1861, including the new tracery in the east window, installed in 1867.

serve as a powerful reminder to the congregation that wealth and status do not guarantee entry into the Kingdom of Heaven.

Further carvings reinforce the Christian message: rising up from Pillar 2, on side *b*, are seven human figures, this time mainly representatives of the labouring classes, many of whom work on the land or with natural materials: (1) a ploughman, a profession made famous (or notorious) by the fourteenth-century *Piers Plowman*, a Middle English narrative poem by William Langland that measured contemporary society against Gospel values and found it wanting, full of injustice; (2) a carpenter, a craftsman like Jesus and the many itinerant tradesmen who worked for so many years on the construction and repair of the chapel; (3) a gardener with his spade, respecting the land and its fruits; (4) a sportsman or hunter; (5) an innocent child; (6) a husband and wife, trying to live out the teachings of Christ in their humble and poverty-stricken lives; (7) a farmer, perhaps exploiting his workers. However, each of these sixteen figures has a grisly skeleton beside it, suggesting that the message contained in the carvings is 'Memento mori' ('Remember, Man, that thou art Dust . . .') – death knows no barriers, observes no human etiquette, but strikes where it will, and only the just will escape the cleansing fires of Hell.

The Revd Robert Forbes, Episcopal Bishop of Caithness, who knew the chapel well, has an alternative perspective on these carvings, as John Thompson scrupulously records.[12] He believed that these figures all 'represent the Resurrection, by people rising out of their graves like skeletons, and improving into proper forms placed close to the skeletons'. However, the general effect seems less about the dead rising to life and taking on new heavenly bodies than the terrifying experience of the Dance of Death – a chilling reminder to the people who worshipped in the chapel that the result of Adam's Fall meant that no rank, class or station could escape the hand of the Grim Reaper, as the Apostle Paul says: 'so death passed upon all men, for that all have sinned' (Romans 5: 12). Perhaps another sobering truth is alluded to – that 'in the midst of life we are in death'.

The opposite sides of the roof provide some respite from this cavalcade of crime and punishment. Here are gentle doves with olive leaves in their beaks. (The olive leaf or branch was the symbol of fruitfulness, warmth, peace and reconciliation, the sign that the pigeon brought back to Noah after the Flood to signal that dry land was

Botanical decoration at Rosslyn Chapel. (By permission of Rosslyn Chapel Trust)

at hand.) Nearby, the theme of hope is continued in a beautiful carving of the glittering Star of Bethlehem, the star that spurred the Wise Men to leave their palaces or observatories near the Tigris and Euphrates and journey west.

We now move on to the fourth compartment of the roof. Over the stairs leading down to the crypt, on a rib springing up from the south-east wall corbel at location *e*, there are four figures: (1) a fierce soldier, armed with helmet, sharp sword and spear; (2) an itinerant monk, caught in the act of drinking; (3) then cunning and secret death, crouching down beside him, unseen; (4) a man with very wide sleeves (perhaps a lawyer or a merchant). On the opposite side at rib *f*, rising up from a stone corbel on the east wall, are four more figures: (1) a proud and stately queen; (2) a rich and fine lady seated comfortably in a chair; and (3) another lady, deep in prayer; finally (4), another aggressive soldier.

Since these eight figures also have skeletons hovering around them, they are probably linked to the series on the north compartment described earlier. These last eight figures require the visitor to scrutinise walls and roof most carefully, as they are not easy to find – they are on the top of the rib near the roof, facing east. However, the series seems incomplete, for it extends over only half of the stone rib, the rest of the structure being decorated with no more than skilfully carved leaves and other intricate foliage. Perhaps the powers that be had become a little tired of the rather negative messages that the themes of Death and Judgement were intended to convey.

In the other compartments of the groined roofs, the stone ribs are covered in yet more stone foliage, but the pendant *S* is very interesting, as it has a large star with eight points on its lower surface, probably, once again, the Star of Bethlehem announcing the birth of Jesus.

Around it is another set of eight figures. On the southernmost point is (1) the Virgin and Child; on the Virgin's right is (2) the simple wooden manger from which the animals ate in the stable but which was later used as an improvised cradle for the Christ-child; then (3) the Three Kings (Magi), each with a long staff or sceptre in his hand, travelling with their gifts from Persia or Mesopotamia; finally, in complete contrast, (4) the Angel of Death and four other figures, all connected with the birth of Jesus at Bethlehem.

On the decorated capitals of the pillars, facing the star, are twelve Angels (standing for the twelve Apostles), singing or playing musical instruments (among them the bagpipes). They represent the Nativity story's heavenly host who rejoiced and praised God at the birth of Christ (Luke 2: 13).

Nearby, on Pillar 2, is the carving of an angel with a book open before him, perhaps symbolising the proclamation of the Good News of the Gospels first announced at the birth of Jesus by an angel. Here are images of birth and death, snapshots of the key moments in the life of Jesus, in the life of a Christian and in the liturgical cycle of the Church's year, all designed to underscore the Christian message.

No tour of Rosslyn Chapel would be complete without a careful inspection of the incredibly carved stone column to the south east, above the steps down to the crypt. Pillar 4, which the Victorians referred to as the 'Prentice Pillar, and the Dutch ordnance engineer Captain John Slezer in the late eighteenth century called the

Timothy Pont and Jodocus Hondius, *A New Description of the Shyres of Lothian and Linlitquo* (1630). Roslin is in the centre. (By permission of the Trustees of the National Library of Scotland)

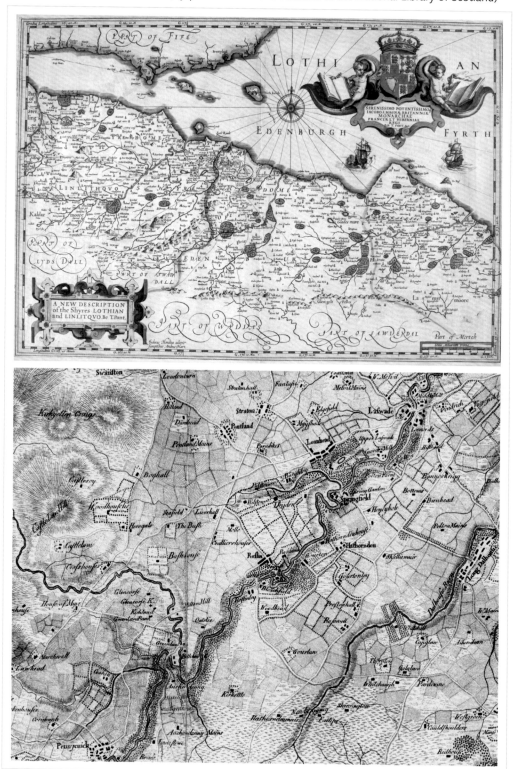

John Laurie, *A Plan of Edinburgh and Places Adjacent* (1766). (By permission of the Trustees of the National Library of Scotland)

A sandstone outcrop in Roslin Glen.

A foot-stile above the river.

Beside the North Esk.

Returning to Roslin and looking back to Bilston Wood.

A Green Man in the roots.   A Green Man on the river path.

A Green Man on the way to Rosslyn Castle.   A young frog on the river path.

Dazzled by sunlight above the river.

Foaming waters.

Glencorse Reservoir, under whose waters lies the chapel of St Catherine in the Hopes, with King's Hill on the left and the Knight's Field on the right.

Soutra Aisle.

St Nicholas, Dalkeith. (By permission of St Nicholas Parish)

Newbattle Abbey crypt. (By permission of Newbattle Abbey College)

Crichton Collegiate Kirk. (By permission of Crichton Parish)

Under the castle arch.

Hart's tongue fern.

Fr Richard Augustine Hay. (By permission
of the Scottish Catholic Archives)   Rosslyn Castle from the river.

Thomas Bonnar, Great Hall ceiling (n.d.). (By permission of Royal Commission on
the Ancient and Historical Monuments of Scotland)

Consecration cross (south end of west transept). (By permission of Rosslyn Chapel Trust)

Old St Matthew's Church in Roslin Cemetery.

John Slezer's view of the chapel (*c*. 1800). (By permission of the Royal Commission on the Ancient and Historical Monuments of Scotland)

Stained-glass windows installed in 1867. (By permission of Rosslyn Chapel Trust)

Detail of the Prince's Pillar. (By permission of Rosslyn Chapel Trust)

The top of the Prince's Pillar. (By permission of
Rosslyn Chapel Trust)

The sacrifice of Abraham and Hart's tongue fern.
(By permission of Rosslyn Chapel Trust)

Dragons at the base of the Prince's Pillar.
(By permission of Rosslyn Chapel Trust)

An hour before the wedding. (By permission of Rosslyn Chapel Trust)

The Eucharist from the Arbuthnot Prayer Book. (By permission of Paisley Museum)

David Roberts, *The Interior of Rosslyn Chapel* (1842), pencil and watercolour.
(By permission of the National Galleries of Scotland)

The east window (1840s), by Hill and
Adamson. (By permission of Glasgow
University Archives)

Stained-glass window in the crypt in memory
of the Fifth Earl of Rosslyn. (By permission of
Rosslyn Chapel Trust)

The grave of the Fourth Earl of Rosslyn. (By permission of Rosslyn Chapel Trust)

The south door. (By permission of Rosslyn Chapel Trust)

Statue canopy (south wall). (By permission of
Rosslyn Chapel Trust)

Window moulding with Green Man.

The chapel roof. (By permission of Rosslyn
Chapel Trust)

The Lady Chapel. (By permission of Rosslyn
Chapel Trust)

College Hill House and the Pentlands beyond. Gargoyle drain-spout at the south door.
(By permission of Rosslyn Chapel Trust)   (By permission of Rosslyn Chapel Trust)

Window mouldings. (By permission of Rosslyn Chapel Trust)

Rosslyn Chapel from the air looking west (1997), with the village graveyard top left. (Crown Copyright: Royal Commission on the Ancient and Historical Monuments of Scotland)

An angel in the village graveyard.

Carved medieval musicians playing the viol and the lute with great enthusiasm. (By permission of Rosslyn Chapel Trust)

Angel pumping the bellows of a portable organ or *portative*. (By permission of Rosslyn Chapel Trust)

Prince's Pillar, has been mentioned above.[13] Briefly, the cruel and gruesome legend concerning this pillar goes as follows.

The master mason, having received from Sir William Sainteclaire the model of a pillar of exquisite workmanship and design, hesitated to carry it out until he had been to Rome and seen the original. Accordingly, he left Scotland and went abroad for many months. In his absence, an apprentice, having dreamt that he himself had finished the pillar, immediately set to work and executed the design as it now stands, a perfect marvel of workmanship. On his return and seeing the pillar completed,

Angels blowing a shawn, beating a drum and holding the music book. (By permission of Rosslyn Chapel Trust)

Angel piping on a shawm on the north exterior side of the chapel. (By permission of Rosslyn Chapel Trust)

A rather more sedate musical angel in King's College Chapel, Cambridge. (By permission of the Dean of King's College, Cambridge)

Dragons twisting on the base of the Prince's Pillar. (By permission of Rosslyn Chapel Trust)

A riot of imagery on the south side of the capital of the Prince's Pillar. (By permission of Rosslyn Chapel Trust)

instead of being delighted at the success of his pupil, the master was stung with envy and demanded to know who had dared to finish the work in his absence. On being told it was his own apprentice, he became so incensed that he struck out at him with his mallet and killed him on the spot.

The Prince's Pillar has a uniquely complex design and a high standard of workmanship. While there are those who claim that it displays a level of skill not visible in any other part of the chapel, this is not strictly accurate, as many of the pendant roof sections, although smaller, exhibit equal skill in design and execution. It is possible that the raised and twisting curves of the pillar were achieved by tying a horizontal piece of cord round its top and bottom, then connecting both with a series of vertical cords tied round the top and bottom. Either the top or the bottom loop would then be slowly turned round the pillar, while the other corresponding horizontal cord would be held in place to stop it from turning. This would then produce the profile for the stonemasons to mark the dynamic 'double helix' feature, as it twisted hypnotically round the stone.

Today, there are parts of the warm red and yellow freestone of the pillar already emerging from under the cold white chemical coating where friction from the constant contact with fascinated and deeply excited visitors has gradually rubbed it away.

At the base of the pillar are eight intertwined dragons. From their mouths issue the stems of four double spirals of foliage in low relief (*basso rilievo*) that wind round the clustered column, still bound to it by ropes, at a distance of some 18 inches apart.

To many who see this extraordinary pillar for the first time, or even those who know it from long and intimate observation, there seems to be nothing but tortuously interwoven leaves. Because there appears to be no visible fruit, some find the pillar has an evil presence. It is as if the dragons, having sucked all goodness out of the stems, are preparing to squeeze the life out of the human race. Fortunately, the dragons come to an end at the top of the pillar.

On the south side of the Prince's Pillar is depicted one of the most poignant episodes in the Bible, in which a father is asked to kill his son to prove his faith in God. We are now confronted with a carving of the terrible sacrifice of Isaac, an Old Testament pre-echo of the ultimate sacrifice Christ paid his Father for the forgiveness of human sin.

Here, above the capital of the Prince's Pillar on the carved stone (facing the south window and above the steps down to the crypt), Isaac lies on an altar, tied up, and nearby a ram is caught by his horns in a bush.[14] But the biblical story in the stone originally ended on a positive note. In Bishop Robert Forbes's day, there was, in the centre of the group, a carving of Abraham with hands uplifted in prayer – but today this carving has completely disappeared.

It is more than possible that the story of Abraham and Isaac was corrupted into that of the master and apprentice. Since the carving of Abraham and Isaac is now virtually obliterated, it may be that the original meaning was lost. Interestingly, there is a curious parallel to this misinterpretation at a tomb in Greyfriars churchyard, Edinburgh, erected around a century after construction at Rosslyn Chapel had ceased.

At Greyfrairs lie buried Commissary Clement Little (d. 1580) and his brother, Lord Provost William Little (d. 1601), two of the three founders of Edinburgh University. Clement Little, an advocate, left 300 books as a generous foundation for the Edinburgh University Library. The monument is certainly curious: four grim-faced women (noses missing and one headless) stand on guard over the roof. The story once went round Edinburgh that these were four cruel daughters who had poisoned their father (now to be seen resting in his tomb). This was a colourful and widely believed way of explaining the eerie-looking monument. The mysterious female figures on the roof seem to threaten the man lying below. But in reality the disturbing statues are far from evil. They portray the virtues Justice, Mercy, Faith, Love: the qualities by which the Little brothers sought to be remembered. Justice has her eyes blindfolded; one of her hands grips a sword, the other holds a set of scales. Another statue is crowned with laurel and clenches squirming snakes in her hand. The elements have not treated them kindly, but they stand erect and silent sentinels on the roof – in spite of popular misconceptions!

Next we encounter a tale that truly pits power against truth. At the east corner, on the south-facing architrave (lintel) connecting Pillars 4 and 5 on the east corner, is a king proudly wearing his crown. This is very probably King Darius of Persia. His story, taken from the Apocrypha (1 Esdras: 3–4), is as follows.

There came a year when King Darius organised a magnificent feast for all his subjects – his household, the princes of the Medes and Persians, his governors and captains and lieutenants, from India to Ethiopia, from 127 provinces.

The Corporal Works of Mercy (the Virtues), the duty of every Christian person. (By permission of Rosslyn Chapel Trust)

When all the king's guests had eaten and drunk their fill and departed for home, Darius went into his bedroom and fell asleep. However, after only a short time he suddenly woke up. Then three young men, members of his bodyguard, said to each other (presumably to help the king fall asleep again): 'Let's each one of us write a letter to the king; the winner will be the one who writes the wisest letter and the king will surely reward him for his wisdom. The winner will be given rich purple clothes, cups of gold to drink from, a golden bed, a chariot with golden bridles, a fine linen head-dress and a chain of office. And he will sit next to Darius and be known as his cousin.'

So each of them wrote a letter, sealed it and decided to place it under Darius' pillow. The first guard wrote: 'Wine is stronger than anything'; the second wrote, 'The King is the strongest of all'; the third, 'Women are strongest, but Truth wins the day.' Then Darius suddenly awoke, so instead the three guards brought their letters and handed them to him to be read aloud. The King then summoned all his princes, governors, captains, lieutenants and senior officers. He sat in the public Seat of Judgement and asked the young men to come forward and read out what they had written.

After the first and second bodyguards had spoken, it was the turn of the third. His name was Zorobabel, a Jew. To his face he calmly told the king that he had watched the royal concubine, Apame, sitting beside the King, in the place of honour. Apame had taken the crown from the King's head, placed it on her own head and then slapped the King. The King pretended to be amused and tried to please her, no matter how insolently she continued to behave.

Zorobabel did not flinch from saying what he felt about Darius' humiliating relationship with Apame. He ended by affirming that, although women were very strong, Truth was the mightiest force in the world. All the people then shouted, 'Truth is great, it is the ultimate power.'

So impressed was Darius by Zorobabel's courage that he offered him anything he wanted. Zorobabel asked the King to enforce an earlier decree of King Cyrus that would allow the Jews to return home and rebuild their Temple. This Darius did and the seventy years' captivity of the Jews was over.

Carved in the Lombardic alphabet on the architrave connecting Pillar 4 with the south wall are the words of the three messages handed to the King. On the

The Sins (the Vices), which lead (on the right) to the gaping mouth of Hell. (By permission of Rosslyn Chapel Trust)

architrave, extending from No. 5 to the south wall, the Contrast between Virtue and Vice is illustrated in a series of nine figures.

On the east side of the lintel at *a* are the Virtues (also known as the Corporal Works of Mercy). These begin from the left, outlining exactly what true Christians had to do to qualify for a place in Paradise. A cardinal bishop is portrayed holding a crozier (pastoral staff) in his left hand and a book with two clasps in his left. This figure symbolises the Church's responsibility for showing its members how to be virtuous and offer every assistance in the form of religious orders to care for the needy, and lay associations that would encourage the practice of the Works of Mercy. One of these would be the practical support that the guild of stonemasons and other early forms of trade union gave their members.

The Works of Mercy carved here in the chapel are: (1) helping the needy (a lame man on crutches, leading the blind); (2) clothing the naked; (3) visiting the sick; (4) visiting those in prison; (5) comforting the fatherless and destitute; (6) feeding the hungry; (7) burying the dead. The reward that virtuous men and women would be given is symbolised by a carving of St Peter at the gates of Heaven, with a key in his hand, waiting to admit those who have practised the works of Mercy.

On the west side of the architrave, at *b*, are the Vices. Again, we see the responsibility of the Church underlined in a carving of a bishop, who holds his crozier in his left hand, while his right hand is raised in warning. The procession of Vices follows this order: (1) Pride: represented by a supercilious Pharisee; (2) Gluttony: a man holding a large jug up to his mouth; (3) Anger: two men drinking, one with his hand raised as if to punch the other; (4) Sloth: a soldier who is too lazy to help the child clinging to his left side; (5) Luxury: a man who has over-indulged, with hands across his chest, surrounded by clusters of grapes; (6) Avarice: a miser, gripping a long purse in his hand; (7) Lust: lovers whose relationship is purely physical. For those who choose to disregard the guidance of the Gospels, the Devil can be seen emerging from the mouth of a monster (Hell) and stretching out a triple hook towards the whole group of vicious men and women.

The remaining pillars bear a variety of religious symbolism: Pillar 6 (on the capital), a head and two birds; Pillar 7 (on the capital) a group of human figures and animals, heavily damaged and broken. On the wall pillar opposite (on the left of the

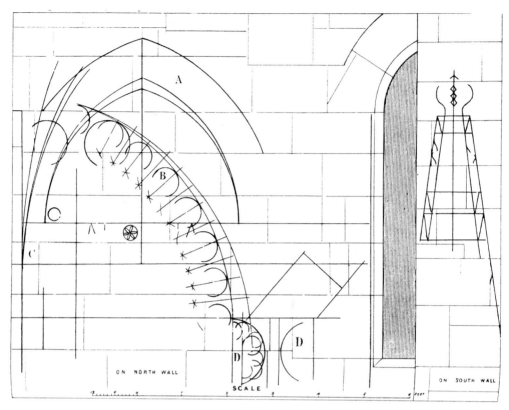

Robert Anderson's copy of the medieval architects' plans scratched into the walls of the crypt. (By permission of the Society of Antiquaries of Scotland)

side door) is a group thought to show the Conception or Annunciation, in the form of an aureole (halo); Pillar **8** on the wall pillar opposite No. **8** (on the right of the south door), the Presentation of the Infant Saviour in the Temple. Other images include: the Crucifixion (high above these, decorating a pillar capital on the north side); Elijah (on a capital at the south side is a group said to represent this Old Testament prophet being taken up to Heaven in a fiery chariot, an event understood as prefiguring the Ascension of Christ, but the carving is so heavily damaged that its subject is difficult to identify with complete accuracy).

THE CRYPT

At the side of the Prince's Pillar are the steps that lead to the crypt (also known as the sacristy or lower chapel). It seems probable that the crypt is the oldest part of the chapel and may have been built to house the remains of members of the Sainteclaire family in a location that predates the chapel's construction; indeed, the crypt may mark the site of the earliest castle built at Rosslyn, either before it was owned by the Sainteclaires or, perhaps, when it was first acquired by them.

The Prince's Pillar, the steps down into the crypt and one of the post-holes used to support the original choir screens. (The London Stereoscopic Company, early 1860s?)

At the south-east corner of the chapel is the stair leading to the crypt, said to have been built by Lady Margaret Douglas, first wife of Sir William St Clair, as the coat of arms on the south side of the window seems to indicate. This building has puzzled historians and archaeologists alike. In the Revd John Thompson's time it was certainly used as a sacristy and, until not long before 1892, as a vestry; but doubtless that was not the original intention. That some other building existed on the site of the chapel seems probable because in his *Theatrum Scotiae* Slezer says that three earls or princes of Orkney and nine barons of Rosslyn were buried here. Since Sir William Sainteclaire, the founder of the chapel, was the third and last Earl of Orkney, his grandfather and father, at least, must be buried there, the latter certainly thirty years before the chapel was begun.

The crypt is entered first down a flight of stone steps and then, from a wooden landing, down wooden steps. To the south is a door to a small room and another door to an even smaller (and later) enclosure is on the north wall.

It has been conjectured that the space was intended as a crypt or burial place for the junior members of the Sainteclaire family, while the vaults under the choir of the collegiate church were to be reserved for the heads of that family. There seems little or no evidence for this suggestion; and from the fact that it contains a fireplace, and what appear to be presses (cupboards) in the wall, besides two doors in the north and south walls, leading to other rooms, it seems more probable that it was at one time intended to serve as the living quarters of the priest custodian of the church, a role that Fr Richard Augustine Hay seems to have quietly continued. Certainly, recent archaeological investigation of the crypt has revealed that the original building was more extensive than it is today, both at the north and south sides and in extent above and below.[15]

However, the principal furniture of the crypt consists now of an altar under the east (and only) window, a piscina (water-basin) and an aumbry (cupboard), which certainly were used for mass during the forty years when the upper chapel was being built, and, no doubt, afterwards by the clergy when the chapel proper was not in use. It is also possible that they were used specifically for the celebration of requiem masses.

Several working drawings, presumably made under the supervision of the original architect and stonemasons and scratched onto the north and south walls of the crypt, were investigated by the architect Robert Anderson in 1873.[16] The first drawing he found was on the south wall and consisted of converging lines with succeeding sectional decorations, capped by a ball shape. These appear to have been measurements incised during the design process for one of the many pinnacles around the roof of the chapel on the south side. Perhaps this was a temporary graphical alternative to Sir William Sainteclaire's Norwegian boarding. Nevertheless, this is also very reminiscent of a drawing of a gable with decorative elements in the Frankfurt Lodge Book of 'Master W. G.' (1560), held today at the library of the Städtlisches Kunstinstitut at Frankfurt-am-Main in Germany.[17]

On the north wall a scribed pointed arch can still be seen, which relates to the window arches of the Lady Chapel; then a vaulted rib with a series of cusps, again associated with the same area, and a number of other lines and circles that have not been identified. Again, these engraved designs bear strong similarities to a sketch for the curvature of diagonal ribs in the Frankfurt Lodge Book of

The Arms of James Francis Harry, Earl of Rosslyn, in Patrick Pollen's stained-glass window in the crypt. (By permission of Rosslyn Chapel Trust)

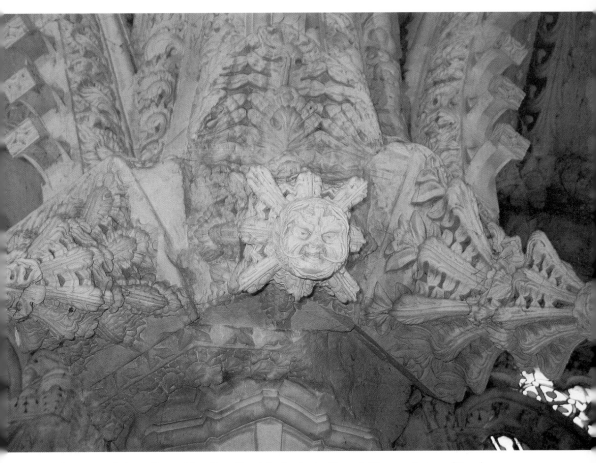

Pendant carved stone Green Man thrusting into the Lady Chapel. (By permission of Rosslyn Chapel Trust)

'Master W. G.'.[18] Anderson judged that the drawings were probably the work of the master mason and predated the construction of the main chapel. This again makes it clear that the crypt was in existence before the main chapel, and the tentative nature of the drawings on the crypt walls leads Anderson to conclude that they were executed while the master mason was examining different strategies for solving specific architectural problems – possibly incised on the wall as a way of demonstrating his solutions to a watching group of masons, much as a blackboard is used today. The Frankfurt Lodge Book also shows that sketches on paper and cut-out paper patterns were used during the medieval period to record the principal design options for windows and vaults, laid out simply as if for the guidance of clients – such as Sir William Sainteclaire.[19]

Above the altar, providing a vivid visual focus for the crypt, is a fine stained-glass window designed by Patrick Pollen and installed in 1954 in memory of the 5th Earl of Rosslyn, James Francis Harry.

THE STAINED GLASS

All the present stained glass at Rosslyn Chapel was installed after 1862 – there is no earlier stained glass whatsoever in the chapel. However, given Sir William Sainteclaire's profound wish that the chapel should be as beautiful as possible, we may fairly assume that there would have been some medieval stained glass at one time, but if so all of it was destroyed, probably at the Reformation.

After the 1560s there was no glass in the chapel and the window openings were protected only by wooden shutters (whose iron hinges can still be seen). Eventually, in 1736, the windows were re-glazed with plain glass by General St Clair, although the Hill and Adamson photographs from the 1840s would suggest that only the simple vertical rectangular lights in the lower section of the windows were glazed; the upper, tear-shaped parts of the windows were not glazed, nor was the east window.

The stained glass visible today in the upper chapel was designed and, according to the Revd John Thompson, installed in 1867 by Messrs Clayton & Bell of London at the request of Francis Robert, 4th Earl of Rosslyn, who intended the windows as a memorial to his parents.

The six stained-glass windows in the Lady Chapel show the twelve Apostles. As we walk from the north side of the Lady Chapel to the south we see: (1) St Peter and St James the Greater; (2) St John and St Andrew; (3) St Philip and St Bartholomew; (4) St Matthew and St Thomas; (5) St James the Less and St Thaddeus; (6) St Simon and St Matthias. In the east aisle (north window): St John the Baptist with a lamb standing on a book; St Paul with a sword. In the corresponding south window are St Mark and St Luke.

In the north aisle (beginning at the west end) we see: (1) the Annunciation and the Nativity; (2) the Presentation in the Temple and the baptism of Jesus; (3) the Sermon on the Mount and the miraculous draught of fishes. In the south aisle are: (1) the miracle at the marriage feast of Cana and the raising of Jairus' daughter; (2) Christ blessing the little children and the Last Supper; (3) The Crucifixion and the Resurrection. The west window above the organ gallery shows Christ in glory, holding a book symbolising the power of the law and the Gospel. These windows comprise some of the most memorable Episcopal Church additions to the chapel.

SERMONS IN STONES

We may hazard a guess as to the reasons why Rosslyn Chapel was named after St Matthew. Over the centuries he has become the patron saint of accountants, bankers, customs officers and tax collectors.[20] Yet, none of these characteristics seems to fit the case of Sir William Sainteclaire. During his own lifetime, however, St Matthew was an apostle, an evangelist and a martyr, and so fitted well with the aims of the St Clairs.[21] As for St Matthew's Gospel itself and its major themes, a rationale can be identified in that the text contains: (1) a vision of the Lion of Judah, and a connection between the Old and New Testaments; (2) a 'majestic and kingly

The choir, furnished and decorated after David Bryce's restoration of 1861 and after the installation of new coloured stained glass in 1867 (early nineteenth-century postcard).

tone', evident in Christ's Sermon on the Mount and his denunciation in the Temple; (3) a brief and condensed narrative (such as we see in the graphic depictions of biblical events in the chapel carvings); and, finally, (4) a 'disclosure of the workings of the Kingdom of Evil' and its attempts to stifle truth (such as Herod's instruction to kill Jesus in his cradle, or the wrong-headed attempts to detain the risen Christ in his tomb).[22] St Matthew, in other words, encapsulated the Gospel values that, in his declining years, Sir William Sainteclaire so dearly wished to embrace and promote.

When we look closely at the carvings in the chapel – perhaps sitting down in recollection at one of the Sunday morning or late afternoon liturgies (rather than following the great swarm of tourists who flow in considerable bewilderment through the chapel or sit silently, listening to the well-rehearsed exposition of the tour guides) – they can be seen to reflect the riches of the biblical tradition of the Psalms.

The visual impact of the chapel is powerful and quickly stimulates in the visitor a sense of awe and even disorientation. Entering the chapel for the first time, the visitor may also be gripped by a feeling of mystery: 'Holiness is the beauty of your house' (Ps 93: 5) or 'Better one day in your courts' (Ps 84: 10). Absorbing the sensuous atmosphere may lead to meditation on the elevation and protection that the chapel offers: 'He folds me on the recesses of his tent, sets me high on a rock' (Ps 27:

5).[23] For someone gazing in wonder at the complex adornments of Rosslyn Chapel, whether in the soaring roof or in the cramped cavern of the Lady Chapel, it would be easy to conclude that 'From the entire earth the design stands out' (Ps 19: 4). The visitor may become like those who say 'I look up at your heavens . . . moon and stars' (Ps 148: 1) and might conclude by whispering: 'Praise Yahweh upon the heavens' (Ps 148: 1).

The Hebrew Old Testament Psalms provided the poetic basis for the devotions in which the canons at St Matthew's collegiate church spent much of their time. Today, thinking of the North Esk River that flows round castle and chapel might promote reflection that 'In the ravines you opened up springs running between the mountains' (Ps 104: 10) and 'Deep is calling to deep, by the roar of your cataract' (Ps 42: 7), while looking at the long low tomb of a Sainteclaire (a medieval warrior like so many of his family in those days) might recall the chivalric ideal of the Christian knight: 'Warrior, strap your sword at your side . . . ride on in the cause of truth, gentleness and uprighteousness' (Ps 45: 3).

In the days of Sir William Sainteclaire, life was cheap. It would be easy to conclude that, as the Psalmist observes, 'As for a human person – his days are like grass, he blooms like the wild flower' (Ps 103: 15). So would come fear of the Lord, visible in the chapel's carved Dance of Death: 'My heart withers within me, the terrors of death come upon me, fear and trembling overwhelm me and shuddering grips me' (Ps 55: 4). It is a cry for help that God answers decisively and with power – 'Smoke rose from his nostrils' (Ps 18: 8). Now, the forces of evil (epitomised by the devils so much in evidence in the chapel) launch their attack, their throats are wide-open graves (Ps 5: 9), but those who lie in wait for God's people are heading for destruction – 'The path of the wicked is doomed' (Ps 1: 6). Like the dragons which curl around the base of the Prince's Pillar, 'They are poisonous as any snake, deaf as an adder that blocks its ears' (Ps 58: 4), and so Yahweh will 'hurl them into a blazing furnace and fire will devour them' (Ps 20: 9). He will split the sea monster, Rahab (representing Chaos), 'in two like a corpse' (Ps 89: 10) and crush the heads of the monster Leviathan (Ps 74: 14).

The theme of many of the chapel's carvings is, however, the fruitful reign of God: 'When the Lord has restored his Kingdom, the Earth will rejoice', as do the many musicians carved in the roof of the Lady Chapel, each one saying: 'I sing for joy' (Ps 81: 1), and 'We will sing and make noise' (Ps 20: 13).

It was impulses such as these that the College of Canons followed in their daily round of praise: 'Let the voice sound for our God, let it sound' (Ps 47: 6), telling their congregations and each other to 'Sing to God, play music to his name, build a road for the Rider of the Clouds' (Ps 68: 4).

CHAPTER 4

Varieties of Speculation

THE BUILDING

Solomon's Temple

It has often been suggested – for example, by Dan Brown in *The Da Vinci Code* – that Rosslyn Chapel was built following the design of the Jewish Temple of Solomon.[1] This, of course, is not unexpected – Jesus was a Jew and so were his earliest followers; he lived and acted in the context and atmosphere of Judaism, within a culture that had inherited the rich history found in the Old Testament.

At the period when Christianity emerged, Jews worshipped at home, at the synagogue (where sacrifice was also permitted) and in the Temple: the ministry of Jesus develops through these structures. He taught in the synagogue and drove the money-changers out of the Temple.[2]

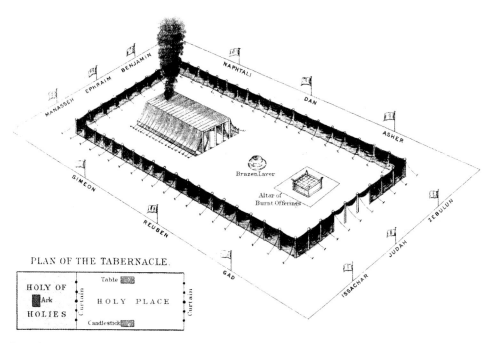

The Tabernacle in the desert. (From *Philips' Handy Scripture Atlas* (London: George Philip & Son, Ltd, 1909))

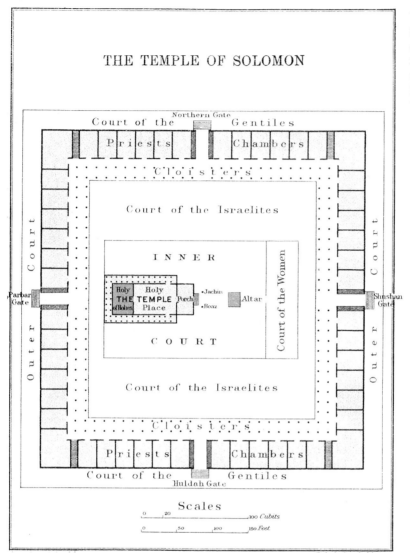

The Temple of
Solomon. (From
*Philips' Handy
Scripture Atlas*
(London: George
Philip & Son, Ltd,
1909))

For the early Christians, emerging out of the life-long practices and customs of
Judaism, it was natural that their styles of prayer and the buildings in which they
worshipped should bear some resemblance to the Temple or the synagogue. But
Christians also made it clear that they had no temples, but were themselves the living
stones of the new Temple.[3]

Comparison of the plan of Solomon's Temple with that of Rosslyn Chapel shows
that the similarities are those one would expect to find within any Christian church,
given that Christianity grew out of the Judaic tradition, which in turn developed
from the Judaic experience of tabernacle worship in desert exile, the Old Testament
priesthood and the rituals such as the notion of sanctuary and sacrifice. There is no
evidence of any deliberate attempt to recreate Solomon's Temple (or Herod's Temple),
nor for any arcane or esoteric symbolism at Rosslyn. The design and function of

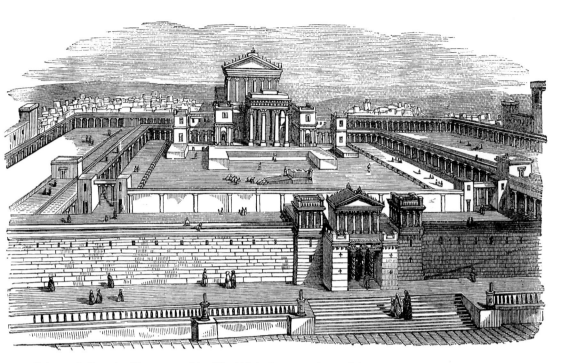

Solomon's Temple. (From an unidentified Victorian encyclopaedia)

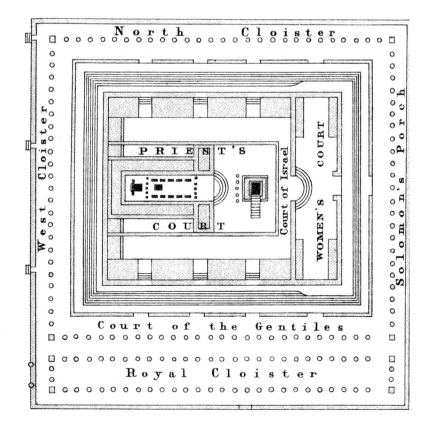

The Temple of Herod.
(From *Philips' Handy
Scripture Atlas*
(London: George
Philip & Son, Ltd,
1909))

Rosslyn Chapel look forward to the development of the Kingdom of God as an ongoing, living process.

Glasgow Cathedral

In his essential guidebook, the Revd John Thompson refers to the opinions of several leading architectural and historical authorities that there is a

> strong resemblance . . . between Rosslyn Chapel and Glasgow Cathedral, in the arrangement of their various parts, and the peculiar feature of the central pillars in the east end, between the Choir and the Lady Chapel – a resemblance so striking that it has been thought to have been intentional, and that Glasgow Cathedral, which was built considerably more than a century before Rosslyn, really formed the model for this Collegiate Church.[4]

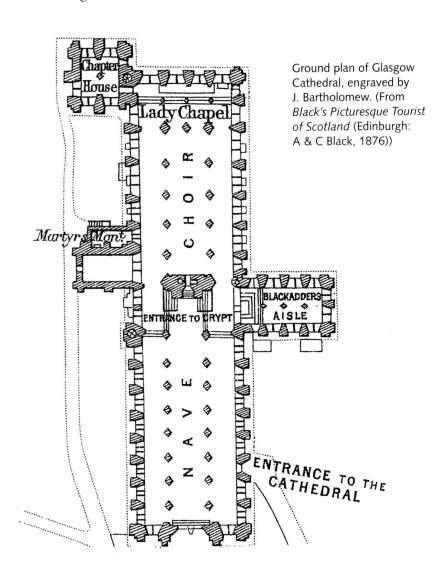

Ground plan of Glasgow Cathedral, engraved by J. Bartholomew. (From *Black's Picturesque Tourist of Scotland* (Edinburgh: A & C Black, 1876))

The choir, Glasgow Cathedral, with its low 'retro-choir' and central pillar with an arch on each side (so allowing a tall east window), clearly showing Glasgow's influence on Rosslyn Chapel. (By permission of Historic Scotland)

Rosslyn Chapel photographed from the same position, showing the striking similarity with Glasgow Cathedral. (By permission of Rosslyn Chapel Trust)

Speaking about Rosslyn Chapel in 1914, the architect Thomas Ross adds that

> After all that has been said and sung in prose and rhyme, in sense and nonsense, it is a very simple building, with some constructional features which are, it may be, departures from the true principles of medieval architecture as applied to the construction of a great cathedral, but hardly so when referred to a tiny church like this. It has been ornamented with a profusion of architectural detail – sculpture and carving – to a degree not seen elsewhere in this country.[5]

Ross goes on to say that the plan of Rosslyn Chapel is identical to that of Glasgow Cathedral – a square east end, an ambulatory all round and chapels to the east. There are other similarities: the roofs of the ambulatories and the chapels were kept low to give added space for lighting the interior. He finds resemblances to Rosslyn in the porches at Trinity College Church in Edinburgh and St Nicholas Collegiate Church in Dalkeith. Ross ends by asserting that 'the theory of its foreign origin is supported neither by documentary evidence nor by probability'. This is an opinion that is largely shared by Andrew Kerr, the architect of the baptistry, who writes that, while Rosslyn Chapel has some French features (the roof) and some Spanish ones (the pillars resembling those of Siguenza Cathedral), 'the distinguishing features of Rosslyn, both externally and internally, will be found to consist chiefly in the richness and variety of the design, and the vigorous execution of the decoration . . .'.[6]

One of the foremost contemporary historians of the medieval period in Scotland, Dr Richard Fawcett, Principal Inspector at Historic Scotland, largely concurs with the views expressed above, writing that the church at Rosslyn follows the plan of Glasgow Cathedral in having aisles on three sides and a series of chapels on the eastern side of the building.[7]

Additionally, there is some evidence that the tracery of the east window as put in place in 1867 owes its design not only to the south window of Melrose Abbey but also to the west window of Glasgow Cathedral.

The east window today, showing the new tracery and stained glass installed in 1867. (By permission of Rosslyn Chapel Trust)

WHERE DID THE STONEMASONS COME FROM?

Historians are generally divided as to the countries of origin of the stonemasons who worked on Rosslyn Chapel. Fr Richard Augustine Hay records that Sir William Sainteclaire 'caused artificers to be brought from other regions and forraigne kingdoms'. However, the word 'region' may mean no more than other parts of Scotland and 'forraigne' may refer principally to England with its long tradition of importing builders, stonemasons and architects from France – a tradition King David I also followed in the twelfth century when he initiated a major programme of monastery construction in the Scottish Borders and at Holyrood, accompanied by the importation of monastic orders from England and France.

Thomas Ross, in a paper read at Rosslyn Chapel in 1914 to the Scottish Ecclesiologial Society, cautions: 'It has been claimed as the work of some unknown Spanish architect, or a Portuguese, or a Frenchman; and there has even been talk of Rome. No Scotchman in this connection has been allowed to have a look in, except the noble Founder, Sir William St Clair.'[8]

The west window of Glasgow Cathedral, with its triangle of glass at the apex of the window, a possible influence on the new tracery and stained glass inserted in the east window of Rosslyn Chapel in 1869. (By permission of Rosslyn Chapel Trust)

BOTANICAL IMAGES

In a series of three articles, 'A Botanist Looks at the Medieval Plant Carvings at Rosslyn Chapel' (2001–2), Dr Adrian Dyer, a professional botanist, now retired but previously a member of staff at the University of Edinburgh, and husband of the Revd Janet Dyer, former Priest in Charge at Rosslyn Chapel, has meticulously examined the botanical carvings in the chapel.[9]

Dr Dyer begins by looking at the carvings of leaves. He lists the plants that the Revd John Thompson identifies in the chapel: hart's tongue fern, curly kale, oak, cactus, sunflowers and three-leaved botanical forms (trefoils). Broadly speaking, Dr Dyer finds the botanical forms in the chapel to be stylised or conventionalised, with the exception of the approximately life-size hart's tongue fern (on top of the Prince's Pillar, immediately below the figure of Isaac), which grew in Roslin Glen in the fourteenth century and still does today.

With respect to the fruits and flowers and their possible symbolism, the three-leaved flowers may be seen as references to the Trinity. However, the flowers in the roof that Thompson and other early guides describe as daisies are not true representations of that flower. There are some carvings that are reminiscent of the Madonna lily and may therefore have religious significance.

Lastly, the repeated assertion that carvings in the chapel show two plants that, in the fifteenth century, were native to North America – maize and aloes – does not bear scrutiny. Dr Dyer finds that there has been no attempt to represent a species accurately or such as can be identified and that the carvings are almost certainly derived from stylised architectural patterns, whose resemblance to recognisable botanical forms is fortuitous.

Much the same conclusion is reached by Dr Brian Moffat, the archaeo-botanist who has, almost single-handedly over many years of excavation, revealed many of the medicinal practices of the monks at Soutra Hospital. In an article entitled 'Magic Afoot: Rosslyn Aloes in Veritas?' he rejects the notion that the chapel is 'a pharmacy in stone', principally because the carvings of botanical forms are neither naturalistic nor accurate.[10] He adds the significant information that there is no citation for either 'maize' or 'aloes' in the *Oxford English Dictionary* before the mid-sixteenth century and suggests that the available evidence makes the arum lily and its highly stylised abstractions the most likely candidate for what has been identified as American maize. As for the aloes sometimes thought to be depicted at Rosslyn Chapel, Dr Moffat points out that the consumer would never have seen the plant, only the sap that was used medicinally and that, in any case, it was not imported to Spain until 1561. He adds: 'In common with the majority of Rosslyn's foliage, little life is on display and precious little nature.'

THE PRINCE'S PILLAR

Although the two studies mentioned above looked at the botanical carvings in Rosslyn Chapel in considerable detail, there is one more component of the carving and the architecture that is derived from natural forms. The design of stone pillars, as the Greek orders (Doric, Ionic and Corinthian) show us – particularly in the least elaborated of the three, the Doric order (the most ancient) – was based on the tree trunks that first supported structures such as temples, before their architecture was systemised in stone construction. In a similar way, one can see how the Tabernacle of the Jews was derived from the simple practicalities of worship in the desert. If the Prince's Pillar is studied as a form derived from the trunk of a tree, its biblical symbolism emerges.

The pillar becomes the 'rod from the stem of Jesse', or the 'root of Jesse' (Isa. 11: 1–10); it is at the same time the 'wood of the Cross', completing the Old Testament in the New, where Christians believe that Jesus suffered the agonies of Roman crucifixion to save the world. The dragons entwined at the base of the pillar are the serpents (representing evil) that may be trodden on with impunity by those whom Yahweh (the saving God of the Old Testament) protects (Psalms 91: 13). The rotating decorative scheme of the pillar can be seen as stylised ivy that wraps and entwines itself around the stone: a symbol of strong attachment and eternal life. Hence, the Prince's Pillar may also be seen as an image of salvation through Christ, a motif echoed in the carved group of figures above the pillar to the south, which shows Abraham, who was prepared to offer his son to God in sacrifice. The popular concept of the 'Apprentice Pillar' is perhaps a folk memory of this biblical narrative.

In spite of the worldwide reputation of the 'Apprentice Pillar', numerous authorities have shown that the story of the apprentice is a familiar fable that was recorded in the popular lore of a number of other medieval buildings.[11] Writing in 1789, Fellow of the Society of Antiquaries Francis Grose dismisses the legend of the disobedient apprentice:

In support of this story, the *cicceroni* of the place shows not only the column, called the apprentice's pillar, but several other heads, supporting brackets in the wall, said to be the heads of the parties; one is called the master's; another that of the apprentice, whose wound is marked with red ochre; and the head of a weeping woman is said to represent the mother. Most certainly this is all fiction: the head pointed out for the apprentice, exhibits an old man. Similar stories are told of different buildings; one, in particular, of the famous rose window at Rouen in Normandy, said to have been built by an apprentice, whose master, out of jealousy, knocked out his brains with a hammer.[12]

In 1877 the architect Andrew Kerr, long associated with the preservation and development of the chapel and a Fellow of the Society of Antiquaries of Scotland, also dismissed the legend of the apprentice:

An almost similar tradition is preserved at Melrose, in connection with the building of the east window of the abbey church. It is curious to find such legends associated chiefly with ecclesiastical buildings, but they are not confined to them. There is one connected with the building of the bridge over the Danube at

Powerfully twisting, the dynamic spiral of the Prince's Pillar. (By permission of Rosslyn Chapel Trust)

Ratisbon, where Satan himself was said to have been employed, his hire being the lives of the first three creatures who crossed the bridge.[13]

The Revd John Thompson also inserts a caveat into his account of the 'Apprentice Pillar'. Having described the traditional tale of the vindictive master and the murdered apprentice, he then (diplomatically) proceeds to add that 'similar legends are repeated in reference to Melrose, Lincoln, Rouen, &c'.[14]

And there are other, more contemporary examples of the 'murdered apprentice' story even closer at hand. Interviewed by Joanna Vallely (*Edinburgh Evening News*, 17 April 2007), Lesley Peebles Brown, one of two Historic Scotland stewards at Seton Collegiate Church, points out that at Seton there are not only several good examples of a 'green man', but also the face of an apprentice mason murdered by his master for (without his knowledge) correctly working out the confidential mathematical calculation needed to fix the angle and the dimension of the church roof.

An alternative title is given to the pillar by John Slezer (d. 1714). Born in a German-speaking part of the Low Countries, John Abraham Slezer, or, as he signed himself, Sletzer, was a gunner, draughtsman and engraver who by 1669 had made his home in Scotland. Having trained as an ordnance engineer, Slezer had a successful career as a topographical illustrator that led to his becoming a burgess of Dundee in 1678. Ten years later he was active as captain of artillery for the Scottish Parliament. Slezer published his *Theatrum Scotiae* in 1693, a large-format book of engraved views of Scottish cities and historic buildings with text originally contributed by the Geographer Royal, Sir Robert Sibbald. However, much to Sibbald's annoyance, his text (after being signed off by himself and Slezer) was considerably altered and expanded by the latter without either Sibbald's knowledge or permission.

One of the views in the book is of Rosslyn Chapel in which Slezer's expanded description refers to what he calls the 'Prince's Pillar'. Slezer, with his military background, was nothing if not organised. As was the case with most of his topographical assignments, Slezer would have come to Rosslyn with a portable reflecting camera obscura, which he set up on the then more open south side of the chapel, prior to the construction of the present stone wall and fence. Sitting in the virtual total darkness of a small canvas tent, Slezer was able to project an image of the chapel onto his drawing board and then trace the outline.[15] His published engraving is, however, a little misleading, as it shows Rosslyn Chapel (quite inaccurately) standing alone in the middle of a picturesque and widespread wasteland and also omits any sign of the crypt.

The design of the Prince's Pillar is not unique, as Thomas Ross reminds us: 'a slight, sunk, twining rope-like moulding is quite frequent in massive Norman pillar.' But he adds that, while 'pillars decorated with carved wreaths are frequent in small architectural details such as balconies . . . I do not remember any structural pillar so decorated as here [Rosslyn]'.[16]

Ross goes on to refer to another example of this feature in Britain – the

Vigorous knots, struts and shooting vegetation: a detail of the Prince's Pillar. (By permission of Rosslyn Chapel Trust)

twelfth-century parish church at Pittington, near Durham, where 'this rope becomes a massive cable of even bulkier form than the Rosslyn wreath'. Other examples are to be found at Romsey (in a Norman doorway) and at Brunswick Cathedral in Germany.

Finally, there is the evidence of professional workers with stone today. Stonemasons contacted in 2006 have expressed serious doubt as to the possible truth of the 'Apprentice Pillar' legend. Joe Lang, stonemason, Freemason, builder and Rosslyn Chapel guide and someone long associated with the repair and care of Rosslyn Chapel, does not believe that an apprentice would have acquired the knowledge or skill necessary to carve the pillar and estimates that it would have taken about a year to carve from start to finish.[17] This also is the considered opinion of sculptor Chris Hall (who spent many years carving new capitals for the pillars at Iona Abbey) and of Jordan Kirk, charge-hand stonemason at St Mary's Cathedral Workshop in Edinburgh.[18] Bearded and fair-haired, Chris Hall spent thirty years (1967–97) regularly returning to Iona Abbey, where he carved forty-seven capitals out of Northumberland blackster stone.[19]

FREEMASONS

In the fifteenth century, when Rosslyn Chapel was constructed, Freemasonry as we know it today did not exist – at that time the working practice of stonemasons was similar to that of other manual crafts. Building, stone-carving and architecture had not differentiated themselves into the separate career paths that emerged in the eighteenth century. While the techniques of building, stone-carving and architecture could be absorbed only through a long and structured apprenticeship (the source of the legend of the disobedient apprentice and the vindictive master), the craftsmen (like most medieval working people) were unable to write (as is evidenced by the widespread use of distinctive masons' marks on building stones) and needed to be able to prove their qualifications and skills as they moved from one part of the country to another. They did this through special signs and passwords (rather like today's credit-card pin numbers and passwords), which they could learn only when they had completed their apprenticeship and mastered their craft. This was, in other words, a practical and sensible way of ensuring that quality-control mechanisms were in place in an industry where many unqualified workers tried to pass themselves off as experienced craftsmen.

The association of craft guilds that had developed in medieval times grew out of the need to protect their members from exploitation by merchants, town councils or wealthy aristocrats. In medieval Scotland such guilds of working masons developed and were known as incorporations. King James I sometimes visited and supported such lodges, on one occasion paying a revenue of £4 Scots to every master mason, and to a grand master whose office was to regulate the fraternity. Scottish Masons' lodges, built where prolonged building activity was taking place, are recorded at Aberdeen and Dundee in the late fifteenth and early sixteenth centuries. However, these seem to have been dissolved around the time of the Scottish Reformation (1560).

Many aspects of the medieval stonemasons' craft would be adopted by later Freemasonry: these embraced the craft history and the connection between construction and mathematics (including secret signs or words and initiation rituals used to protect standards of workmanship). After 1200 architecture was increasingly governed by theoretical rules derived from geometry.[20] Critical to this application of theory to construction was the geometrical square, which would be used in architecturural design by being superimposed or rotated.[21] The master masons also carried with them their own personal sketchbooks, which would later develop into more formal written texts for public dissemination.[22]

By 1475 the masons and wrights (carpenters) of Edinburgh had enough collective power to be able to obtain a 'seal of cause' (charter) from the city of Edinburgh allowing them to act as an incorporation, an early form of trade guild that set out the craft regulations. In 1489 coopers and other tradesmen joined the incorporation, whose function was to rule on disputes, supply charity and also control apprenticeships and entrance to the trades.

Although most trades had such incorporations, the stonemasons had a unique feature – namely, the lodge. In 1491 Edinburgh's burgh authorities gave the stonemasons the right to have recreation in their common lodge, suggesting that the lodge was more than a place for storing tools and also had a social function.

In 1583 King James VI appointed William Schaw (even though he was a Roman Catholic) as master of the work and warden general, with a commission to reorganise the stonemasons' craft. Accordingly, in 1598 he issued the Schaw Statutes setting out the rights and obligations of the stonemasons. Penalties were to be imposed for poor

workmanship or for any breaches of safety codes. A further statute was drawn up by Schaw in 1599, which referred to esoteric knowledge and confirmed the fact that in Kilwinning, Ayrshire, the mother lodge of Scotland, Lodge Mother Kilwinning No. 0, was already in existence.

Schaw instructed all lodges to keep written records, fix the times of regular meetings, test members on their knowledge of the craft and record the attendance and progress of apprentices. For this reason William Schaw is looked upon as the founding father of modern Freemasonry.

In the sixteenth and seventeenth centuries men of importance were admitted to the Scottish lodges (even if they were not craftsmen), and soon the membership changed in nature. Among the first non-stonemasons to join (1598) a

The name and monogram of master stonemason William Schaw (1550–1602), carved on a marble slab at his tomb in Dunfermline Abbey. (From David Murray Lion, *History of the Lodge of Edinburgh* (Edinburgh: William Blackwood & Sons, 1873))

Scottish lodge was James Boswell of Auchinleck, the biographer of Dr Samuel Johnson.

In 1634 William Lord Alexander, his brother Lord Anthony and Sir Alexander Strachen of Thornton were initiated into the Lodge of Edinburgh (St Mary's Chapel) No. 1. From Schaw's time to the early eighteenth century Freemasonry evolved to become an organisation led not by craftsmen but by men totally untrained in working stone.

In 1717 there were at least two lodges in Edinburgh, and others in Kilwinning, Inverness, Dundee, Stirling, Aberdeen and Glasgow. On 30 November 1736 representatives from thirty-three lodges met in Edinburgh: the Grand Lodge of Scotland was formed and William St Clair of Roslin was elected the first Grand Master Mason.

Although modern Freemasonry is a product of the post-Reformation period, the St Clairs undoubtedly had an early and important role in the support and protection of stonemasons and hammermen as part of the craftsmen's long struggle to impose quality control and independence in their industry by ensuring an effective apprenticeship structure. By charters of *c.* 1601 and 1628, the 'Free Masons of Scotland' are reputed to have recognised that the St Clairs and their ancestors had been hereditary 'Grand Master Masons of Scotland' from the time that the title was granted by King James II in 1441, the original charter having been destroyed in a fire at Rosslyn Castle.

However, these two seventeenth-century charters (now held in Edinburgh by the Grand Lodge of Scotland) show conclusively that it was the poverty and helplessness of the stonemasons that were the catalyst for the attribution of this title to the St Clairs: they were appealing to Sir William to help them adjudicate in their internal disputes and seem to have invented the title and its hereditary derivation in order to persuade him.[23]

While there is no connection between modern Freemasonry and the medieval craft of the stonemason, the earlier charters (however spurious) had some bearing when it came to the choice of a Grand Master. At the time when the Grand Lodge of Scottish Freemasonry was formed, members of Canongate Lodge Kilwinning decided to invite Sir William St Clair (the nineteenth baron) to be Grand Master, and he was accordingly initiated in the spring of 1736.[24] However, when it came to electing him as a non-hereditary Grand Master, he first had to resign his position as hereditary Grand Master.

Thereafter, Sir William's descendants maintained a close relationship with Scottish Freemasonry: Sir James St Clair Erskine (d. 1837), 2nd Earl of Rosslyn, was Grand Master Mason of Scotland. The 4th Earl, Francis Robert St Clair Erskine, was elected sixty-ninth Grand Master Mason of Scotland in 1871. The previous year he had held a Grand Masonic fête at Rosslyn attended by over a thousand Freemasons.

The 4th Earl died in 1890 and was buried at the south-west of the chapel gardens, the first St Clair of Rosslyn to be buried outside the chapel. He and his wife are commemorated by a handsome red sandstone monument designed by W. Birnie Rhind.[25] He was succeeded by James Francis Harry St Clair Erskine, 5th Earl of

Francis Robert, fourth Earl of Rosslyn and Grand Master Mason of Scotland. (From David Murray Lion, *History of the Lodge of Edinburgh* (Edinburgh: William Blackwood & Sons, 1873))

Rosslyn, whose love of horses and gambling, and work as a war correspondent and, later, as a repertory actor, drew on his innate charm and his somewhat reckless nature.

In June 1897 he was installed to the office of Provincial Grand Master of Fife and Kinross shires at Rosslyn Chapel, in the presence of 500 Masons. After arriving at Roslin railway station, the visiting Masons processed to Rosslyn Chapel, headed by the Roslin band. Some 250 Masons were admitted to the chapel for the ceremony.[26] Afterwards white blooms were placed by the members on the Past Grand Master's grave, and Lord Rosslyn also laid a wreath of white flowers.

The company were photographed by W. Drummond Young, and then all adjourned to a marquee 'in a beautiful spot not far from the Chapel', where nearly a thousand Masons and their friends had luncheon. Meanwhile, at the invitation of Lord Rosslyn, the members of the Grand Lodge assembled in the town hall for a private lunch.

Margaret Place – Roslin's only genuine Masonic symbol: a stone plaque (1894) high on the frontage of a residential block in Manse Road.

Past Freemasons of note have included the Lord Provost of Edinburgh, George Drummond (Grand Master Mason of Scotland, 1752–3), the architect Robert Adam (1728–92), the poet Robert Burns (1759–96), the novelist Sir Walter Scott (1771–1832) and, in the twentieth century, King George VI (1895–1952) and the entertainer Sir Harry Lauder (1870–1950). Today there are some 665 active lodges in Scotland and 499 overseas.

The 4th Earl died in 1890 and was succeeded by the 5th Earl, James Francis Harry St Clair-Erskine. He in turn died in 1939, and was succeeded by the 6th Earl, Anthony Hugh Francis Harry St Clair-Erskine, who took considerable responsibility for seeing that the chapel was properly conserved. The present (7th) Earl of Rosslyn, Peter St Clair Erskine, as Commander Peter Loughborough, is a senior officer with the Metropolitan Police.

As to the relationship between modern Freemasonry and Rosslyn Chapel, it is highly probable that the restorations by David Bryce in 1861 involved some redesigning of the stone carvings to fit the Masonic interests of the Earl of Rosslyn, and that the 'restoration' of the great east window, along with the installation of new stained glass, also included some reworking of the symbolism (particularly in the stone tracery of the east window) to allow a Masonic interpretation. In reality, the only genuine and original Masonic carving in Roslin is a plaque above a door in Manse Road.

Robert L.D. Cooper, Curator of the Grand Lodge of Scotland Museum and Library in Edinburgh, states (2006) quite categorically that 'the chapel is, and always has been, a Christian edifice . . .'.[27] He goes on to assert that the misguided assumption that there is some connection between Rosslyn Chapel and Scottish Freemasonry is a myth constantly elaborated without critical examination.[28]

TEMPLARS

The order of the Temple has the distinction of being the first Christian military order. It was founded by knights who had come to the Holy Land on pilgrimage and were tasked by the patriarch of Jerusalem with protecting pilgrims from the very real danger of marauding bandits who preyed on them.[29] In return, the members of the order could expect absolution for their sins. Templar knights took vows of poverty, chastity and obedience, but, like a number of other orders (such as the Cistercians and Franciscans), the order enjoyed certain financial privileges, such as freedom from ecclesiastical dues. They did not pay teinds (tithes) and were also independent of the authority of the bishops.

The order of the Temple was first recognised as a religious order by Pope Honorius II in 1128. In the same year King David I granted the chapelry and manor of

Looking down into Temple Village in the valley of the North Esk River.

Balantravach (Temple), a sheltered enclave deep in the valley of the South Esk River in what is now Midlothian, to the 'poor fellow soldiers of Christ' (the Knights Templar).[30] By royal charter Balantravach (also known as Balantradoch) became the first and chief preceptory in Scotland. There the brothers dedicated themselves to worship, prayer and preparation for the Crusades.

The Templars in Europe were organised into ten provinces (nations), each province being headed by a prior (master) who controlled the individual houses. England, Scotland and Ireland were not separate nations but were administered from London, first at the Old Temple, then at the New Temple. In 1180 the 'master of the house of the Temple in the land of the Scots' was Ralph Corbet; there was also a second preceptor at Maryculter near Aberdeen and three other brethren and four other clerics attached to the order. However, there were never more than five or six Templars in Scotland and most of them of the second or third rank – chaplains (*capellani*) or serjeants (*servientes armorum*).[31]

The Abbey Church, Holyrood.
(From James Grant, *Edinburgh Old and New* (London: Cassell, Petter, Galpin, 1880?–1883?))

The roofless shell of Temple Old Kirk.

The Templars collected revenues annually in the form of rents, cattle and grain, as well as income from teinds, from churches, burying grounds and pious donations. Virtually no active warriors were ever based in Scotland.

There seems, therefore, to be little factual basis for the traditions, first, that a number of Templar knights escaped from France to Scotland in 1304 to avoid persecution and, second, that Robert the Bruce had elite troops trained at Balantradoch (today known as Temple village) who went on to play a crucial role in the defeat of the English forces at Bannockburn.

The Templars were the subject of repeated accusations of heresy, idolatry and excessive secrecy. Urged on by King Philip IV of France, the Catholic Church authorities put the order of the Temple on trial between 1307 and 1312. At the trial of the Templars in Scotland (held at Holyrood Abbey in December 1309) two knights based in Scotland were examined (both of them English).[32] The trial, which could not be conducted with full solemnity because of the daily attacks of the Scottish patriots under Robert the Bruce, was held before Master John de Soleure, a chaplain to Pope Clement V, and William Lamberton, Bishop of the diocese of St Andrews.

Swearing on the Gospel book, Walter de Clifton, who had served ten years in the order, was the principal preceptor in Scotland, living at Balantradoch (Temple). His predecessor, John of Husefleet, had thrown off his habit and left the order. There was also another fugitive from the order, whose whereabouts were equally unknown, the Englishman Thomas Totti and two others (both Englishmen). William of Middleton, a Newcastle man, who had spent seven years as a Templar (five of them at Maryculter), was also examined, dressed in the habit of the order. Although forty-one witnesses were summoned to appear, sworn to tell the truth and legally examined (including abbots, priests, Sir Henry St Clair along with other men of rank and even domestic servants of the Templars), their summarised statements did not testify to any significant evidence of heresy or immorality, only to a culture of excessive secrecy, a tendency to avarice and an uncaring attitude towards the poor, whom they neglected in favour of the great and the wealthy.[33]

By a decision of the Council of Vienne (1311–12) and the papal bull *Vox clamantis* (1312), the Order of the Temple was suppressed; the property of the Templars was then transferred to the Order of St John of Jerusalem. The Templars' reputation for ruthlessness, however, persisted: Sir Walter Scott based his evil Templar, Brian de Bois-Gilbert in his novel *Ivanhoe*, on Brian de Jay, once preceptor of the Templars' house at Temple, Midlothian. While master of the Temple in England, de Jay led a band of marauding Welshmen into Scotland to join the forces of King Edward I, but died at the battle of Falkirk (1298), fighting against Sir William Wallace.

While the Templars' practice of secret reception and initiation into the order led to gossip and wild speculation, the Templars' power and property meant that they acquired a reputation for financial greed, best exemplified in a case, details of which are to be found in a charter of 1354.[34]

In this charter, the story of Christiana, daughter of Robert the Scot, emerges. She had fallen heir to landed property at Esperstoun near Balantradoch. She was married

The carved stone floreate Crusader cross on the gravestone of William de St Clair, who was killed (1330) in battle at Teba in Spain, while taking the heart of King Robert the Bruce to the Holy Land in 1869. This stone was originally located near the Old St Matthew's Church, in what is now Roslin Cemetery. (By permission of Rosslyn Chapel Trust)

to William, son of Galfrid (a man with little appetite for work), by whom she had three sons. Her husband had conveyed his wife's land to the Templars for his lifetime, apparently in return for bed and board in the house of the Templars at Balantradoch.[35] This had the effect of leaving his wife with little to support herself or her sons. When her husband died, the Master of the Temple tried to evict Christiana from the property, claiming it belonged to the Templars. When she objected, he ordered his followers to drag her out of her house. Christiana locked the door and resisted the Templar men with all her strength. She managed to reach the door and clung on to the arch above it, so that they could not pull her away. One of the Templar men pulled out his knife and, to make her let go, cut off one of her fingers, whereupon she was dragged out of the house, sobbing and shrieking. The Master of the Temple then took possession of the property.

However, Christiana appealed to King Edward of England when he was at Newbattle Abbey in 1296 and won her case: her land was returned to her. Some years later, after Christiana's death, her land was seized once more and her eldest son deceitfully murdered. The Templars held the land up until suppression in Scotland (November 1309), when Christiana's second son claimed it and was given it as being rightfully his.

As for the St Clairs, were any of them members of the Templar order, vowed to chastity, poverty and obedience? Eighteen years after the suppression of the order, Sir William Sainteclaire, in the role of Crusader (not Templar), made a brave and honourable bid to fulfil the wishes of his late monarch, King Robert the Bruce.

Sir William Sainteclaire died a Crusader on pilgrimage at Teba in Spain: his memorial tombstone in the north-west corner of Rosslyn Chapel, with its sword and radiating floreated (that is, shaped like a flower) cross, commemorates a fine and honourable knight who set out on pilgrimage to the Holy Land and whose marriage to Lady Margaret Ramsay of Dalhousie produced a son (also Sir William) to succeed him as 8th Baron of Rosslyn. His father could never have been a Knight Templar, as his wealth and marriage would have broken two of the three Templar vows – poverty and chastity.

Nor is the mere possession of land that had once belonged to the Templars evidence of direct transfer between the St Clairs and the Templars (who had possessions in almost every county in Scotland). Four charters transcribed by Fr Richard Augustine Hay confirm the transfer of ownership of 6 acres of land that 'Thomas de Temple' had originally been given by the chaplain Gregory de Lisours. These had reverted to William de Lisours and were then rented out to Stephen de Melville, a clerk. Sir William Sainteclaire bought these 'Temple Lands of Gourton' from Stephen de Melville's son. As Sir John Preston acquired the estate of Gortoun (Gorton) in 1342, these charters must have been signed before that date.[36] The transfer of the land from Gregory de Lisours to de Temple, then to William de Lisours, to the de Melvilles and finally to the St Clairs, is evidence that there was no direct transfer of property between the Templars and the St Clairs.

The position of the St Clairs was not like that of Mark Ker, Commendator (lay administrator) of Newbattle Abbey; although a Commendator could have a legitimate son, the latter could not be heir to his father's monastic office without a fresh grant of commend. However, Ker (the only case of a legitimate son being born to a Commendator before 1560), took 'extraordinary measures to retain his abbacy after contracting marriage'.[37] The Revd J.C. Carrick, minister of Newbattle, explains:

> Mark Ker, son of Sir Andrew Ker of Cessford, was lay Abbot at the Reformation of 1560. He became a Reformer at the dissolution of the monasteries, and was made Commendator of the lands, and thus became the founder of the House of Lothian. He was among those lords and barons who subscribed the 'contract to defend the liberty of the Evangell of Christ' at Edinburgh on the 27th April, 1560. In the roll of the Parliament on the 1st August of that year which ratified and approved 'The Confession of the Faith and Doctrine believed and professed by the Protestants of Scotland, he is styled 'Commendator' [or caretaker until the troubles of the time

The Temple Lands in the Grassmarket, Edinburgh. (From James Grant, *Edinburgh Old and New* (London: Cassell, Petter, Galpin, 1880?–1883?))

had passed over] of Newbottle.' In course of time he married Helen Leslie, of the House of Rothes, and died in 1584.[38]

Mark Ker left the abbey and its properties to his son, having also cleverly taken care to have been 'provided' (i.e. granted entitlement) to them by the Roman Catholic Mary Queen of Scots in 1567. His son became the 1st Marquess of Lothian. This bold and unique legal strategy was not employed by the St Clairs, who remained Roman Catholics for many years after the Reformation.

Neither was the St Clairs' situation similar in these respects to that of the (equally unique) Sir James Sandilands, last Grand Prior of the Hospitallers, who also joined the Reformers in 1560: 'The Order was [by] then suppressed, and Sir James, on paying a sum down, and engaging to pay an annual rent to the Crown, entered into possession of the remaining estates in that quarter as a temporal barony, and was created Lord Torphichen.'[39]

It is important to emphasise that the St Clairs possessed the lands and titles that the monarch gave as a reward for their defence of the realm and person of the king or queen. Sir William Sainteclaire, for example, demonstrated his ultimate loyalty to the monarch by signing a bond of man-rent to Queen Mary of Guise as late as 1546.[40]

Map of Edinburgh published in 1575. (From James Grant, *Edinburgh Old and New* (London: Cassell, Petter, Galpin, 1880?–1883?))

The story of the hunt over the Pentlands is indicative of the ways in which the kings of Scotland cleverly encouraged and reinforced feudal loyalty – what several charters refer to as 'service of the body'. Like any of their peers, the St Clairs had to put their bodies on the line, and their reward for this potential self-sacrifice was ownership of land, titles and property. Hunting was not just an idle or cruel pastime: a day's hunting was a bonding exercise, designed to allow the king to assess the characters of his principal subjects, their strengths and weaknesses, while under the pressure of the hunt. It also gave him an opportunity to talk to them as individuals in an informal setting, man to man, to gather information on his kingdom and the interpersonal relationships between his nobles. Finally, it was also good exercise and an opportunity to let off steam for the more headstrong; killing defenceless animals was preferable to killing one another.

It should not be forgotten that Rosslyn Chapel was the religious expression of a rich and powerful man, actively engaged in the public affairs of the kingdom. The most convincing evidence of the orthodoxy and loyalty of the Sainteclaires is the tight control that the kings of Scotland maintained over their subjects, no matter how high born or wealthy. Apart from the fact that there is no valid evidence of subversive or irregular practices by the Sainteclaires, it is inconceivable that men of their stature could have concealed huge fortunes or major relics from the king or even indulged in covert irregular religious rites.

A glance at the Sainteclaire charters shows that their affairs were very public and witnessed by many of the most powerful figures in the country. The confirmation of castleguard (feudal service), for example, to Henry de Sinclair by King Robert in 1404 was witnessed in Edinburgh by the Bishop of Aberdeen, the Chancellor of Scotland, the Sheriff of Bute and a number of knights, as well as a secretary and a clerk. A charter of 1476 dealing with the ownership of lands at Roslin required that £5,000 be paid annually at the high altar of the Abbey of Holyrood; the document was signed at Rosslyn Castle before more than nine witnesses.

The loyalty of the St Clairs was continuously witnessed and guaranteed by the highest in the land, as the signatures on their charters prove: the successful kings of Scotland derived their power partly by keeping a tight rein on their subjects, no matter what their status in society. The charter made in 1357 by King David II confirming the gift of the lands of Morton and Merchiston to Sir William St Clair was written at Edinburgh in the presence of the Bishop of St Andrews, the Bishop of Brechin (the Royal Chancellor) and other great men of the kingdom. The charter drawn up in 1476 by Sir William St Clair in favour of Sir Oliver St Clair, for example, confirms that Sir William will submit himself to penalties should he break his word. This is defined as wounding or hurting his solemn oath and faith in Christ, and the penalty is the payment of £5,000 to the Bishop of St Andrews and his successors at the high altar of St Andrews Cathedral.

Following the dismantling of Roman Catholic canon law at the Reformation, papal authority ceased to be recognised in Scotland, although much of the legal framework and legal technical vocabulary that had been developed over many centuries by the Roman Catholic Church was adopted and adapted by the Reformers, such as the College of Justice or the office of notary public, leaving the Latin legal terminology almost intact. The Order of the Temple was suppressed in 1309 in Scotland but was revived as a Romantic lay Protestant organisation for gentlemen in 1805 by Alexander Deuchar (1777–1844), a seal-engraver and herald at the court of the Lord Lyon in Edinburgh, with the archaic Latin title of *Ordo supremis militaris templi hierosolymi militari*. Its true origins lay within the fellowship of modern Freemasonry. Today, there are several orders of Knights Templar not formally connected to each other.

CHAPTER 5

Contemporary Attitudes

ROSLIN HERITAGE SOCIETY

In late 1967, when Roslin village was under threat of unprecedented expansion from a planning application submitted by a speculative building contractor, many people in the village became so incensed that the Roslin and District Amenity Society was formed to coordinate public objections. This primary aim was later extended to safeguarding and improving village amenities. The planning application was rejected by Midlothian Council and, following a lengthy public inquiry, an appeal by the contractor to the Secretary of State for Scotland was also dismissed.

Accordingly, the Roslin/Bilston Community Council was inaugurated in October 1974 and took over a number of the objectives of the Amenity Society; however, the latter continued as a supplementary body to the Community Council. A subcommittee of the Amenity Society was then formed to put together a history of Roslin. In May 1981 a *History of Roslin Churches* was produced, followed by a *History of Parish Schools 1929–1980*.

After 1981 the Amenity Society changed its name to the Roslin Heritage Group and began to hold regular local history meetings. During a 1988 'Clean-up Forth' campaign inspired by *UK 2000 Keep Scotland Beautiful*, over a hundred volunteers from local youth organisations and the Round Table picked up 10 tons of paper and metal scrap, which were then removed by Midlothian Council.

During this operation it was noticed that many paths were overgrown and other local amenities sadly dilapidated. It was decided that urgent remedial work was necessary. With the help of Lothian Regional Council, the 72 wooden steps leading from the River Esk (known as 'Jacob's Ladder') and which had been installed by boy scouts in 1913 were replaced by 136 steps securely anchored with wooden blocks made from old railway sleepers and recycled kerb stones.

The Roslin Heritage Group changed its name to the Roslin Heritage Society in 1988, with 60–80 members who came regularly to the monthly meetings. In 1991, having spent a number of years restoring the right of way between Rosslyn Castle and Hewan, with additional public access at Roslin Glen, the society was named Scottish winner of the Shell Better Britain Award. For the award, members of the society had had to renovate the walk, drain boggy sections, lay pipes and restore old bridges. This they achieved with the help of a grant of £500 provided by Shell.

Among the other core activities of the society have been the publication of *Old Roslin*, a Roslin Gunpowder Mills CD Rom, two booklets (*Battle of Roslin* and *Roslin*

Soutra Aisle, not part of the original monastic hospital but built in 1686 from the ruins of the hospital as a burial place for the Pringle family.

Rambles) and the tireless work of the teams of the 'Recording Angels', volunteer historians who are in the process of compiling a list of Roslin's gravestones and monumental inscriptions.[1]

SOUTRA AISLE

Digging of another kind is also a familiar sight at Soutra Aisle, which stands on a windswept hill (1,209 feet) looking west to Rosslyn and the Pentland Hills beyond, high above the B6368 road to Kelso, some 12 miles from Edinburgh. To the north there are unrivalled views of the expanse of the River Forth, with Fife and its hills easily visible on a fine day. Today part of the Borders, the chapel was originally in Edinburghshire and therefore once part of Midlothian.

Once a year in the autumn a Church of Scotland service is held at this tiny chapel, today a family vault for the Pringle family, using the old Pringle family bible. The low but sturdy stone structure of Soutra Aisle is all that is left of the extensive medieval hospital of Soltre, believed to have been founded by King Malcolm IV around 1164 and dedicated to the Holy Trinity.[2]

Granted the privilege of providing sanctuary to the indigent, the infirm, to pilgrims and other travellers, the hospital was strategically placed on the main northern invasion route from England and hence inundated, at times of conflict, with the wounded and the dying. Here, the canons of the Augustinian order tended to the sick, using skills that had been refined over centuries of medical practice, preparing the medicinal herbs grown in the hospital gardens as ingredients for their therapeutic treatments.

The little we know today about the hospital is due to the labours, the unquenchable enthusiasm and determination of one man – Dr Brian Moffat – an archaeo-botanist who has meticulously excavated a small section of the sprawling site, searching for evidence of the medical techniques employed by the Augustinians. Much of what he has found has escaped destruction only because it was preserved by water and the clay soil.[3] In the late 1980s Dr Moffat helped set up SHARP (Soutra Hospital Archaeo-ethnopharmacological Research Project), a project sponsored by the Royal College of Physicians of Edinburgh and the British Pharmacological Society to discover the ingredients used in treatments at Soutra and evaluate them by reference to medieval medical textbooks.[4]

The archaeological evidence seems to suggest that the dedicated Augustinian doctors and nurses also treated psychological conditions such as depression with the medicines they prescribed, as well as more life-threatening diseases such as cancer. Dr Moffat found 'blood-dumps' (the product of blood-letting), traces of locally grown opium and of herbal preparations – which appear to have been used for easing the pains of childbirth – while the presence of tar deposits confirms that amputations were practised.[5] Dr Moffat was able to distinguish more than 200 herbs and spices: he believes that a mixture of black henbane, opium and hemlock anaesthetised the hospital's patients before surgery, ergot and juniper berries were also given to pregnant women to induce labour and St John's Wort prescribed to ease 'melancolia' (depression).[6]

In 1462, while Rosslyn Chapel was still in the throes of construction, the Hospital of Soltre was annexed by Queen Mary of Gueldres to her foundation of the Collegiate Hospital and Parish Church of the Holy Trinity in Edinburgh. This was originally located on the present site of Waverley Station. In 1667 Drs Robert Sibbald and Andrew Balfour formed a Town Physic Garden in addition to their Royal Physic Garden (1670) at Holyrood Palace. In 1761 the two gardens were united by Dr John Hope on a new site at the top of Leith Walk. This, in turn, was moved to its present position at Inverleith in 1820, so completing a long historical link between the Augustinian canons at Soutra and the Royal Botanic Garden at Inverleith in Edinburgh.

ROSSLYNLEE

In the nineteenth century the Midlothian and Peebles District Asylum Board of Lunacy accepted patients from the extensive area around Edinburgh – Cramond, Ratho and Musselburgh – as well as Midlothian and Peebles (in the Borders). By the

The seal of Queen Mary of Gueldres in the Bannatyne Club's charters. (From *Charters of the Hospital of Soltre, of Trinity College, Edinburgh and other Collegiate Churches in Mid-Lothian* (Edinburgh, 1861))

Rosslynlee Hospital (1874). (By permission of Rosslynlee Hospital)

1860s the Royal Edinburgh Hospital, which treated paying and pauper lunatics, had reached its capacity and was unable to accept any more patients.

A search began for a site suitable for a new facility. It had to be easily accessible, located in an area where land was cheap and where there would be a good supply of water. The estate of Whitehill, to the south-west of Roslin, was chosen for these reasons and because it was close to an existing railway line, the Roslin station of the Peebles Railway, from which a siding and a branch would be constructed leading to the asylum grounds.

Known originally as the Midlothian and Peebles District Asylum, it opened in 1874 to serve the landward parishes of Edinburgh and Midlothian with a capacity for 200 patients of both sexes and was provided with a laundry for the women patients and workshops for the men. It became known as Rosslynlee because of its proximity to the local railway station.

Patients were admitted with 'lunacy', or what we would now call mental illness. The definition was flexible and included those with dementia, learning disability or even odd behaviour who could not be coped with in the poorhouse (at Dalkeith or Inveresk), or in the Institutions for Mental Deficiency that sprang up in the 1920s (Gogarburn, for example, or St Joseph's Hospital in Rosewell).

As a former private farm standing as it did deep in the countryside, Rosslynlee had access to more than 500 acres of land and two farms, rearing sheep with lambs that gained prizes at agricultural shows such as those at Peebles and Ingliston.

The therapies offered changed over the years, beginning with moral therapies in Victorian times that employed a system of regular occupational routines. Faradic techniques were also used that depended on electrical stimulation of the skin, and hydrotherapy with baths of various temperatures – water at body heat for the depressed, lukewarm for the manic and cold baths for other conditions. Aversive therapy also had its place, and some degree of (non-physical) reward and punishment was also practised as part of the treatment.

As well as in-house entertainment, the patients enjoyed annual picnics to local beauty spots and historic buildings such as Dalhousie Castle, Loganlea Reservoir and Habbie's Howe in the Pentlands. On Sundays they were expected to take part in a religious service conducted by the Church of Scotland minister from Rosewell.

In 1948 Rosslynlee became part of the Board of Management of the Royal Edinburgh Asylum and Associated Hospitals under the South Eastern Hospital Board.[7]

Today, a history of Rosslynlee Hospital is nearing publication, the work of Dr James Craig, who was employed as a consultant psychiatrist at the Hospital between 1980 and 2005.[8] Now retired from full-time practice, Dr Craig is preparing his history based on forty-one casebooks that cover the period from 1874 to the 1940s and also on recorded interviews with members of staff with long experience of the hospital.

There is little doubt that the unspoilt beauty of the countryside in and around Roslin Glen and its magnificent chapel played a supportive part in the success of the therapeutic regimes at Rosslynlee.

TEMPLE

Not far from Roslin, the tiny village of Temple, once a centre for the Templar knights, has its main street flanked by cottages and, down in the valley, the fourteenth-century church, restored in 1984.

In recent years Temple has been more closely associated with the arts: the journalist, playwright and novelist George Scott-Moncrieff (1910–74) lived there for a time. His daughter Lesley was born in Temple and is proud to have been baptised at Rosslyn Chapel. Among his many works, her father wrote *Hogmanay in a Midlothian Village*, designed as an hour-long BBC Radio broadcast.[9] In this nostalgic look back at the skills and pastimes of previous generations, Scott-Moncrieff has a dyker (stone-wall builder) describe his craft in language that immediately suggests the work of the stonemasons at Rosslyn (albeit at a more rudimentary level) and their pride in working the stone:

> when you build a dyke right it's not so easy. Now, say you were building a dyke at four feet six, that's one of the finest dykes that can be built. You make a gauge with wooden spars. In the middle of the gauge you have a plumb, and that keeps your lines level. They you lay the bottom of your dyke, building first one side and then the other, and build as carefully in the middle as at the sides – for if a man or a dyke has a bad heart there's no good in him . . . When you get the dyke up to two foot, you put a stone right through from one side to the other – a band-stone. That holds it. You need a band-stone every three feet along the dyke. Then you put on your top-course . . . a top band of bit stones and finish the dyke with a cope, and that makes a fine beild [shelter] and it's well worth the work.

In 1939 Scott-Moncrieff sold his house in the main street to the East Lothian-born painter Sir William George Gillies (1898–1973), later to become one of Scotland's foremost landscape artists. Gillies was to make the house his home to the end of his life. After war service, Gillies graduated from Edinburgh College of Art

Above left: The writer George Scott-Moncrieff in his home at Temple Village. (By permission of Mrs Lesley Findlay) *Above right:* The house at Temple Village that George Scott-Moncrieff sold to the artist Sir William Gillies.

Harpist, clarsach player and glass-artist Alison Kinnaird MBE. (Photograph © Colin Clark)

Musician and song collector Robin Morton, a founder (1967) member of the 'The Boys of the Lough'. (Photograph © Pete Heywood)

Sir William Gillies at work in his house at Temple. (By permission of William J.L. Baillie)

and, along with Sir William MacTaggart and Robert Crosier, formed part of the 1922 Group. In 1923 Gillies went to Paris on a travelling scholarship to study with the Cubist painter André Lhote and then joined the staff of Edinburgh College of Art, commuting between Temple and Edinburgh on his beloved motorbike. He became Head of Painting in 1946 and later Principal of the College (1960–6). Gillies continued to paint his characteristically subtle forms and colouring until his death.

Down in the valley, below the main street of Temple and facing the roofless medieval church, is the former Temple Kirk. Since 1976 this has been home to the (small) Scottish harp and clarsach (the Gaelic wire-stringed instrument) player and glass-artist Alison Kinnaird and her husband, Ulster-born former psychiatric social worker Robin Morton. Kinnaird took her degree in Celtic studies and archaeology. She was later introduced to glass-engraving by Harold Gordon at his studio in Forres, subsequently attending classes with Helen Munro Turner at the Edinburgh College of Art, but is largely self-taught. Her work is to be found in many important international collections, and she has a major installation in the permanent collection of the new Scottish Parliament building in Edinburgh. In 1997 Alison Kinnaird was awarded an MBE for services to Scottish music and art.[10]

Today a key figure in Scottish folk music, Morton read Social Sciences at Queen's University, Belfast, followed by economic and social history and studies as a postgraduate at Edinburgh University.[11]

Aside from their impressive academic training, they both share a passionate love of music. Morton was, with Tommy Gunn and Cathal McConell, one of the founder members of the original The Boys of the Lough (1967), with whom he played and toured the United States. During the 1960s Morton spent a number of years collecting songs, mostly in his native Ulster, and in the early 1970s published two books relating to this work.[12]

In 1979 Temple Records was formed (based at Morton's recording studio at Temple) to provide an outlet for the rich heritage of Scottish folk music that was being ignored by the established record companies; a year later he became manager of the Battlefield Band. Morton also found time to be director of the Edinburgh Folk Festival (1986–8).[13]

THE DISRUPTION

In May 1843 under an ancient elm tree at the centre of Roslin's old cemetery, minister the Revd Mr David Brown preached to the people who had followed him in his departure from the Established Church of Scotland. Some 474 ministers (out of a total of 1,200) signed the Deed of Demission and formed the Free Church of Scotland. Here, under the elm tree in the grounds of what was the medieval Roman Catholic church of St Matthew, Mr Brown preached to his people. He did this for eighteen successive Sabbaths, the first three in the open, the remainder in a tent.

On one of these later Sundays, it is recorded that three elderly men, who appeared to be 'gentlemen', spent the day in a variety of amusements. Having dined at the

Interior of the Free Kirk, Roslin, constructed in 1881. (Bryce Collection by permission of Midlothian Library Service)

Roslin Inn, they went down to the old graveyard, overturned the tent placed there for Mr Brown's service, left it lying in pieces and then escaped in a hurry to Edinburgh. Fortunately for Mr Brown and his congregation, even when the week was wet or windy, the day of his service always turned warm and fair.[14] Of the 240 parishioners, some 200 went with Mr Brown out of the Church of Scotland, leaving only 40 behind. When the colder weather came, the new 'Free Church' congregation worshipped in a local schoolhouse. In spite of determined opposition from the local landowners, Mr Brown was eventually able to buy a piece of ground in the middle of the village. The Free Church opened its doors on Christmas Eve 1843.[15]

After his death, Mr Brown's congregation erected a monument to him in the old graveyard under the large elm tree (in the 'Church under the Trees'), which reads:

In memory of Revd David Brown. Died 3rd March 1870, aged 76 years. As a testimony of his faithful services as a minister of the Gospel, this stone is erected

Roslin Cemetery from the chapel. (Bryce Collection by permission of Midlothian Library Service)

by members of his congregation and other friends on the spot where he preached for six months, and dispensed the communion after the Disruption in 1843. 'He being dead yet liveth.'

Not far off was the grave of the 'Big Wife' who had been hostess to Robert Burns at the Roslin Inn, while on a neighbouring stone the following curious lines are engraved:

> Underneath this stone doth lie
> As much virtue as could die,
> Which when alive did vigour give
> To as much beauty as could live.

ST MATTHEW'S, ROSEWELL

To the east, not far from Roslin, the Roman Catholic church of St Matthew's, Rosewell, was built to minister to the needs of a large mining community, many of whom were Irish. The rows of compact red-brick houses reflect the solidarity and closeness of the men and women who worked in the local industries, in the local coalmines or in the nearby paper mills.

For these Catholics, a 'neat and substantial chapel' was opened in February 1889, named, appropriately, after its older and more famous neighbour at Roslin. The first church of St Matthew's, Rosewell was also built in the Gothic style but in local red and white brick with stone facings. It had ten pointed windows, a roof open to the ridge and lined with wood. Above the altar was a triangular stained-glass window showing the figure of St Matthew.[16]

Within forty years this first church had become too small for the size of its congregation. In November 1923 another and larger church was opened, built almost entirely of yellow brick, with a large brick cloister and wall enclosing the parish grounds. To celebrate the opening of the new church a dance was held at the institute nearby, where the dancers twirled and spun to the strains of Mr C. Foster's band.[17]

In 1917, when she was 17 years of age, Margaret Sinclair, an Edinburgh working girl who lived in Blackfriars Street (where once had stood the town house of the St Clair family), came with her sister to spend a summer holiday at Rosewell, boarding with a local family, and Rosewell soon became a favourite holiday resort for the Sinclairs. Margaret was for some time concerned at the lack of a proper Catholic church at Rosewell and attended the laying of the foundation stone of the present building on 9 October 1922. The country lane along which she used to walk to mass in the original school chapel was once known as 'Margaret Sinclair's Walk'.[18] Many years later these visits would sow the seeds of an extraordinary devotion.

As a young girl in St Patrick's parish (a former Episcopal church in the Cowgate), Margaret attended St Patrick's School. After leaving school, she studied for certificates in dressmaking, cooking and sewing at the prestigious Atholl Crescent School of Domestic Economy, qualifications that would help her find a job as a housemaid.

Margaret also worked part-time as a commercial messenger to help support her family. Then she took up full-time work as a French polisher, becoming an active trade-union member.

When the Waverley Cabinet Works closed in 1918 she found employment at McVitie's biscuit factory. But another calling was awakening in her. She thought long and hard about the direction her life was taking and then decided to dedicate herself to God by becoming a nun. In 1923 she entered the convent of the Poor Clares at

Margaret Sinclair. (By permission of Fr Ed. Hone, St Patrick's, Edinburgh)

Notting Hill in London and was professed as a nun in February 1925. Her name in religion was Sister Mary Francis of the Five Wounds.

However, she was subsequently diagnosed with incurable tuberculosis of the throat and, after a long and painful illness, died that November at a sanatorium in Essex and was buried at Kensal Green cemetery, London. In 1927 her remains were transferred to a marble tomb at Mount Vernon cemetery in Edinburgh, close to a convent of the Poor Clares. Over the ensuing years a number of miraculous cures were reported by those who prayed in her name.

By 1931 popular devotion to Margaret Sinclair was such that Archbishop Andrew J. McDonald instituted an 'informative process' of investigation, involving in-depth interviews with people who had known her and could vouch for her lifestyle. This was followed by her cause (the ongoing process to show that a person deserves to be declared a saint) being introduced to the Vatican's Sacred Congregation of Rites by Pope Pius XII. Margaret Sinclair was declared a 'Servant of God', the first step on the road to eventual canonisation (which includes 'Venerable', 'Blessed' and finally 'Saint'). In August 1952 Archbishop Gordon J. Gray presided over an apostolic process (a legal tribunal) in Edinburgh, in the presence of officials from Rome, which closed that October.

In 1961 a film produced by Bert Mocogni and recreating Margaret Sinclair's life was released; *The Story of Margaret Sinclair* dramatised her early years and included scenes of a visit to Rosslyn Chapel.[19] With the arrival in 1965 of Fr Denis O'Connell (vice-postulator of Margaret Sinclair's cause) as parish priest at Rosewell, efforts were made to provide a focus for popular devotion to her Cause for Beatification. A National Margaret Sinclair Centre was opened at St Matthew's Church, Rosewell, on 29 June 1965, housing her domestic relics in a small parish room: a table, chairs, pictures, a lamp, a coat and a bed taken from Margaret's own room in Blackfriars Street.

As well as organising an annual pilgrimage to Rosewell, St Matthew's generated much public interest in the Scottish nun, who had by now become known as 'The Edinburgh Wonder Worker'. There were, too, more claims of miracles, among them that of the recovery from the crippling effects of a fall at the age of 2 years of the mother of TV personality Sir Jimmy Saville OBE, who attributed his mother's cure to prayers she had said after seeing a photograph of Margaret Sinclair at Leeds Cathedral.

In 1978 Margaret Sinclair was declared Venerable by the Roman Catholic Church – the next step towards canonisation. On 6 October 2003 her body and its marble monument were brought together at a new place of rest in a side-chapel of her own parish church of St Patrick's in the Cowgate, to which her former belongings were also brought from St Matthew's, Rosewell.

THE COMMUNITY OF THE TRANSFIGURATION

With the Community of the Transfiguration we come to a contemporary and experimental religious community. It is easy, perhaps, to forget that the Collegiate

Fr Roland Walls outside the former miners' institute, now the Community of the Transfiguration.

Church of St Matthew was also something of an experimental community in the 1440s. While it is not easy to reconstruct the lives of the canons of St Matthew, today it is nevertheless still possible to learn a little of what it means to live in community.

Not far from Rosslyn Chapel stands a weather-beaten green tin shack, a former miners' institute saved from demolition in 1965 only by the last-minute donation from a kindly local benefactor. Today, the building is still set back from the road but shaded by mature trees. Brother John Halsey (an Anglican priest) and Father Roland Walls (an Anglican priest who became a Roman Catholic) live there in what they called the Hermitage of the Transfiguration.

Both Father Roland and Brother John had been priests in charge of Rosslyn Chapel, the former from 1962 to 1968, the latter succeeding him for a period in 1968. In 1965 they had, along with several others, set up an experimental religious community in Roslin, not far from the rectory. During these early years, following the promptings of the Second Vatican Council, Abbot Columban Mulcahy of the Cistercian Sancta Maria Abbey (at Nunraw in East Lothian, not far from Haddington) was the driving force behind the ecumenical movement in Scotland. On one occasion, while Brother John and Father Roland were on retreat at Nunraw, Abbot Columban directed them to spend the first day meditating on the fact that 'God loves you'. On the following day the Abbot proposed that they think about a truth that 'You can love God'; on the final day, he suggested they concentrate on the hardest truth of all – 'Love one another', the injunction of Jesus to his disciples.[20] This was a moment of enlightenment, as Abbot Columban had made them realise that these three truths were the foundations of religious life.

A recent biography of Father Roland by Ron Ferguson and Mark Chater describes how he came to be in Roslin. Father Roland was originally invited in 1962 by his friend Kenneth Carey, Scottish Episcopal Bishop of Edinburgh, to be priest in charge at the Rosslyn Chapel and to act as chaplain to the Earl of Rosslyn. At first Father Roland recoiled from the suggestion, as the chapel was used only on Sundays and for a few holy days a year. The congregation was also very small – it was a *museum*, he protested.[21] However, after spending some weeks with the late Brother Roger at Taizé (on whose Rule that of the Hermitage of the Transfiguration would be based), he accepted the charge and took up his duties at the chapel. In 1981, however, Father Roland became a Roman Catholic and was, as he put it, subsequently 're-ordered' as a Catholic priest in 1983.

The author interviewed Father Roland some years ago at Roslin in glorious sunshine and was welcomed by his mischievous (and at the same time serenely cherubic) smile. He leaned over the wooden gate, drawing meditatively on his pipe. Behind him on the gable end of the Houses of the Transfiguration (which was founded to promote Christian unity) hung a sign in Gaelic, *Comaraich*, meaning 'sanctuary'. It dangled below the gnarled wish-bone branch of an ancient tree from a bog in Sutherland. This was, and still is, his 'Buddhist garden' ('The Lord is the gardener,' he added). He then pointed out an even more twisted antique root, shaped like a man. 'That's what we call the Devil,' smiled Father Roland. 'He's fleeing – I hope!'

Inside the main communal house, coffee was on the boil. Here was not only a community that was ecumenical and open to all, but one able to reaffirm the value of the discarded and the decayed, an oasis of reality in a world of polystyrene.

Before he retired, Brother John Halsey – an Anglican priest and now Prior of the house – worked as a labourer in a local garage stripping down cars for repainting. Father Roland, an Anglican priest for over forty years, has the gift of prising people open with the challenge of his insight and humour. His community, basing their lives on the rules of St Benedict ('sobriety') and St Francis ('that's where the wildness comes in!'), have their cells and their chapel in the back garden of the house, where silence is maintained at all times. A key public event in the life of the Houses of the Transfiguration was the celebration of the community's twenty-fifth anniversary on 16 August 1990, held at Rosslyn Chapel, with leaders of the different denominations – the Episcopal primus, Bishop Richard Holloway, the Greek Orthodox Archimandrite, John Maitland-Moir, and members of the Roman Catholic hierarchy, Cardinal Gordon Joseph Gray and Archbishop Keith O'Brien. The celebration came as part of a wider international plenary of *Faith and Light* attended by its founder, Jean Vanier.

Set in the shade of the Houses of the Transfiguration are the community's cells, garden sheds of treated wood with roofs of black roofing felt; the hermits' mattresses lie on stout wooden doors. In the chapel with its 'feminist icon' showing the valuable role of women in the Church, was the most telling example of the community's cherishing of the ordinary things in life – Stations of the Cross, each made from two used matchsticks pierced through by a pin. The overwhelming impression of Father Roland and the Houses of the Transfiguration was of a community at the leading edge of the religious life.

Perhaps it is possible to understand a little of what the biblical carvings in Rosslyn Chapel meant those long centuries ago by listening to Father Roland's theology:

If he's really the God of the Bible, God is interested in the pluralism of love. Love not only endures but rejoices in diversity – as in the Blessed Trinity itself. I'm more and more inclined to go back to avoiding the word 'God' as often as possible, because I notice that in the Fathers of the Church (the early Greek Fathers and the Latin Fathers) they like to call God by his proper name of 'Father, Son and Holy Spirit' (or the *Trias* – Trinity).

We've got to get into the habit of doing this because it immediately points out what He's up to. It's the Trinity of a love relationship whose essence and unity is love in a diversification of persons. So it gives us some clue as to what He does and what He is. As I've lived in Roslin for many years, I believe that one of the attractive sides of Midlothian is that, unlike some other rather overtly touristic counties, Midlothian contains this extraordinarily rich diversity. But it also has its struggles towards unity which is always fraught and always has to be remade again and again (rather like love-affairs anywhere).

I'm interested in the *county*-God, and this particular effort of trying to get people to – not just tolerate diversity – but rejoice in it. It is a stage of maturity in the human person that he or she can do this.

Normally speaking, our adolescence includes a certain intolerance. You bolt yourself down into a certain class or educational or economic background. You find yourself a comfortable nest in whatever you've been born into and fall into the routine of getting it going.

Whereas the world at large, in this county in particular – its future and its happiness and its viability, is going to depend on whether we've got enough people working away to change what persons in society look like.

It's only when we're persons in society, in community, that we're going to reflect, as the Bible says, 'The image of the God who made us'. It's only thus that we're going to understand what He's up to (and always has been up to).

It is very important, it seems to me, that we localise very particularly and rejoice when people are going to write or speak or work for a particular 'locality'. I'm very optimistic about the present situation because in this sort of homelessness, exile and alienation (that have been going on at least from the Industrial Revolution) there's been a reaction in the past thirty years: people speaking on the media and writing about 'locality' and 'characters' have become very popular. Such books and programmes have a good commercial selling-value which indicates to me that there's a need for roots and a seeking for roots.

In my own life, I was born into a very rooted family in the Isle of Wight and for the first part of my life I wandered from work in Leeds, Sheffield and Cambridge. Then I found myself up in Midlothian in a broken-down mining village. I've now lived years here and my need for roots isn't to return to my original soil in the Isle of Wight. I've found myself joining little families and in the things that go on in a Midlothian village and finding my rootedness in this.

If anyone asks me what I've been thankful for, it is that I found myself in such a place. It's very important that people should be affirmed not only in their jobs and their activities, but in their locality. It's to do with faith.

'Home' is one of the most powerful words you can use in a sermon. However dreary you are in a sermon, if you use the word 'Home' you get attention for that sentence.

This homelessness (for lots of people, a will-o' the wisp image at the back of their minds, something that corresponds to the open fire and the slippers), I think can be healed in a locality. That locality is the place where you can think about a God who is Home because He's love, who is love because He's diversity in unity. Wherever these two words 'God' and 'Home' appear (whether in economics, social developments, family problems or successes, in the Church and in the Church's unity and disunity) they are of paramount importance.

If you want a laboratory where you can look at these words in detail, then this county is as good as any in Britain.

CHAPTER 6

Castles and Houses

ROSSLYN CASTLE

Today, after many centuries and vicissitudes, Rosslyn Castle itself is not open to casual visitors, but members of the public can walk across the arched stone bridge, into what is now a forecourt, admire what remains of the tall structure that towers precariously above them like a miniature Old Man of Hoy and even peer cautiously over the parapets down past the sheer drop of the castle foundations into the wooded paths and the North Esk River even further below.

According to an anonymous manuscript (collected and quoted from at length by Fr Richard Augustine Hay), the 'History of the Sainteclaires', the stronghold of Rosslyn 'is said to have been founded by the Pictish leader Asterius, whose daughter, Panthioria, married Donald the First'.[1] Today, the latter is better known as Domnall (d. AD 862), who succeeded his brother Kenneth mac Alpin as King of Alba in AD 858.[2]

An early nineteenth-century postcard by Alex A. Inglis showing Rosslyn Castle from the river, with, on the left, the ancient yew tree and the gardens that supplied celebrated strawberries and vegetables and, to the right, Rosslyn Chapel upon the hill.

The Revd John Thompson follows Hay in saying that it was William Sainteclaire (the so-called Seemly Sainteclaire) who was the first of his line to be associated with Rosslyn, a barony given to him in 1070 by the king as a *liferent* (having the use of its income during his lifetime). However, Thompson also adds that it was only some forty years later that the first of the Sainteclaires came to settle permanently at Rosslyn, a Sir Henry Sainteclaire. Thompson very sensibly adds that Hay's sources appear to confuse three different men called Henry Sainteclaire. Whatever the dating, all sources agree that Rosslyn came into Sainteclaire hands as a reward for services rendered to the Crown.

On a much smaller scale, the Sainteclaire colonisation of Rosslyn's glaciated rock, which rises so steeply out of the glen, bears some similarities to the way in which Edinburgh developed out of a castle on a glaciated crag and tail hill and a religious foundation below, the Canongate (the *gait* of the canons), but in reverse. In those days power had two contrasting expressions – fortification and prayer, gunpowder and incense.

Thompson quotes Hay in saying that, after the triple battle of Roslin on 24 February 1302, and in return for the honourable and generous way in which Sir William had treated him, an important English prisoner of Sir William Sainteclaire gave him some useful advice on fortification. He observed that Sir William's castle, at that time almost certainly located on the glacial deposits on the hill where Rosslyn Chapel stands today (probably over what is now referred to as the crypt and, allegedly, as deep as the future Rosslyn Chapel would be high), was defensively weak and exposed. He strongly advised Sir William to build a new castle on the site with which we are now familiar, constructed on an almost impossibly steep rocky promontory above what was at the time a small loch.

Evidently, the flat piece of land that exists at the bottom of Roslin Glen, part of which is known as the Stanks (from *étang*, French for a pond or pool) and near where the linen-bleaching, carpet-weaving and gunpowder factories would later be situated, was at that time flooded, forming a marsh or stagnant pool, a feature of which was the Goose's Mound where waterfowl used to nest.

The earliest part of the present castle, continues Thompson, would appear to have been the tower (now in ruins) on the north-east corner, and some other buildings behind. This was known as the Lantern, and also as the Lamp Tower (presumably because it was equipped with a light to guide visitors in the dark) and was constructed some two years after the battle of Roslin.

At the base of the high wall which adjoins it on the south-east were the remains of a staircase of nine steps cut out of the face of the rock and probably leading to a terrace above. This feature would have been in place before the vaults were built and the rock cut away on the south-east.

At the south-west corner of the castle is the Great Dungeon (*donjon* in French), also known as the Keep, built (according to Hay) by Sir William's great-grandson, Sir Henry, the second Prince or Earl (*jarl*) of Orkney, around the year 1390. The dungeon is some 50 feet long, of unrecorded width, and has five storeys. Access to it

Rosslyn Castle, seen from the river walk.

was apparently at the furthest side of the bridge, where one of the jambs of the doorway could still be faintly seen.

The next major development of the castle came when Sir William Sainteclaire, founder of the chapel, who succeeded to the estate in 1417, spent a number of years enlarging and strengthening it. Hay states that for thirty-four years before Rosslyn Chapel was completed, Sir William (a man who took much pleasure in erecting buildings for the common good) employed enormous numbers of craftsmen and labourers at the castle, both to strengthen the defences and to improve the accommodation. These projects included the construction of the first chapel at Rosslyn (at the castle), that of the castle's forward defences facing to the north-east, of the arched bridge below the castle and of various rooms to house administrative offices. At the south-east (above the North Esk), opposite what was the wall of the first chapel, he had the rock face on which the castle sits cleared and smoothed out in order to make it more difficult for potential attackers to gain a foothold. This area of improved defences extended from the keep (the south-west tower) northwards, turning along the north-east front by the drawbridge to the original tower of 1304.

This section of the reconstructed defences clearly differs from the older part, as it is made from polished stone. At the north-west, the unusual feature known as the 'rounds' (circular alcoves with defensive wedge-shaped external profiles) can still be seen, but to the north-east only massively towering fragments remain. What were once the inner walls near the courtyard have been demolished and their foundations dug up. At the north-west side the rounds, with their series of alcoves pierced by spy windows, were constructed as a buttress to strengthen the high wall to which they were attached and upon which the galleries and fine chambers were built. Some historians believe that this was also the location of the first chapel, which was inside the castle. Certainly, the shape of the windows that still flank the site of the high altar at the thirteenth-century Dunstaffnage Chapel in Argyll bears a remarkable resemblance to what remains of the rounds at Rosslyn Castle.[3]

Between the rounds is a series of openings, with recesses for shutters cut into the stone. Although it had been suggested that these were cannon emplacements or rooms in which cattle were kept, the Revd Thompson had not 'the slightest doubt that this lower apartment, with the windows as described, was the original Chapel itself'. Moreover, Fr Hay records that the rock at the south-east side of the castle was smoothed out to make it more difficult for assault troops to scale and that these improved defences stood opposite the first chapel.

The style and luxury in which Sir William, his wife and family lived mark this period as the highpoint in the history of the Sainteclaires, after which their dignity and wealth began to decline. A number of features that are essentially French were added to the castle – galleries, projecting chambers and turrets. Of the various administrative buildings constructed by Sir William nothing remains. Perhaps the many dependants with whom the Prince habitually surrounded himself lived instead at the old cottages that stood on the left-hand side of the roadway down to the castle and in which Mr Purves, the castle-keeper, lived in the 1890s, or in what was known as the Orchard (the wide slope below the east end of the chapel) where foundations have been uncovered from time to time.

As has been noted previously, fire broke out at Rosslyn Castle on 6 November 1447, when a candle accidentally set a bed alight. In spite of the dramatic circumstances of the fire, little of any great importance appears to have been damaged or destroyed. Certainly, the precious charters and other documents of Sir William Sainteclaire were saved by the presence of mind of his chaplain. By 1455 Sir William

The intriguing Midway Cottages and Rosslyn Chapel from the gate to Rosslyn Castle, *c.* 1903. (Postcard printed by Valentine & Sons Ltd, Dundee)

Hamilton is recorded as having been imprisoned at the castle for taking part in the Douglas rebellion against King James II. Nevertheless, he was soon released and accepted back into the King's favour.

However, very much worse was to come in 1544 when Henry VIII attempted to force Scotland to accept a marriage between his son Prince Edward (later King Edward VI) and the infant Mary Queen of Scots. The Earl of Hertford (later Duke of Somerset) crossed the Border in what became known as the 'Rough Wooing' (1544–7), which caused much destruction but merely served to drive the Scots into an alliance with France against the English.

King Henry, aggravated by his failure to bring the Scots into line, lashed out in all directions: he organised plots against Cardinal David Beaton, tried to bribe disaffected members of the nobility, encouraged Protestants, gave support to a pretender to the Lordship of the Isles and launched a succession of Border raids.[4] The destruction was on a massive scale: 'Edinburgh was sacked, Dundee reduced to rubble, the Border zone savaged, tens of thousands killed . . .'.[6] The Border abbeys, once the linchpin of David I's strategy for economic and social regeneration, were systematically vandalised and looted.

The Earl of Hertford attacked Rosslyn Castle and then set it on fire, almost completely destroying it. (The effects of the fire can still be seen on the walls to the north-west.) In spite of this, the castle was rebuilt again.

Following the resignation of the collegiate clergy and other widespread changes introduced by the Reformers in Scotland after 1560, the castle and chapel passed into new ownership in 1580, when Sir Edward St Clair, having fathered no children, made his estate over to his brother, Sir William Sinclair of Pentland (the fourteenth baron), who accordingly succeeded in 1582.

Sir William built the vaults and the Great Turnpike – the large 4-foot-wide stone staircase that leads from the basement of the castle up the storeys of the building. He is also credited, adds the Revd John Thompson, with constructing one of the arches of the drawbridge and a fine house near the mill, as well as the dungeon tower (where the clock was located). The mill was near the Lynn, where the watercourse cut into the rock, and could still be seen in Mr Thompson's day. Today no trace of either house or mill remains.

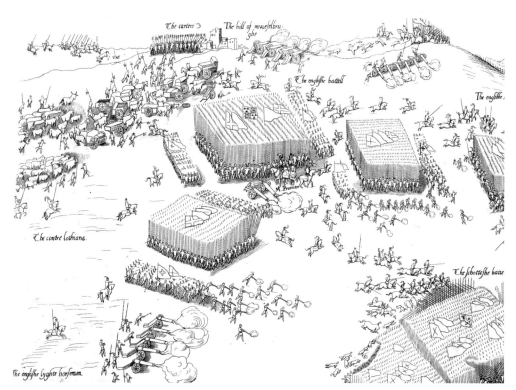

The 'Rough Wooing' - the defeat of the Scots at Pinkie near Musselburgh by the Earl of Hertford in 1547. (From the Bannatyne Club, *Récit de l'expedition en Écosse l'an MDXLVI* (Edinburgh: D. Constable, 1825))

His unwavering support of the King and his keen desire to follow the King's lead encouraged Sir William to make a continuous series of improvements. However, the frequent rebuilding, the extensions to the castle and other modifications constituted a major drain on his resources, so much so that he was forced to sell large parts of his estates in Stirling, for example, and at Mortonhall in Edinburgh.

His son (also Sir William) inherited his father's passion for construction: he completed building over the vaults (which his father had begun on a foundation of solid rock), carrying the work right up to the level of the courtyard, having his initials carved over the door: '*S.W.S* [Sir William Sainteclaire] *1622*'.

One of the curiosities of the castle is the dining-room ceiling. Made of plaster, it is divided into nine panels decorated with hunting and hawking scenes and, as in Rosslyn Chapel, with a profusion of floral ornamentation. In the centre panel are the arms of St Clair: the engrailed cross, with, on the right, a mermaid holding a comb in one hand and a bunch of seaweed in the other; to the left are a griffin and a dove, with the motto *Credo* ('I believe' – the opening Latin word of the Christian profession of faith) and the date, 1622.

This was probably the period when the castle was at its most complete. Sir William, the 16th Baron of Rosslyn, was the last to be buried in full armour, being interred in the chapel on 3 September 1650, the same day as the battle of Dunbar. At

Oliver Cromwell, who led his forces in Scotland (1650–1) against the supporters of King Charles I – a nineteenth-century engraving by Edward Scriven (1775–1841).

General George Monck, a lieutenant-general of Cromwell's ordnance in Scotland who was given the task of reducing fortresses in the winter of 1650–1 – an early nineteenth-century engraving by Phillippe Benoist.

Dunbar, under their commander David Leslie and in spite of superior numbers, the Scots were defeated by Oliver Cromwell; the Scots suffered 4,000 casualties, with 10,000 prisoners taken and the remainder fleeing to Edinburgh.

For a time, Sir William's son John held the castle in the face of the Cromwellian army. However, a force of 600 men under General George Monck attacked the Castle, using four pieces of ordnance and a mortar. 'Monck's Battery', with perfect command of the north-east end of the Castle, was some 20 yards square, placed near what was to be Rosebank House, the future residence of the Dowager Countess of Rosslyn.

The besieging forces battered down the north-west and the west sides of the castle, which was then pillaged. Everything that was worth removing was taken away and Sir John despatched to Tynemouth Castle, where he remained a prisoner for many years, only returning to Rosslyn to die in 1690.

Two years before his death, at the time of James II's flight and the accession of King William, on 11 December 1688, the castle and chapel had been looted by a mob from Edinburgh, helped and encouraged by inhabitants of Rosslyn and the Laird's tenants.

The new laird at Rosslyn was James St Clair (the future stepfather of Fr Richard Augustine Hay); unlike his predecessors, he did not immediately restore and rebuild the castle. The financial resources available to him were much more restricted than theirs had been. However, Hay records that his stepfather bought a brae (hill or hillside) just over the river at Gorton, with the intention of fencing off its wooded areas. In a similar spirit of conservation he had a wall built around the chapel and landscaped a garden beside the Linn (waterfall). He constructed the forward section of the castle at the left where the drawbridge is now crossed, and arranged for his coat of arms to be placed there, carved in stone and gilded, along with those of his mother. He ordered parapets to be added to the bridge over the River Esk (a broken bridge that today is dangerous and therefore blocked off). The parapets can still be seen below the south walls of the castle; at that time there was a stout gate to keep out walkers.

James St Clair arranged for the Dutch engineer Peter Brusche (who had in 1681 installed a new 3-inch lead-piped water supply system in Edinburgh, bringing the sweet water of Comiston to the heart of the city) to install a water supply for the castle, bringing it into the inner courtyard with the same type of lead pipes. A few years later, Brusche would not only establish a paper mill at Canonmills but also be appointed by King James VII as printer to the Royal Household at Holyrood, where he is said to have been one of the first printers in Scotland to produce playing cards.[6]

Unfortunately, all this engineering and structural work at and around the castle and chapel depleted St Clair's financial resources to the extent that after his death his widow was so impoverished she was forced to petition the King and Queen for help in bringing up and educating her large family.

From this point very little was done to either the castle or the chapel to preserve or protect the buildings, so that by the 1890s, when the Revd John Thompson wrote his invaluable guidebook, Rosslyn Castle was pretty much as James St Clair had left it – except that the ruins had become more ruinous. Indeed, the historian Francis Grose (1731–91), writing in 1788, a century after the pillaging, describes it as 'haggard and utterly dilapidated – the mere wreck of a great pile riding on a little sea of forest – a rueful apology for the once grand fabric whose name of "Roslin Castle" is so intimately associated with melody and song'.[7]

The bridge across the North Esk mentioned above was a continuation of the road under the drawbridge. By 1893 it had almost disappeared. The centre of the arch had collapsed around 1700, but some 70–80 feet of masonry remained at each end until about 1868, when the part at the south fell into the river. The stonework at the north side still stands today and can be seen through the thickly growing bushes, and also from the castle garden.

In earliest times the only route to the castle was by a slender rocky ridge that was later opened up from beneath to create a narrow roadway high above the deeply sloping ground, reinforced with a solid double sustaining stone arch. The bridge itself is 50 feet above the ground and today remains the only entrance to the castle. The first arch was built by Sir William Sainteclaire in c. 1446 and the second by another Sir William in 1596 or 1597. The roadway above was once also protected by a drawbridge, long since demolished.

To reach the castle today the visitor has to walk down from the car park past the cemetery. The path slopes and curves steeply down to the bridge, from where the first view of the castle is a little disappointing. However, the views to the south into the heavily wooded glen and the North Esk River at the bottom of the ravine are

The ruins of Rosslyn Castle from the river walk, early nineteenth century.

Old stone bridge over the North Esk River. (Bryce Collection by permission of Midlothian Library Service)

The stone arch supporting the entrance to Rosslyn Castle.

stunning: it is a landscape of high romance. Across the drawbridge, on the left, is what remains of the fortified construction – a larger and heavier upper section, which now seems precariously balanced on a spindly lower base.

The view of the castle that most visitors have today is difficult to set in its historical architectural context. As one enters what is now a courtyard, to the right is what remains of the rounds, today a curious wall of red stone arches. In front is a hedge, behind which the upper section of the main domestic lodging can be seen. It is very hard to imagine what the castle must have been like in its heyday – now it resembles a jigsaw with many of the main pieces missing. However, the castle as a whole is around 200 feet in length, with a breadth of 90 feet, its walls in some places being 9 feet thick.

The Revd John Thompson adds that during the summer months the building of 1622 was inhabited and visitors could gain admission to the lower tiers of the vaults by a doorway in the garden wall to the left. In front of the entrance to the vaults, near the base of the clock tower, stands an ancient yew tree of immense size, which must have been planted around the time the castle was built at the beginning of the fourteenth century – if not earlier.

Were we able to examine the plan of the castle in section, we should see that there are five storeys, three of them below the level of the courtyard, tentatively identified (starting at the lowest) as kitchen, bakehouse and servants' quarters; above the courtyard level are two more floors that house the dining room and bedrooms. At the

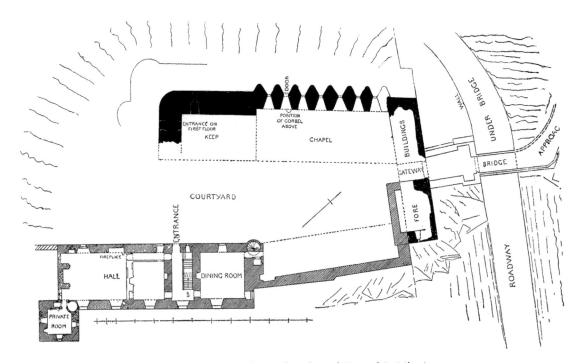

Ground plan of Rosslyn Castle showing the wedge-shaped 'Rounds' at the top.

lowest level the underfloor contains the kitchen, which features a very large fireplace and a small window in the corner; space at this level is also taken up by the Great Turnpike, which connects the floors, and there are four cellars (or dungeons), only one of which has a fireplace. Above this level is the bakehouse, whose main feature is a large oven. Both these levels are connected with each other by the Great Turnpike and with the garden to the south-west by means of a passage on the second floor, the entrance to which is near the ancient yew.

At the bottom of the Great Turnpike, noted the Revd John Thompson, on the right hand, between the stairs and the kitchen, is a doorway that leads down a few steps under the stairs – how far it is impossible to say, as it appeared to be filled up with earth. It might have led to a vault or vaults further down, as there were remains of strong iron hinges on which a heavy door had once been hung. Or it may simply have been a cupboard or recess for using up the space under the stairs.

At the foot of the Great Turnpike was an aperture or hatch in the roof, around 3 feet square (but now filled up), which was clearly to allow a lift or hoist to pass from the kitchen and bakehouse to the Great Hall above, or to the ante-room that adjoins it. In the kitchen, and also in the bakehouse, there is a smaller aperture about 8 or 9 inches square, which was probably used as a speaking-tube or shaft, for communication with the Great Hall.

The third or upper tier of compartments can now be entered only from the house above, the entrance from below being bricked up. Not many years before the Revd Thompson's time these compartments were inhabited by the castle's administrative staff.

Near the bottom of the stairs, in the passage, is a doorway that once led to the vaults that are said to be under the courtyard. Here, apparently, was a vault or dungeon that was called 'Little Ease'. It was a pit (rather like the bottle dungeon at St Andrews Castle) into which a prisoner was let down with ropes, where no ray of sunlight ever penetrated.

Above the third tier, at the south-west end, is the Great Hall, part of which forms the kitchen of the modern dwelling house (the other half being partly in ruins and roofless). The Great Hall must have been a fine room some 53 or 54 feet long and 23 feet wide, well lit on three sides by large windows. The ruined part contained a handsome moulded fireplace. Over the fireplace are the heraldic arms and initials of Sir William St Clair and his wife, Jean Edminston, dated 1597. At the south-west end there seems to have been a raised dais or state seat in a recess, with a window on each side. There are also some ruins on the steep bank below the Great Dungeon to the north-west. It is not clear exactly what purpose these outworks served, but they were probably the remains of the two towers, 'Robin Hood' and 'Little John', which Sir William St Clair allowed the gypsies to inhabit around 1559 when they came to perform their plays in the castle and in the stanks.

The Revd Thompson concludes his description of the castle by regretting its state of decay in the 1890s and suggesting that one solution might lie in the curious legend that surrounds the building. According to John Slezer in his *Theatrum Scotiae* (1693), the legend runs as follows:

The stanks (former river ponds) on the banks of the North Esk.

A great treasure, we are told, amounting to some millions, lies buried in one of the vaults. It is under the guardianship of a lady of the ancient house of St Clair who, not very faithful to her trust, has been long in a dormant state. Awakened, however, by the sound of a trumpet, which must be heard in one of the lower apartments, she is to make her appearance and to point to the spot where the treasure lies.

An eloquent memorial to Rosslyn Castle and the pastoral beauties of Roslin Glen are the cheerful verses of Richard Hewitt (d. 1794), which Robert Burns evidently admired. The song 'Roslin Castle' was at first known as 'The House of Glammis'; an earlier song (with the same title) was printed in the collection of David Herd (1732–1810):

> 'Twas in that season of the year
> When all things gay and sweet appear,

That Colin, with the morning ray,
Arose and sung his rural lay.
Of Nanny's charms the shepherd sung:
The hills and dales with 'Nanny' rung;
While Roslin Castle heard the swain,
And echoed back his cheerful strain.

Awake, sweet Muse! The breathing Spring
With rapture warms: awake and sing!
Awake and join the vocal throng,
And hail the morning with a song.
To Nanny raise the cheerful lay;
O! bid her haste and come away;
In sweetest smiles herself adorn,
And add new graces to the morn!

A pastoral view of Rosslyn Castle from the south by S. Bowers.

A dancing couple. (From Hector McNeill, *Scotland's Skaith* (Edinburgh: Mundell & Son, 1795))

O look, my love: on every spray
Each featured warbler tunes his lay:
'Tis beauty fires the ravished throng,
And love inspires the melting song.
Then let the raptured notes arise,
For beauty darts from Nanny's eyes,
And love my rising bosom warms,
And fills my soul with sweet alarms.

O come, my love! Thy Colin's lay
With rapture calls, O come away!
Come while the Muse this wreath shall twine
Around that modest brow of thine.
O hither haste, and with thee bring
That beauty blooming like the Spring –
Those graces that divinely shine,
And charm this ravished heart of mine!

The melody and the words were enthusiastically reworked in a number of popular versions: 'In Heav'n we'll meet' by T. Welsh (1825), a song by Sir Henry Bishop (1830); a part-song by H.A. Lambeth (1887), subsequently arranged by Sir A.C. Mackenzie (1906) and, most notably, in an arrangement by Franz Joseph Haydn (through his contacts with George Thomson, the Scottish song-collector).

A WALK THROUGH ROSLIN GLEN

On a fine day, a walk through Roslin Glen often brings contentment and even a half-remembered song of interior joy. After leaving the castle, walk down to the left along the broad steps secured with wooden boarding. At the bottom the path curves left again under the trees and the vaulting arch of the drawbridge. Steps lead down the slope onto the path below, from which the walker has a magnificent view of the towering defensive walls of Rosslyn Castle. Here you may, if you are lucky, find the long green-leaved hart's tongue fern, the only plant to be positively identified in Rosslyn Chapel at the top (south side) of the Prince's Pillar.

Here, unlike his studies of Rosslyn Chapel, the normally highly reliable guidance of the Revd John Thompson is only partly relevant today. His gentle and affectionate description of the routes that the Victorian walker could take when going along the side of the North Esk River from Rosslyn Castle to Polton provides little support to the modern-day rambler.

It would appear that his route, while matching everything Mr Thompson has to say about scenic beauty, demands a more cautious approach than in Thompson's more sedate era. The route can be muddy, slippery, even treacherous – mainly because of the hidden but sudden precipices from whose imminent threat the stunning scenery only too easily distracts the eye. The Revd Thompson's instructions to walkers now have mainly curiosity value, as an interesting example of Victorian tourism.

Many centuries of visitor activity have resulted in a multiplicity of paths along the route, some old and made dangerous by landslides or the fallen trunks of trees. In general, the sensible walker should keep as far away as possible from the river and its plunging ravine, and children, in particular, should be taken there only when they are of a sufficient age to appreciate the dangers. It is far better to err on the side of caution: stout walking boots with soles that grip must be the order of the day, and long protective trousers, as nettles and brambles abound. The best map to take is the Ordnance Survey Explorer 344 (*Pentland Hills, Penicuik and West Linton* at a scale of 1:25 000), which covers not only the Pentland Hills Regional Park but also Roslin and Roslin Glen. In addition, the

Hart's tongue fern near Rosslyn Castle.

The sun falling on the river.

Midlothian Ranger Service's leaflet, *Roslin Glen Country Park* (which, however, does not cover the whole of the walk), is also invaluable as a starting-point and as a guide to flora and fauna. Roslin Heritage Society's *Roslin Rambles* is specifically designed for walkers who have an interest in history; Midlothian Council's thirty-page leaflet *Exploring Midlothian* not only contains copious information (including maps) but lists sixteen trails, one of which is a 12-mile route of six hours over the Pentland Hills and another, one of 5 miles of approximately three hours duration in Roslin Glen.

However, a more modest walk is also possible from Rosslyn Castle along the bank of the North Esk to Bilston Wood, returning via Mountmarle to Roslin. This is the Rosslyn Castle to Hewan walk described in the Roslin Heritage Society's *Roslin Rambles* leaflet.

The walk starts from under Rosslyn Castle drawbridge (or further back, at the car park in the heart of the glen). You will see the remains of a bridge over the river as you pass. Walk on in an easterly direction, past the end of the castle and parallel to the north bank of the river, which, depending on the season, gurgles (to use an expression of Mr Thompson) or foams far below. As you walk forward, the chapel comes into view up above to the left, with what was once known as the orchard sloping down from the small and ancient sacristy building, and Rosslyn Chapel itself towering on the hilltop. There are still some old pear and apple trees below the castle, just outside what would have been the medieval kitchen.

As you walk, your eye will inevitably be drawn across the river to the high, steep banks opposite with their rugged cliffs of deep-red sandstone carved by the river, but also undoubtedly quarried for the construction of Rosslyn Chapel.

It is no longer possible, as it was in the Revd Thompson's day, to walk by the water's edge along a path that gradually rises far above the river, in some parts with steps cut into the solid rock. Nor can we any longer see the river as it flows down from the ravine below the castle, as he once did, nor take the narrow, steep path and clamber down to the water's edge, where a small waterfall that issues from a drinking fountain in the path above comes tumbling above our heads. Today there is no path and, alas, no (visible) waterfall!

Where giant flat boulders form a level platform was once a favourite resting place for Victorian picnic parties. As we pass on, the path descends from this rocky height into wooded glades, still some distance above the river, the opposite bank of which is

The path along the ledge down by the by-now shallow river's edge.

densely packed with trees and the damp slopes thickly covered with moss and ferns, allowed to grow in wild profusion as they are inaccessible to the improving hand of mankind. In this respect, added the Revd Thompson, the north bank contrasts with the south side, where wild flowers or ferns were less easy to find. Today, however, the north bank is no longer short of either.

Now the banks of the river narrow and the rocks on each side seem to close in on the walker. On the north side of the river, a small waterfall gushes down out of a cleft in the rock. After passing a large cave-like hollow in the rocks to the left, the path continues to descend until it is no more than a narrow ledge. However, here the river is not deep at all, so there is no longer any danger.

For the more daring, the route branches down to the right. We eventually come to a curious rock jutting up, carved all over with graffiti and even the heads of small Green Men. Go round the rock and press on. To the left, above our heads, but out of sight, once stood Rosebank House, formerly the residence of the Dowager Duchess of Rosslyn. To the right, almost opposite Rosebank, is Gorton House, only the roof of

The exposed sandstone outcrops overlooking the channel of the river.

which could be seen by the Revd Thompson, but which is quite invisible today on account of the massive trees. On the cliff face below the house the dark entrance can be seen to the Caves of Gorton, which, in 1338, formed the hiding place of Sir Alexander Ramsay of Dalhousie and his band of patriots.

The caves have two compartments, able to hold sixty or seventy men. From where we stand on the opposite bank, the caves appear inaccessible, but they are not. A path runs along the top, with steps cut into the rock at the back, and a good safe path leading right down to the entrance. But that side of the river is today all private property.

A little further on, the path was once barred by a substantial wall that divided the Rosslyn and Hawthornden estates. In the early nineteenth century, tourists could get no further, as the door in the wall was locked against them. They then had to retrace their steps to Rosslyn Castle – at that time, the only place to cross the river. This wall, therefore, marked the end of Rosslyn Glen, but today no visible trace of it remains.

'Hawthornden proper', wrote the Revd John Thompson, 'begins on the other side of the wall.' Some years before his guidebook was first published (1892), somewhere to the east of this wall, both sides of the river were claimed as the private property of Hawthornden, with the two banks connected by an elegant swing bridge. The public argued that this was still a historic right-of-way. The case was tried in the House of Lords, who decided in favour of the public. The door was then removed, leaving access free. However, the bridge was also then removed to prevent people getting to the opposite side (which remained private). The stone supports of the bridge, with its iron connections, could still be seen in 1892, along with a swinging wooden gate reaching down almost to the edge of the river.

HAWTHORNDEN CASTLE

Today, however, since there is no wall to bar the way, we can press on again, passing a substantial outcrop of red freestone on our left, hanging down over a wide but shallow cave, more a rain shelter than a hiding place. Now we have an option to take the path that leads down to the water's edge. This is only 2–3 feet wide and so unsuitable for small children or the elderly, though the water is very shallow here. There is even an old convenient blue metal handrail further on set into the rock face.

We have to follow the path ahead for some further distance, through what Mr Thompson called 'a delightful ravine', at times below steep, deeply wooded banks, at others under the looming shadows of towering rocks over which shrubs and climbing plants hang down like torrents of water. The only major hurdle is a fallen tree that lies across the path, giving agile walkers just enough room to pass if they duck their heads.

The lie of the land has changed since 1892 and so has the transport system and local industry. In his guidebook Mr Thompson told his readers that a path branched off to the left and then rose up to the top of the high bank, challenging the tourist to do his best to climb it. This path (as finger-posts once indicated) led to Polton by way of the Hewings Cottage, the walker always keeping to the left bank of the river. The path led on to a narrow ridge that in the nineteenth century overlooked a number of paper mills but also had a fine view of the valley past Polton and on to Lasswade. Just as the nineteenth-century tourist reached the top of the hill, from what was then a small grassy plot at the corner of the cottage, there was an impressive view of the upper part of the valley of the Esk with Hawthornden Castle (also known as Hawthornden House) on the rock in the foreground. After getting out into the lane, the tourist would turn right and, along another narrow ridge that overlooks the river and the site of the vanished paper mills, descend to what was once Polton railway station.

However, if, instead of going to Polton, the tourist wanted to approach Hawthornden, it was necessary to keep to the other path, which goes straight on, staying close to the river, under the shelter of magnificent rocks, to a footbridge across the River Esk by which the grounds of Hawthornden could once have been entered. Walking along the Hawthornden side of the bridge, always ascending, the visitor could have caught dramatic glimpses of the castle, perched on the edge of a steep cliff to the left, and could have taken advantage of the projecting rocks to get the best possible views of the river, flowing some hundred feet below, and of the steep, well-wooded banks and rocks by which it was contained, above and below the castle.

Hawthornden House, once home of the poet William Drummond, now a writers' retreat. (Bryce Collection by permission of Midlothian Library Service)

The poet William Drummond of Hawthornden. (From George Aikman, *The Mid-Lothian Esks and their Associations* (Edinburgh: David Douglas, 1895))

Things are different today. There is no bridge across the river, and Hawthornden Castle is a writers' retreat not open to the general public.

Even so, it is instructive to recall why Hawthornden Castle had such interesting historical connections. First are the two tiers of the Caves of Hawthornden in which Sir Alexander Ramsay of Dalhousie and his men are said to have concealed themselves in 1338. Second, Hawthornden was the home of the poet William Drummond (1585–1649), who entertained the English poet, playwright and former bricklayer Ben Jonson for some days at the end of 1618. When Jonson, who had been visiting his friend James Taylor (the 'Water Poet') in Leith, arrived at Hawthornden, Drummond was sitting in front of the house under the 'Corvine Tree' (the Company Tree).

There was also another important landmark that the Revd John Thompson recommended to the attention of tourists – Gorton House, in the woods of Hawthornden, opposite Rosslyn Chapel and Rosebank, with what Thompson describes as a 'commanding view of the Pentland Hills'. There is a link here with another collegiate church and its religious practices. In the fourteenth century Sir

John de Preston, a fine soldier, acquired the estate of Gorton. In 1452 William Preston of Gorton brought back the arm-bone of St Giles from the Continent. After his death in 1454, he was buried in the Preston Aisle at St Giles's Cathedral in Edinburgh. The Preston Aisle contained the grave of William Preston, whose foundation, just as Sir William Sinclair's at Rosslyn, funded daily masses for the repose of his soul.

Enclosed in a richly decorated golden shrine, with a diamond ring on one of its finger-bones, the relic of St Giles was annually carried in solemn procession through the streets of the Old Town until the Reformation, when the statue of the saint was unceremoniously burnt and drowned in the Nor' Loch. The relic itself was destroyed and its jewels sold off by the bailies.

In autumn, in the heights of the path opposite Hawthornden Castle, the walker is surrounded by rowan trees with their red berries, oaks in leaf and the ubiquitous brambles, which tug and tear at clothes and skin like barbed wire. The path slopes quickly under an overhanging tree down to a wooden stile, after which it becomes stone covered, still high above the river in its descent.

Beside the path are giant trees, while across the river are Scots pine and fir trees. Still the path descends, now with the Hewan Bog to the left, a wide open valley, once one of the 'killing zones' at the battle of Roslin, today populated by grazing sheep. Here, the river runs gently, but, as the path descends again, the waters become shallow and the flowing river faster and noisier, accompanied by the raucous crowing of rooks.

Approaching Bilston Wood we reach a gate and turn left, uphill along the edge of the field. There are three sets of wooden steps to negotiate on the climb. The path turns left again and eventually emerges at the top, from where the valley is spread out below. This path leads to another gate, with a signpost that reads 'Roslin 1¼ miles' pointing to the left. There are trees to the right and fields to the left. Here a magnificent view is to be had of the Pentland Hills far to the right and then the path descends to the remains of an old railway bridge before swinging up to the left past the monument to the battle of Roslin, past two agricultural research stations and into Manse Road. From Manse Road we turn down left into the carpark at Rosslyn Chapel.

THE PENTLANDS

'The Pentland Hills offer almost everything that is wanted by the seeker after health, the seeker after beauty, and the lover of Nature.' So confessed William Anderson in the preface to his *The Pentland Hills* (1926). He continues by saying that writing his book on the Pentlands has been 'a thanksgiving for many days of rare enjoyment, many nights of consequent dreamless sleep; perfect health; sound digestion; much moral and intellectual stimulus; many friendships made; fellowship with Nature – in fact, for most things which tend to make life pleasant and profitable. All of these have been attained by persistent tramping over the Pentlands.'[8]

The village of Pentland and the Pentlands have a special place in Sinclair history. What is today Old Pentland village with its now-vanished parish church was part of

The tiny graveyard at what was once Pentland church, with the Pentland Hills in the background.

the Sinclair estates, served by one of the canons from Rosslyn Collegiate Church, two of whose provosts were Sinclairs: John (1542–56); and Henry (1601–6). Other Sinclair property lay even further west, in the heart of the Pentland Hills with the now submerged church and manse of St Catherine in the Hopes. The Pentlands also figured largely in Sinclair family history as it was played out on the slopes of the King's Hill and the Knightfield Rig – a hunting contest in which Sir William Sainteclaire won his life against the wager of King Robert the Bruce.

Linking the Pentland Hills and Rosslyn Chapel and Castle is the North Esk River, whose source and direction Alexander McCallum described in 1912: 'The Esk is formed by the junction near Dalkeith of the North and South Esks. The North Esk rises near the Boarstone on the northern slope of the East Cairn Hill in the parish of Linton, Peebleshire. For two and a half miles it forms the boundary between that county and Midlothian, and then turning to the north-east it flows 17 miles to its junction with the sister stream.'[9]

The Pentlands are at once beautiful and harrowing: the wig-maker poet Allan Ramsay (1686–1758) was desperate to preserve his political neutrality. A closet Jacobite, he fled his octagonal 'goose-pie' love-nest just below Edinburgh Castle to allow the occupying Jacobite forces to commandeer it and take pot-shots at the castle, whose governor had refused to surrender. In the libretto of his early pastoral

The Farm House, Swanston, photographed by James Patrick in the early twentieth century.

The sweep of the road up to Swanston village and the T-shaped (or Anchor) wood a century later.

opera, *The Gentle Shepherd* (1720), Ramsay lovingly describes the rural idyll he experienced in the valley of the River Esk at Carlops.

During his youth, Robert Louis Stevenson (1850–94) lived at Swanston Cottage (which the family bought in 1867 and inhabited every March to October), just above a Pentland hill farm on the slopes of Cairketton Hill with its distinctive T-shaped wood. The Stevenson family lived at Swanston for some fifteen years, and a letter from Stevenson written in June 1870 recorded a visit he made to Rosslyn Chapel (family visitors to Swanston were regularly taken there). It had poured with rain on that particular occasion (as he told his mother, with a mock frisson of excitement at deserting the Established Church of Scotland and attending an Episcopalian service, even going to the extreme of dropping money in the offertory plate).[10]

His interest in the Midlothian countryside and its monuments continued during this formative period, when Stevenson's imaginative sensitivity was awakened to landscape, flora, fauna and history, a quality that would be vital for the future poet and novelist: 'The air comes briskly and sweetly off the hills, pure from the elevation and rustically scented . . . Straight above, the hills climb a thousand feet into the air. The neighbourhood, about the time of lambs, is clamorous with the bleating of flocks; and you will be awakened, in the grey of early summer mornings, by the barking of a dog, or the voice of a shepherd shouting to the echoes . . .'[11]

Swanston and the Pentlands also held other memories for Stevenson, of struggles against the Established Church by the Covenanters. When Swanston was his home, he could walk over the hills to the memorial to a Covenanter wounded at Rullion Green on 28 November 1666 and who died the day after and was buried in the hills; or he could wander further still to Glencorse Kirk (to which Stevenson frequently tramped of a Sunday to hear the minister's sermon).

Today, access to the Pentlands can be had by two main routes. Visitors to Rosslyn Chapel can leave Roslin by the B7006 and then turn right at the roundabout on the A701, heading straight north towards Edinburgh until the next roundabout, where the route heads west down the Pentland Road. This runs past Old Pentland Cemetery (on the right), which is well worth a visit. Then the route continues to the busy (and dangerous) triple junction with the A702 (T). Turn sharp left and head south towards Carlops and West Linton. Do not take the A703, which is on your immediate left.

Coming from Edinburgh, the approach is very much easier (and safer). Simply drive south out of town, through Morningside and up to Fairmilehead. Follow the road up as it skirts the east side of the Hillend Ski Slope (with Swanston Village to your right, accessible from Oxgangs Road via Swanston Road over the city by-pass).

Then the same potentially confusing and dangerous three-way junction presents itself. Keep always to the right, following the A702 (T) towards Carlops and West Linton. After a number of bends follow the signs for Flotterstone on the right. Turn in past the Flottersone Inn and make for the Pentland Hills Ranger Information Centre, where there is a carpark.

Alternatively, a helpful leaflet, *How to Get to the Pentland Hills by Bus*, lists the buses that stop at Flotterstone. In fact, the leaflet advises 'leave your car at home and come to the Pentland Hills by bus'. The leaflet *Explore Midlothian* describes in detail three possible Pentland Walks; of these, 'The Hillend Trail' (3½ miles over three hours) is the most relevant to those interested in the Sinclairs and Rosslyn Chapel. There are also two much shorter routes: a strenuous one that takes the walker slightly to the left straight up to Turnhouse Hill. From here there is a magnificent view of Rosslyn Chapel far to the east in the expanse of Midlothian but also a bird's-eye view of Glencorse Reservoir, the King's Hill and the Knightfield Rig (where the celebrated hunt with King Robert the Bruce took place) and the submerged location of St Catherine in the Hopes.

Another option is much less strenuous. This route goes to the right and involves walking through a gate beside a stream, past the disused filter beds and then up to the right to the eastern edge of Glencorse Reservoir. From here the walker can follow the road round the edge of the reservoir to Kirkton to arrive under the Knightfield Rig with the King's Hill ahead. There are other options, such as climbing up from the eastern edge of the reservoir to the prehistoric Castlelaw souterrain (underground dwelling), taking care to avoid the well-flagged army firing ranges.

The grave of the Covenanters at Rullion Green Farm, buried not far from where they were killed in battle, fighting for their beliefs.

To visit the Covenanter memorial at Rullion Green, starting at the Pentland Hills Ranger Information Centre, walk south along the right kerb of the A702 (1) until on your left you see a small wooden signpost for Rullion Green Cottage. Walk up the private road, taking care not to interfere with the working of the farm. From the farmhouse, cross the large field on the left to reach the small wood at the other side. The memorial, a headstone protected by iron railings, is at the edge of the wood.

VISITING POETS AND NOVELISTS

One of the earliest and most famous celebrity travellers in Britain was the London literary critic and novelist Samuel Johnson, who was accompanied by his biographer, James Boswell of Auchinleck (1740–95), on his tour to the Hebrides. On their return from the north of Scotland, the pair prepared to take the coach for London on Monday 22 November 1773, but decided instead to make a lingering and nostalgic detour. Boswell wrote:

> I resolved that, on our way to Sir John's [Dalrymple], we should make a little circuit by Roslin Castle and Hawthornden . . . it was, I believe, one o'clock before we got into our post-chaise. I found that we should be too late for dinner at Sir John Dalrymple's . . . but I would by no means lose the pleasure of seeing my friend at Hawthornden, – of seeing *Sam Johnson* at the very spot where *Ben Jonson* visited the learned and poetical Drummond. We surveyed Roslin Castle, the romantick scene around it, and the beautiful Gothick Chapel, and dined and drank tea at the inn; after which we proceeded to Hawthornden, and viewed the caves . . .[12]

To such an extent did Johnson and Boswell drag out their literary sight-seeing that they arrived at their host's far too late for dinner, much to Sir John Dalrymple's barely concealed displeasure.

On 13 June 1787, shortly before he left Edinburgh for ever, the poet Robert Burns with the painter Alexander Nasmyth (1758–1840), who had been working on a portrait of Burns, set off for the Pentland Hills after a session at an Edinburgh hostelry that lasted into the 'wee, sma' hours'. Nasmyth's son James, the inventor of the steam hammer, writes of that early morning expedition:

The poet Robert Burns, who walked early one morning to Roslin in the company of the painter Alexander Nasmyth.

At that time of the year the night is very short, and morning comes early. Burns, on reaching the street, looked up to the sky. It was perfectly clear, and the rising sun was beginning to brighten the mural crown of St Giles Cathedral. Burns was so much struck with the beauty of the morning, that he put his hand on my father's arm and said, 'It'll never do to go to bed on such a lovely morning as this! Let's awa' to Roslin Castle.' No sooner said than done. The poet and painter set out. Nature lay bright and lovely before them in that delicious summer morning. After an eight-miles' walk they reached the castle at Roslin. Burns went down under the great Norman arch, where he stood rapt in speechless admiration of the scene. The thought of the eternal renewal of youth and freshness of nature, contrasted with the crumbling decay of man's efforts to perpetuate his work, even when founded upon a rock, as Roslin Castle is, seemed greatly to affect him. My father was so much impressed with the scene that, while Burns was standing under the arch, he took out his pencil and paper, and made a hasty sketch of the subject. This sketch was highly treasured by my father, in remembrance of what must have been one of the most memorable days in his life.[13]

Burns was so taken with the wholesome fare the landlady of Roslin Inn provided that he scratched the following verses on a pewter plate:

> My blessings on you, sonsie wife!
> I ne'er was here before;
> You've gi'en us walth for horn and knife,
> Nae heart could wish for more.
>
> Heaven keep you free frae care and strife,
> Til far ayont forescore;
> And while I toddle on through life,
> I'll ne'er gang by your door.

Lasswade Cottage, the picturesque honeymoon home of Sir Walter Scott and his bride. (Bryce Collection by permission of Midlothian Library Service)

The writer Thomas De Quincey. (From John Ritchie Findlay, *Personal Recollections of Thomas De Quincey* (Edinburgh: Adam & Charles Black, 1886))

It was Sir Walter Scott, however, whose summer home was only a short walk away, who would use Rosslyn Chapel as a more powerful inspiration for his fiction and poetry. In the early 1800s Scott rented Lasswade Cottage with its quaintly thatched roof from the Clerk family of Penicuik. There Scott wrote the opening stanzas of 'The Lay of the Last Minstrel' (also known, from its last line, as 'The Dirge of Rosabelle') and 'The Gray Brother' (which featured the countryside near Lasswade), which referred to the popular tradition of the chapel appearing to be on fire when any member of the St Clair family died.

Soon after their honeymoon Scott brought his wife, Charlotte, to Lasswade. He had many friends living nearby: the writer Henry Mackenzie, his old teacher Alexander Fraser Tytler, and the 'Opium-Eater', the novelist Thomas De Quincey.

Scott's novel *The Talisman* includes a description of the chapel of the hermit of Engaddi, which Sir Kenneth visits (and which is clearly based on Rosslyn Chapel):

The door opened spontaneously . . . and his senses were at once assailed by a stream of the purest light, and a strong and almost oppressive sense of the richest perfumes . . . When he entered the apartment in which this brilliant lustre was displayed, he perceived that the light proceeded from a combination of silver lamps, fed with the purest oil, and sending forth the richest odours, hanging by silver chains from the roof of a small Gothic chapel, hewn . . . out of the sound and solid rock . . . the invention and the chisels of the most able architects. The groined roofs rose from six columns on each side, carved with the rarest skill; and the manner in which the crossings of the concave arches were bound together . . . were all in the finest tone of the architecture, and of the age. Corresponding to the line of pillars, there were on each side six richly wrought niches, each of which contained the image of one of the twelve apostles.[14]

Scott walked from Lasswade along the North Esk on many occasions. On one such outing he was trying to make his way up to a cave to sit down for a moment with his companions, when his footing gave way under him and he began to slide down the bank towards the river below. One of his fellow walkers vividly recalled the incident:

Had there been no trees in the way, he must have been killed, but midway, he was stopped by a large root of hazel, when, instead of struggling, which would have made matters greatly worse, he seemed perfectly resigned to his fate, and slipped through the tangled thicket till he lay flat on the river's brink. He rose in an instant from his recumbent attitude, and with a hearty laugh, called out 'Now, let me see who else will do the like.' He scrambled up again with alacrity, and entered the cave, where we had a long dialogue.[15]

Scott's residence at Lasswade Cottage was an added attraction for many of his literary friends and distinguished visitors such as the poet William Wordsworth and his sister Dorothy, whom Scott entertained in 1803. Dorothy's journal tells the story of their encounter:

Friday 16 September 1803 So at about six o'clock in the evening we departed, intending to sleep at an inn in the village of Roslin, about five miles from Edinburgh. The rain continued till we were almost at Roslin; but then it was quite dark, so we did not see the Castle that night.

Saturday 17 September The morning very fine. We rose early and walked through the glen of Roslin, past Hawthornden, and considerably further, to the house of Mr Walter Scott at Lasswade. Roslin Castle stands upon a woody bank above a stream, the North Esk, too large, I think, to be called a brook, yet an inconsiderable river. We looked down upon the ruin from higher ground. Near it stands the Chapel, a most elegant building, a ruin, though the walls and roof are entire. I never passed through a more delicious dell than the glen of Roslin, though the water of the stream is dingy and muddy. The banks are rocky on each side, and hung with pine wood. About a mile from the Castle, on the contrary side of the water, upon the edge of a very steep bank, stands Hawthornden, the house of Drummond the poet . . . After Hawthornden the glen widens, ceases to be rocky, and spreads out into a rich vale, scattered with gentlemen's seats.

Arrived at Lasswade before Mr and Mrs Scott had risen, and waited for some time in a large sitting-room. Breakfasted with them, and stayed till two o'clock, and Mr Scott accompanied

Sir Walter Scott. (From James Grant, *Edinburgh Old and New* (London: Cassell, Petter, Galpin, 1880?–1883?))

The poet William Wordsworth. (After the portrait by Benjamin Robert Haydon)

us back to Roslin . . . We ordered dinner on our return to the inn, and went to view the inside of the Chapel of Roslin, which is kept locked up, and so preserved from the injuries it might otherwise receive from idle boys; but as nothing is done to keep it together, it must in the end fall. The architecture within is exquisitely beautiful. The stone both of the roof and walls is sculptured with leaves and flowers, so delicately wrought that I could have admired them for hours, and the whole of their groundwork is stained by time with the softest colours. Some of those leaves and flowers were tinged perfectly green, and at one part the effect was most exquisite: three or four leaves of a small fern, resembling that which we call adder's tongue, grew round a cluster of them at the top of a pillar, and the natural product and the artificial were so intermingled that at first it was not easy to distinguish the living plant from the other, they being of an equally determined green, though the fern was of a deeper shade.[16]

Her brother William, impressed by the carved stone foliage in the chapel (hart's tongue ferns, curly kale, trefoil, oak leaves, cactus leaves), later wrote his 'Sonnet Composed in Rosslyn Chapel' (1831):

> The wind is now thy organist; a clank
> (We know not whence) ministers for a bell
> To mark some change of service. As the swell
> Of music reached its height, and even when sank
> The notes in prelude, Rosslyn! to a blank
> Of silence, how it thrilled they sumptuous roof,
> Pillars and arches – not in vain time-proof,
> Though Christian rites be wanting! From what bank
> Came those live herbs? by what hand were they sown
> Where dew falls not, where rain-drops seem unknown?
> Yet in the Temple they a friendly niche
> Share with their sculptured fellows, that, green-grown,
> Copy their beauty more and more, and preach,
> Though mute, of all things blending into one.

Perhaps more than any poem it was Scott's 'Lay of the Last Minstrel' that broadcast the name of Rosslyn Chapel and Castle most widely:

> O listen, listen, ladies gay!
> No haughty feat of arms I tell
> Soft is the note, and sad the lay,
> That mourns the lovely Rosabelle.
>
> – Moor, moor the barge, ye gallant crew!
> And, gentle ladye, deighn to stay,
> Rest thee in Castle Ravensheuch,
> Nor tempt the stormy firth today.
>
> The blackening wave is edged with white;
> To inch and rock the sea-mews fly;
> The fishers have heard the Water-Sprite,
> Whose screams forbode that wreck is nigh.
>
> Last night the gifted seer did view
> A wet shroud swathed round ladye gay;
> Then stay thee, Fair, in Ravensheuch:
> Why cross the gloomy firth today?
>
> 'Tis not because Lord Lindesay's heir
> Tonight at Roslin leads the ball
> But that my Ladye-mother there
> Sits lonely in her castle-hall.
>
> 'Tis not because the ring they ride,
> And Lindesay at the ring rides well
> But that my sire the wine will chide
> If 'tis not fill'd by Rosabelle.
>
> O'er Roslin all that dreary night
> A wondrous blaze was seen to gleam;
> 'Twas broader than the watch-fire's light,
> And redder than the bright moon-beam.
>
> It glared on Roslin's castle rock,
> It ruddied all the copse-wood glen
> 'Twas seen from Dryden's groves of oak,
> And seen from caverned Hawthornden.

Seem'd all on fire that chapel proud,
Where Roslin's chiefs uncoffin'd lie,
Each Baron, for a sable shroud,
Sheathed in his iron panoply.

Seem'd all on fire, within, around,
Deep sacristy and altar's pale,
Shone every pillar foliage-bound,
And glimmer'd all the dead men's mail.

Blazed battlement and pinnet high,
Blazed every rose-carved buttress fair –
So still they blaze, when fate is nigh
The lordly line of high St Clair.

There are twenty of Roslin's Barons bold
Lie buried within that proud chapelle;
Each one the holy vault doth hold –
But the sea holds lovely Rosabelle!

And each St Clair was buried there
With candle, with book and with knell;
But the sea-caves rung, and the wild winds sung,
The dirge of lovely Rosabelle.

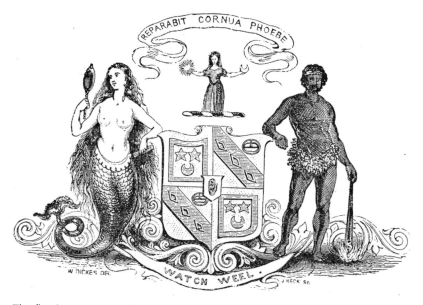

The flamboyant Arms of Sir Walter Scott. (From James Grant, *Edinburgh Old and New* (London: Cassell, Petter, Galpin, 1880?–1883?))

Writers of slighter literary merit but with a keen appreciation of church architecture also waxed lyrical. The clergyman Edward Bentley (1827–89), writing under the pseudonym Cuthbert Bede, describes Rosslyn Chapel in his rather garishly titled *A Tour in Tartan-Land* (1863) as

> an unfinished thought in stone; one of those architectural wonders, whose intricate beauties and peculiarities extort our admiration, while they baffle description. One of its chief characteristics is its bewildering variety. There are thirteen different kinds of arches: while endless diversity marks the prolific ornamentation of the architraves, the capitals of the pillars, window traceries, crocketed pinnacles, flying buttresses, and the five compartments of the vaulted roof. Canopied niches and bracket pedestals are lavishly scattered over the exterior and interior, but display great variety in their decorations.[17]

PAINTERS AND PHOTOGRAPHERS

Over the centuries Roslin Glen, its chapel and castle have attracted artists who came to sketch and paint the wildness and the charm of the landscape and the picturesque architecture. The future architect of the Scott Monument, George Meikle Kemp (1790–1844), the son of a shepherd born at Ninemileburn in Midlothian, came to Rosslyn in his youth, and 'gazed with wonder and admiration on the exquisite details of the architecture of the chapel'; during the second year of his apprenticeship he 'studied the beauties and construction of the buildings, their style' and made rough sketches.[18] He drew the 'Apprentice Pillar' and his brother, evidently, was the draughtsman responsible for a fine drawing of Rosslyn Chapel, rendered as it might have appeared, had it been completed.

In the 1820s the great English painter Joseph Mallord William Turner (1775–1851) came to Edinburgh to capture in paint the triumphal visit of George IV (masterminded by Sir Walter Scott) and found time to draw and sketch at Roslin.

For Edinburgh-born David Roberts (1796–1864), employed in his early days as a theatre scenery painter, Rosslyn Chapel held an abiding attraction – in spite of Roberts's travels to the more exotic parts of the East such as Egypt. But there are clues also to be found in his water colour *Apprentice Pillar* (1830), where (using his theatrical experience) he deliberately exaggerates the scale of the building, making the pillar three times the height of the male bonneted figure and the woman he can be seen talking to below it. At the back of the picture, however, can be seen the gaping holes in the chapel windows, where the small leaded panes have apparently simply been punched out.

Another view of much the same scene and dated 1843, *The Entrance to the Crypt*, shows two (different) figures, this time seated, and the windows at the rear now securely barred and glazed. In a less dramatic watercolour, *The Interior of Rosslyn Chapel* (11 October 1842), outlined in pencil, with yellow and blue-white highlights on brown paper, Roberts depicts the view from the centre of the Lady Chapel looking south, with the demolished altars clearly visible.

Roberts, however, was by no means enamoured of the Earl of Rosslyn's well-intentioned plans for widespread 'restorations' and wrote to *The Scotsman* in December 1843 warning that they would lead to disaster:

> By the removal of the roof from above the aisles, together with the opening of the great east window, this solemn effect is now completely destroyed; while, at the same time, by the window being thrown open, an immense body of air is admitted, which will, in all probability, dry up and destroy the vegetation which has tended so much towards the preservation of the building . . . The *restoration*, as it is called, of the east window, *is not a restoration*, but a monstrous blunder, being nothing more or less than an enlargement of one of the smaller windows of the aisles to three or four times its proper size, destroying the whole symmetry and beautiful proportions of the chapel. From the very exposed position of the building itself . . . the opening of this window facing the east renders the whole building (necessarily, from its great age, in a very tottering condition) liable to be shaken to its foundation, if not to be hurried to total destruction . . .[19]

At about the same period David Octavius Hill (1802–70) and Robert Adamson (1821–48), pioneers of photography, were also at work fixing images of the chapel for posterity, and their paper negatives capture it with greater accuracy than the work of even the finest painters. Their images show the east window and its muscular (and surprisingly well-preserved) stone tracery totally open to the elements.

The chapel, for all its antiquity, continued to fascinate. In his *Præterita: Outlines of Scenes and Thoughts* (1886), discussing the relationship between architecture and the character of landscape and scenery, the artist and art historian John Ruskin identified the Trossachs as a case in point and condemned the destructive tourism of his day: 'And all the nineteenth century conceived of wise and right to do with this piece of mountain inheritance, was to thrust the nose of a steamer into it, plank its blaeberries over with a platform, and drive the populace headlong past it as fast as they can shuffle . . .'[20] Ruskin goes on to say that, fortunately, there were other better sustained and better conserved scenic experiences to be had in Scotland – he had given himself some writing to do, and the sight of Melrose Abbey and then Rosslyn Chapel had further inspired him.

TOURISTS

Rosslyn Chapel, Rosslyn Castle and Roslin Glen have long been magnets for visitors. The Revd John Thompson, writing in the second (1893) edition of his highly popular guide, thoughtfully supplied a written route (but no map to get there).

He recommended a journey by train, taking one of two routes. The first, from Edinburgh's North Bridge, to Newington Station, to Liberton and then Straiton, also went past Roslin Moor (the site of the triple battle); the second went from Lothian Road to Morningside Station, then out under the end of the Pentland Hills to Seafield. Alternatively, visitors could take a coach that travelled past Dalkeith once or

twice a week and stopped to set its passengers down, first at Hawthornden Lodge and then at Roslin.

The chapel was not open all year round to the general public: signed with the name of the seat of the Earl of Rosslyn (Dysart House in Fife), a notice in *The Scotsman* (20 July 1866) advised that, although the chapel was open 'every lawful day to the public on and after Saturday, 21 July', it was accessible '*by Ticket only*', tickets being available at Messrs Edmonston & Douglas, Robert Grant & Sons, Booksellers in Edinburgh's Princes Street, or from Mr Purves at the chapel. Visitors were also sternly warned to 'remove their hats' by a notice that hung in a conspicuous place at the chapel – which prompted the aside from the *Dalkeith Advertiser* in August 1877 that 'it is strange that Scotchmen have a tendency to retain their coverings when in places of worship'.

Parked horse buses waiting for their passengers to return at Main Street, Roslin. (Bryce Collection by permission of Midlothian Library Service)

Today it is astonishing to hear that annual visitor figures for Rosslyn Chapel in 2006 were around 120,000. On 27 August 1870 a landmark for the period was reached with a figure of a mere 614 visitors in one week – as the curator John Thomson wrote with surprise and pleasure to the Fourth Earl of Rosslyn. The figure represented the largest ever number of visitors in a week, he added, and included the appearance of some Indian princes, whose stay in Edinburgh had already attracted favourable comment in the press.[21] The daily tally of tickets sold that week at £1 each were: 22 August (29 visitors), 23rd (112), 24th (116), 25th (111), 26th (104), 27th (142), giving a grand total of £30 14s taken at the door. The battered visitors' book for the chapel warned visitors that they should write nothing more than their name and address, as the Earl of Rosslyn had asked that the book be available to consult so he could gauge the level of public interest. The Earl's stern instructions seem to have been taken as a challenge by a number of wags who were moved to insert fictitious and ridiculous names tucked away at the bottom of each page plus a few covert examples of playful obscenity.

By the late nineteenth century visiting the countryside had become a national pastime. Hugh Jamieson, an Edinburgh publisher of Scottish vocal music, brought out his *Guide to Roslin and Suburban Beauties of Edinburgh* for the 'excursionist'. He strongly recommended the journey to Hawthornden Station (11¼ miles from Edinburgh), which 'gives access to the wild and romantic scenery lying between Roslin on the west and the roadway leading south from Bonnyrigg', adding that 'it is often visited by excursion parties in brake conveyances'.[22] At that period the chapel was open for divine service on Sundays; during the week the cost of admission for an excursion party was 1s 6d.

Cycling was also highly popular with tourists. James Horne published his *Fifteen One Day Cycle Tours from Edinburgh with Description of the Roads and Objects of Interest in the Vicinity*, which supplied concise altitude and mileage charts, and wrote of his Route No. 6 (Edinburgh to Roslin, Leadburn, Peebles and Innerleithen) that 'ever since the dawn of cycling this has been a favourite route with Edinburgh votaries of the wheel', adding that 'Roslin is a favourite spot with cyclists, especially in early spring and late autumn'.[23]

An elegant dog cart waiting outside the original Roslin Hotel. (Bryce Collection by permission of Midlothian Library Service)

In Harry R.G. Inglis's *Short Spins round Edinburgh* (1897) highly detailed maps and routes are sandwiched between advertisements that give an insight into the fashionable world of the gentleman and lady cyclists on day excursion (who can be seen pedalling nonchalantly on the cover). The advantages of waterproofs, capes and ponchos were extolled, as well as the Woodley pneumatic tyre, Sibbald's new safety cycling skirt and 'cameras for the pocket, the hand and the stand'.[24] Writing of the chapel (to which the admission charge was now 1 shilling), Mr Inglis concluded somewhat lamely: 'Perhaps its greatest peculiarity is that nearly every part is different, and the carving of one part is never repeated in any other.'

Visitors to the chapel continued to come in satisfying numbers, but there were some curious incidents, as the chaplain Mr Alexander Thomson Grant was quick to tell the Earl: 'On Sunday the 10th Mrs Cornwallis Weet was in the Chapel with the Clerks [of Penicuik]. She created what is called a *Sensation*, when in the middle of the service, and while standing, she let fall from her shoulders a fur cloak and appeared arrayed in a bright geranium costume.'[25]

In 1880, replying to complaints in the letters column of *The Scotsman*, the Revd Mr Grant explained that no visitors were admitted to the chapel on Sundays unless they came to attend divine worship and that 'the inconvenience of visitors leaving during the service has been found to be so great, and so disturbing to the regular

A four-in-hand on the final stretch, crammed with visitors anxious to see the famous Rosslyn Chapel. (Bryce Collection by permission of Midlothian Library Service)

congregation, that I have been obliged to place printed notices in each seat, requesting such visitors to remain until the conclusion of the service'.[26] He went on, 'I cannot imagine this to be a great hardship as sermons are rarely prolonged beyond a quarter of an hour, and the offertory is of course entirely voluntary'. The Chaplain ended by assuring his readers that both the offertory collection and the admission fee to the chapel charged on weekdays were spent on the chapel and on the expenses of the priest.

With the agreement of the Earl of Rosslyn various learned bodies were also regularly given special permission to visit the chapel. Seventy members of the Edinburgh Architectural Association came on a Saturday afternoon in early April 1885 under the guidance of the architect Andrew Kerr, who read a paper on the history of the chapel and the castle, informing his listeners (among many other matters) that the small room to the south of the crypt had been a priest's chamber.[27]

A service commemorating the dedication of Rosslyn Chapel at the conclusion of the restoration undertaken by Francis Robert, the late 4th Earl of Rosslyn, was held on Tuesday 31 March 1891. The altar of the chapel was decorated as for Easter, and among the congregation (which filled the chapel) was the 5th Earl of Rosslyn. The chapel choir was augmented by a number of choristers from Christ Church, Trinity in Edinburgh.[28]

The Roslin Tour charabanc, with passengers, driver and conductor, waiting by the monkey-puzzle tree. (Bryce Collection by permission of Midlothian Library Service)

The restoration of the chapel was again celebrated at its jubilee in September 1912. In the presence of the Earl of Rosslyn, the Primus of the Episcopal Church in Scotland, the Most Revd W.J.F. Robberds, referred to the state of the Episcopal Church in 1862 when there were 7 bishops and some 150 clergy. By 1912 there were still 7 bishops but nearly 350 clergy, while church membership had risen from 40,000 in 1862 to 142,000 in 1912.[29]

Throughout this time the chapel also continued to be used for funerals. On 7 March 1914 a large congregation of mourners attended the chapel for the funeral of the 43-year-old brother of the Earl of Rosslyn, the Hon. Alexander Fitz Roy St Clair-Erskine, who had died at Maidenhead. The coffin, which had been brought from the south, lay overnight on a bier in the chapel. The general public were excluded from the chapel grounds during the ceremony. This rule had also been enforced two or three days before, and only the mourners, the choristers and the officiating clergy were present at the services.[30] Many of the deceased's close family were unable to be present: the Earl of Rosslyn had been detained in Marseilles on his way home from Egypt, and the deceased's mother, the Dowager Countess of Rosslyn, his sisters and his niece were unable to attend because of illness.

At the conclusion of the service, the bier was taken from the chapel as the choristers sang a hymn, and interred in the grave a few yards away in the grounds,

Fresh air, countryside and sensible romance on the cover of Harry R.G. Inglis's *Short Spins round Edinburgh* (Edinburgh: Gall & Inglis, 1897).

adjoining that of the deceased's sister, the Countess of Westmoreland (who had died in 1910), and also close to that of the late Earl (who had been buried there in 1890).

A handsome red sandstone neo-Gothic monument by W. Birnie Rhind stands not far from the chapel baptistry, marking the burial place of the 4th Earl and that of his wife, Blanche.

The power of Rosslyn Chapel to attract visitors remained as high as ever. Some one hundred ladies and gentlemen of the Scottish Ecclesiological Society visited Rosslyn Chapel on Saturday 10 October 1914, having travelled by train from Waverley Station. After a short service, a paper was read by Mr Thomas Ross on the history of the building. He reminded his audience that 'few buildings in the country had been so much written about, and talked about, and visited from far and near as Rosslyn Chapel'.[31] The former priest at Rosslyn Chapel, the Revd John Thompson, recalled that some years earlier, after he had shown Lord Rosebery over the chapel, the latter commented that it was 'a perfect pocket cathedral'.

Rosslyn Chapel was again the scene of mourning on Thursday 8 August 1929, when the funeral of Lord Loughborough was held. He had had a tragic accident and had died the previous Sunday in London. Inside the chapel, Lord Loughborough's father, the Earl of Rosslyn, led the mourners. 'The oak coffin', reported *The Scotsman* (9 August 1929), 'rested on a bier draped in purple and white. Candles around the bier added light to the dim interior of the chapel.' Two wreaths had been placed on the coffin, and when the service had ended the coffin was taken from the bier to the family burial ground on the lawn beside the chapel. Fittingly, a number of people from Roslin village had been invited to the service.

As it is the function of a place of worship to support its congregation in times of happiness as well as sadness, there was a warm welcome from the villagers accorded King George V and Queen Mary when they visited Roslin in July 1931, along with the Duke and Duchess of York. Their Majesties had expressed a wish to visit Rosslyn Chapel. The royal car drove up the Vennel (the roadway leading to the chapel).

Although the King had never seen the chapel before, the Queen had, as had the Duchess of York. After visiting the chapel, the royal party paused at the grave of the 4th Earl of Rosslyn, whom both had known well.

Before the royal party left they visited Collegehill House (formerly the Roslin Inn) and were shown a link to their family's past. On 24 May 1859, King Edward VII, while still Prince of Wales, had dined with his mother Queen Victoria at the inn – Queen Victoria had already visited Roslin in 1842 when the Prince Consort was a baby. In 1859 the Prince was 17 years old and, as *The Scotsman* (13 July 1931) admitted, young enough to want to scratch his name on the glass of the window: 'He scratched it, presumably with a diamond ring or brooch, on the window of an upper room, where he wrote "Albert Edward dined here on the anniversary of his mother's birthday, 1859".' The royal party were conducted to the upstairs room of what had been the inn (now a bedroom in what was the house of the curator, Mr Charles Taylor) to see the window pane with its inscription. As soon as the King saw the window he exclaimed 'Yes, that's my father's writing.' Before they left, the royal party all signed the visitors' book.

THE DA VINCI CODE

Probably the most revolutionary event in the recent history of Rosslyn Chapel was the publication of Dan Brown's novel *The Da Vinci Code*, named after the Italian Renaissance artist and engineer born in 1452, seven years after building had started at Rosslyn Chapel. The novel, along with the motion picture of the book (partly filmed at Rosslyn Chapel, which featured strongly in the climactic and tempestuous final stages of the story) and the appearance of the DVD of the film in October 2006, has prompted an unprecedented rise in visitor numbers. *Monthly* visitor statistics at the chapel since publication of *The Da Vinci Code* match the previous *annual* total.

Because of Dan Brown's book (and because it features Rosslyn Chapel as a key location), by 2007 the chapel had changed from being a slightly obscure hidden gem in an out-of-the-way part of Scotland to a 'must-see' pilgrimage destination that attracts tourists for many different reasons – history, religion or philosophy, or a combination of these. VisitScotland, Scotland's national tourism agency, has calculated that Scotland has already received over £6 million of publicity around the world as a result of its unique partnership with Sony Pictures. Earlier, in 2006, VisitScotland joined forces with Sony Pictures, VisitBritain and the French tourist board, Maison de la France, to promote the locations in the film in forty countries around the world. The promotion included a joint website, competitions, press and TV advertising in both established tourism markets such as the United States and Germany and emerging markets such as China, India and Russia. VisitScotland has also used *The Da Vinci Code* website (www.visitdavincicode.com) to promote Rosslyn Chapel and other locations in Scotland, and around half a million people visited the joint website in the five months from May to September 2006.

In addition, in order to tap into the interest in *The Da Vinci Code*, VisitScotland hosted over 150 journalists from 18 countries on press trips to Scotland: their articles

The magnificent red Gothic stone pinnacles of the monument at the grave of the Fourth Earl of Rosslyn and his wife to the west of the chapel, designed by William Birnie Rhind, 1899. (By permission of Rosslyn Chapel Trust)

A 1913 Siddeley-Deasy 24 horsepower Landaulet (with a removable roof) parked at College Hill outside the entrance to Rosslyn Chapel. (Bryce Collection by permission of Midlothian Library Service)

about Scotland have reached an estimated 100 million people around the world. VisitScotland also used *The Da Vinci Code* as a central theme in its £1.3 million European Touring Campaign of early 2006. The campaign, which encouraged visitors to travel around Scotland to different locations, targeted potential visitors in Germany, France, the Netherlands, Spain and Sweden. Touring packs included three *Da Vinci Code*-inspired itineraries, 'Mystery and Legends', 'Scotland's Literature' and 'Scotland in Film and TV', which were requested by 161,000 consumers, well in excess of VisitScotland's target of 100,000.

Ben Carter, VisitScotland's area director for Edinburgh and the Lothians, speaking in the official VisitScotland press release on 16 October 2006, commented:

The Da Vinci Code was a massive opportunity for the tourism industry in the Lothians, in Edinburgh and in the rest of Scotland. By working in partnership with a major international player like Sony Pictures, we have benefited from worldwide exposure for Scotland that we could not have achieved alone. Tourism businesses have also taken the initiative themselves and reaped the benefits of tapping into the global interest in the movie. With the DVD coming out, interest in *The Da Vinci Code* will continue, bringing benefits to Scotland for a long time to come.

Meanwhile, in a press release of 16 October 2006 Rosslyn Chapel Trust's director Stuart Beattie commented: 'We have seen visitor numbers increase from 38,000 (before the book and the film came out) to 160,000 this year. *The Da Vinci Code* raised awareness of Rosslyn, which was already on the ascendancy as a destination that many find attractive for a raft of different reasons.'

Debbie Taylor, General Manager for the Balmoral, one of Edinburgh's premier hotels, revealed:

Since the launch of *The Da Vinci Code* the number of our guests visiting Rosslyn Chapel has risen by around 50 per cent. As a result we introduced The Balmoral's overnight 'Da Vinci Code Experience', which includes a champagne picnic in the picturesque grounds of the Chapel. The package has proved very popular with our guests who enjoy the special touches we provide, such as the private transfer. The number of individual tours we are organising for guests has also soared. During the summer we were sending on average ten groups a week to Roslin. The film has certainly proven to be beneficial to The Balmoral and Edinburgh as a whole.[32]

Meanwhile, post-*Da Vinci*, researchers and conspiracy theorists continue to find more evidence in the chapel to support their instinctive conclusions: in 2005 Edinburgh composer Stuart Mitchell finally achieved his twenty-year quest to crack the musical code hidden in the 213 squares of the chapel roof when he identified what he intends to call 'The Rosslyn Canon of Proportions', a musical composition covering two pages of manuscript that Mr Mitchell has arranged for the instruments shown carved into Rosslyn Chapel's historic stones.[33]

The Vennel (passageway) at College Hill House (formerly the Old Roslin Inn). (Bryce Collection by permission of Midlothian Library Service)

Epilogue

The Revd John Thompson ends his best-selling guidebook with an appendix that records an intriguing mystery. He quotes William Stephen's *History of the Scottish Church* (1894–6), where, in a footnote on the reconciliation of Churches, Stephen observes: 'William Scheves, second Archbishop of St Andrews, had the privilege, while residing at the Papal Court, of reconciling Churches by proxy. In right of this he commissioned certain clerics of his diocese to reconcile the Collegiate Church of Rosslyn, which had been stained with blood.'[1]

Thompson notes that Scheves was created Archbishop of St Andrews at Holyrood in 1478 and died on 28 January 1496 (or 1497). According to *Lesley's History of Scotland*, 'the King now' (i.e. after 1486) sent to Rome the Archbishop of St Andrews 'to require of the Pope's holiness certain privileges; which freely, and with all humility, shortly were granted'.[2] Thompson continues by telling us how *Lyon's History of St Andrews* records that 'Scheves performed various journeys into England and its dependencies. In 1485 we find him obtaining a safe-conduct from Richard III to proceed to England with forty persons; from whence it is probable he went to Rome, in order to obtain the papal sanction to the alliance recently concluded between Scotland and France.'

Thompson concludes that, while Rosslyn Chapel took some forty years to build (1446–86), the Archbishop's visit to Rome must have been about 1486, for in 1485 he obtained a safe-conduct to travel to England, and from there probably to Rome. While he was in Rome in 1486, Rosslyn Chapel was finished and ready for consecration, but, evidently, the shedding of blood in the chapel was an obstacle to its solemn consecration, an obstacle that could be removed only by an act of reconciliation. This would explain, adds Thompson, the privilege obtained by the Archbishop (then at the Papal Court) of reconciling Churches by proxy: the Archbishop would then commission certain clerics of his diocese to reconcile the collegiate church at Rosslyn, as it had been stained by the as yet unexplained shedding of blood.[3]

Whatever the precise details of this still mysterious act of blood, Rosslyn Chapel today is a place of prayer and reconciliation. As the Revd Michael Fass, priest in charge at Rosslyn, noted in a sermon preached there in the spring of 2003:

There are no secrets here. Here we celebrate the story of the life and death of Jesus and we commemorate his Resurrection in our lives through the Eucharist. We are a

St Peter's Basilica, Rome.

community which tries to live using guidelines established by a loving God which were lived out best in the example of Jesus. We acknowledge that we can get things horribly wrong in our own lives. We say sorry and we promise to try our best to do better. None of this is secret; there are no secrets here; anyone and everyone has access to the Good News and we welcome them in God's name to share in it with us.[4]

Furthermore it is worth focusing on exactly where Rosslyn Chapel is today. *Inspires*, the magazine of the Scottish Episcopal Church, explains:

The Scottish Episcopal Church congregation holds regular public worship at the Chapel on a 'grace and favour' basis by verbal agreement with the present Earl of Rosslyn who is, with the Bishop of Edinburgh, the joint Patron of the Charge. The Chapel is privately owned by the Settlement of the Earls of Rosslyn . . . The present Earl and Countess are the original and settler trustees of Rosslyn Chapel Trust, a private limited company with charitable status created by the Earl to manage the site on a lease from the Settlement for 99 years from 1917. No member of the Congregation is a trustee of the Rosslyn Chapel Trust Ltd. The Congregation does not receive any of the revenues generated by the Trust from entrance ticket sales, the purchase of souvenirs or income from grants and loans from public bodies, but neither is it concerned with the physical upkeep of the Chapel, which is cared for by the Trust. The Congregation's annual income comes solely from planned giving by its regular worshippers and occasional fund raising activities, collections, donations, and legacies . . . In short, the Trust looks after the physical upkeep of the Chapel, and the Congregation cares for the spiritual wellbeing of the community and visitors, keeping the Chapel alive with worship. Both tasks are vital for Rosslyn to serve as a Christian place of worship.[5]

Votive candles at Rosslyn Chapel.

Appendix I

EPISCOPAL PRIESTS IN CHARGE

1862–8	Revd Robert Cole
1868–86	Revd Alexander Thomson Grant
1886–1913	Revd John Thompson
1914–22	Revd Ernest Frederick Morison
1923–8	Revd William Hardy Johnson
1928–61	Revd George Hebb Taylor
1962–8	Revd Roland Charles Walls
1968	Revd John Halsey
1968–73	Revd Robert Neil Russell
1974–5	Revd David Leonard Mealand
1977–92	Revd Edward Nalder Downing
1993–7	Revd Janet Dyer
1997–2006	Revd Michael John Fass
2007–	Revd Joseph Roulston

Appendix II

Rosslyn Chapel Trust
Rosslyn Chapel
Roslin
Midlothian
EH25 9PU
tel: + 44 (0) 131 440 2159
email: mail@rosslynchapel.com
web: www.rosslynchapel.com

Local Studies Centre
Midlothian Library Headquarters
2 Clerk Street
Loanhead
Midlothian
EH20 9DR
tel: + 44 (0) 131 271 3976
email: local.studies@midlothian.gov.uk
(for The Midlothian 2000 CD Rom (cost £15 each)
email: alan.reid@midlothian.gov.uk),
web: http://www.midlothian.gov.uk/library/Local.htm

Pentland Hills Regional Park
Boghall Farm
Biggar Road
Edinburgh
EH10 7DX
tel: + 44 (0) 131 445 3383
email: pentlands.enquiry@edinburgh.gov.uk
web: www.pentlandhills.org

The Landmark Trust
(bookable accommodation at College Hill House or Rosslyn Castle)
Shottesbrooke
Maidenhead
Berkshire
SL6 3SW
tel: + 44 (0) 1628 825925
email: bookings@landmarktrust.org.uk
web: www.landmarktrust.org.uk

Historical Search Room
National Archives of Scotland
HM General Register House
2 Princes Street
Edinburgh
EH1 3YY
tel: +44 (0) 131 535 1334
email: enquiries@nas.gov.uk
web: www.nas.gov.uk

West Search Room
West Register House
Charlotte Square
Edinburgh
EH2 4DJ
tel: +44 (0) 131 535 1413
email: wsr@nas.gov.uk
web: www.nas.gov.uk

General Register Office for Scotland (for births, marriages, deaths)
New Register House
3 West Register Street
Edinburgh
EH1 3YT
tel: +44 (0) 131 334 0380
email: records@gro-scotland.gov.uk
web: www.gro-scotland.gov.uk
web: www.scotlandspeople.gov.uk (parish register, civil registration, census)

Scottish Genealogy Society Library and Family History Centre
15 Victoria Terrace
Edinburgh
EH1 2JL
tel: +44 (0) 131 220 3677
email: info@scotsgenealogy.com
web: www.scotsgenealogy.com

Edinburgh City Archives
City Chambers
High Street
Edinburgh
EH1 1YJ
tel: +44 (0) 131 529 4616
web: www.edinburgh.gov.uk

Edinburgh Room
Edinburgh City Libraries
George IV Bridge
Edinburgh
EH1 1EG
tel: +44 (0) 131 242 8030
email: eclis@edinburgh.gov.uk
web: www.edinburgh.gov.uk/libraries

Royal Commission on the Ancient and Historical Monuments of Scotland
(RCAHMS)
John Sinclair House
16 Bernard Terrace
Edinburgh
EH8 9NX
tel: +44 (0) 131 662 1456
email: nmrs@rchams.gov.uk
web: www.rchams.gov.uk

Scottish Catholic Archives
Columba House
16 Drummond Place
Edinburgh
EH3 6PL
tel: +44 (0) 131 556 3661
email: sca@catholic-heritage.net
web: www.catholic-heritage.net/sca/

Cappella Nova (CDs of Scottish Polyphony)
1/R, 172 Hyndland Road
Glasgow
G12 9HZ
tel: +44 (0) 141 552 0634
email: rebecca@cappella-nova.com
web: www.cappella-nova.com

Historic Scotland
Longmore House
Salisbury Place
Edinburgh
EH9 1SH
tel +44 (0) 131 668 8600
email: hs.friends@scotland.gsi.gov.uk
web: www.historic-scotland.gov.uk

National Museum/Museum of Scotland
Chambers Street
Edinburgh
EH1 1JF
tel: +44 (0) 131 247 4422
email: info@nms.ac.uk
web: www.nms.ac.uk

National Gallery of Scotland: The Mound, Princes Street
Scottish National Portrait Gallery: 1 Queen Street
Scottish National Gallery of Modern Art: 75 Belford Road
Dean Gallery & 73 Belford Road
A free shuttle bus runs between the galleries
tel: +44 (0) 131 624 6200
email: enquiries@nationalgalleries.org
web: www.natgalscot.ac.uk

National Library of Scotland
George IV Bridge
Edinburgh
EH1 1EW
tel: +44 (0) 131 623 3700
email: enquiries@nls.uk
web: www.nls.uk

Notes

Abbreviations

NAS — National Archives of Scotland
NLS — National Library of Scotland
RCAHMCS (RCAHMS) — Royal Commission on the Ancient and Historical Monuments of Scotland

1. The Landscape of Midlothian

1. *The Edinburgh Evening News*, 24 May 2006.
2. Scottish Wildlife Trust: Roslin Glen Wildlife Reserve Management Plan, 1993–8.
3. Nigel Buchan, 'A History of Woodland in the North Esk Valley' (unpublished BA thesis submitted August 1979, Department of Landscape Architecture, Heriot-Watt University), 2.2.
4. *General View of the Agriculture of the County of Mid-Lothian* (Edinburgh: J. Ruthven & Sons, 1795), 25.
5. *Memoirs of the Geological Survey, Scotland: The Geology of the Neighbourhood of Edinburgh* (2nd edn, Edinburgh: HMSO, 1910), 245.
6. Telephone call to author from quarry-owner Brian Caulfield, 25 August 2006.
7. Daniel Wilson, 'The Queen's Choir', *Ane Auld Prophecie* (1853), 21.
8. Robert W. Billings, *The Baronial and Ecclesiastical Antiquities of Scotland*, vol. 4 (1845), 2–3.
9. Buchan, 'A History of Woodland in the North Esk Valley'.
10. Richard Augustine Hay, *Genealogie of the Sainteclaires of Rosslyn* (Edinburgh: Grand Lodge of Scotland, 2002), 6.
11. David Turnock, *The Making of the Scottish Rural Landscape* (Aldershot: Scolar Press, 1995), 152.
12. Hay, *Genealogie of the Sainteclaires of Rosslyn*, 7.
13. I am indebted to Susan Orlowski of the Edinburgh Room, Edinburgh Central Library, for this information.
14. Turnock, *The Making of the Scottish Rural Landscape*, 184.
15. G.G. Coulton, *Scottish Abbey and Social Life* (Cambridge: Cambridge University Press, 1933), 136.
16. RCAHMCS, Tenth Report (1929), 142.
17. William Camden, *Britannia* (Edinburgh: Andrew Anderson, 1695), 903.
18. Email from Nick Majer, House of Commons Information Office, 1 August 2006.
19. Sir John Sinclair (ed.), *The Statistical Account of Scotland* (Edinburgh: William Creech, 1794), 277.
20. Sue Tranter, 'Gardens', *Scotland on Sunday*, 26 March 2000.

21. Sinclair (ed.), *The Statistical Account of Scotland*, 280.

22. *Ibid.*

23. *Ibid.*

24. *The Statistical Account of Edinburghshire* (Edinburgh: William Blackwood & Sons, 1845).

25. *Ibid.*, 338–9.

26. *Ibid.*, 339.

27. *General View of the Agriculture of the County of Mid-Lothian*, 27.

28. John Thompson, *The Illustrated Guide to Rosslyn Chapel and Castle, Hawthornden &c.* (11th edn, Edinburgh: MacNiven & Wallace, 1934), 16.

29. NAS GD 164/970, account of mason work at Rosslyn, *c.* 1660.

30. Cairns, *Bright and Early* (Edinburgh: Cairns Bros, 1953), 134.

31. *Ibid.*, 134.

32. See Winnie Stevenson and Veronica Meikle, *Roslin Gunpowder Mills*, CD Rom (Roslin Heritage Society), and Ian McDougall, *Oh, ye had tae be careful* (East Linton: Tuckwell Press, 2000).

33. *Edinburgh Evening Courant*, 3 October 1805.

34. *Dalkeith Advertiser*, 30 January 1890.

35. Midlothian Ranger Service, *Roslin Glen Country Park*, n.d.

36. Report: Pentland Hills Regional Park, 2005–2006.

37. See also Richard Augustine Hay, *Genealogie of the Hayes of Tweeddale*, ed. James Maidment (Edinburgh: Thomas G. Stevenson, 1835); Will Grant, *Rosslyn, The Chapel, Castle and Scenic Lore* (Kirkcaldy: Dysart and Rosslyn Estates, 1947).

38. Hay, *Genealogie of the Hayes of Tweeddale*, ed. Maidment; see also Mark Dilworth, 'Richard Augustine Hay', *Dictionary of National Biography*.

39. Hay, *Genealogie of the Hayes of Tweeddale*, ed. Maidment, 50.

40. Email from Brian Canon Halloran, 27 August 2006; see also B.M. Halloran, *The Scots College, Paris, 1603–1792* (Edinburgh: John Donald, 1997).

41. *Historical Notices of Scottish Affairs* (Edinburgh: Bannatyne Club, 1848), ii, 763; quoted in David McRoberts and Charles Oman, 'Plate Made by King James II and VII for the Chapel Royal of Holyroodhouse in 1686', *Antiquaries Journal* (1968), 286.

42. Hay, *Genealogie of the Hayes of Tweeddale*, ed. Maidment, 54.

43. Halloran, *The Scots College, Paris, 1603–1792*, 62.

44. Hay, *Genealogie of the Hayes of Tweeddale*, ed. Maidment, 57.

45. *Ibid.*

46. John Cunningham, *The Church History of Scotland*, vol. 2 (Edinburgh: Adam & Charles Black, 1859), 259–60.

47. Hay, *Genealogie of the Hayes of Tweeddale*, ed. Maidment, iv.

48. *Ibid.*, vii

49. NLS Adv. MS 33.4.18.

50. NLS Adv. MS 34.6.9.

51. NLS Adv. MS 34.1.10 (i–iii).

52. NLS Adv. MS 34.1.8.

53. NLS Adv. MS 34.1.9.

54. NLS MS 6316.

55. NLS MS 2936, fols 155–64, dated *c.* 1712.

56. NLS MS 2933, fols 53–64, 70–7.

57. NLS MS 10285, fol. 50.

58. NLS MS 10284.

59. NLS Acc. 5022.

60. NLS Acc. 5694.

61. NLS Adv. MS 32.6.2.

62. Richard Augustine Hay, *Genealogie of the Sainteclaires of Rosslyn*, ed. James Maidment (Edinburgh: Thomas G. Stevenson, 1835), i.

63. Anthony Ross, 'Some Scottish Catholic Historians', *Innes Review*, 1 (1950), 19.

64. NLS Adv. MS 34.1.9, Hay's Memoirs, vol. 2.

65. Hay, *Genealogie of the Hayes of Tweeddale*, ed. Maidment, xxv.

66. Walter Scott, *Prose Works*, vol. 3 (Paris: A. and W. Galignani, 1834), 369.

67. E.R. Lindsay and A.I. Cameron (eds), *Calendar of Scottish Supplications to Rome 1418–1422* (Edinburgh: T. & A. Constable, 1934), 304.

68. Hay's manuscript source seems to have been mistaken about the name of Sir William's wife, which it gives as Margaret.

69. Scott, *Prose Works*, vol. 3, 369.

2. The History of Rosslyn Chapel

1. Roddy Martine, *The Secrets of Rosslyn* (Edinburgh: Birlinn, 2006), includes a very useful family tree.

2. Thomas Ross, 'Rosslyn Chapel', *Transactions of the Scottish Ecclesiological Society* (1914–15), 239, n. 1.

3. François Bucher, *Architector: The Lodge Books and Sketchbooks of Medieval Architects*, vol. 1 (New York: Abaris Books, 1979), 13.

4. *Ibid.*, 170–1.

5. John Harvey, *Medieval Craftsmen* (London: Batsford, 1975), 43.

6. Alexander Grant, *Independence and Nationhood, Scotland 1306–1469* (Edinburgh: Edinburgh University Press, 1996), 95.

7. Michael Lynch, *Scotland: A New History* (London: Century, 1991), 193.

8. Richard A. Hay, 'Scotia Sacra', NLS Adv. MS 34.1.8, fol. 380.

9. Richard A. Hay, 'Hay's Memoirs', vol. 2, NLS Adv. MS 34.1.9.

10. D.E.R. Watt, *Fasti Ecclesiae Scoticanae Medii Aevi*, second draft (St Andrews: Department of Medieval History, 1969), 371.

11. John Durkan, 'Foundation of the Collegiate Church of Seton', *Innes Review*, 13/1 (Spring 1962).

12. James Kirk, Roland T. Tanner and Annie I. Dunlop, *Calendar of Scottish Supplications to Rome*, vol. 5, *1447–1471* (Glasgow: Scottish Academic Press, 1997), 374–5.

13. John Thompson, *The Illustrated Guide to Rosslyn Chapel and Castle, Hawthornden &c.* (11th edn, Edinburgh: MacNiven & Wallace, 1934), 38–9.

14. NAS GD 164/1019/15, Andrew Kerr to Earl of Rosslyn, 8 October 1880.

15. Bannatyne Club, *Charters of the Hospital of Soltre, Trinity College, Edinburgh and other Collegiate Churches in Midlothian* (Edinburgh: Bannatyne Club, 1861), 327–32.

16. Earl of Rosslyn, *Rosslyn Chapel* (Rosslyn: Rosslyn Chapel Trust, 1997), 19.

17. J. Maitland Anderson (ed.), *Early Records of the University of St Andrews: The Graduation Roll 1413–1579* (Edinburgh: Scottish History Society, 1926). Annie I. Dunlop (ed.), *Acta Facultatis Artium Universitatis Sanctiandree, 1413–1588* (Edinburgh: London: published for the University Court of the University of St Andrews by Oliver & Boyd, 1964).

18. Simon Ollivant, *The Court of the Official in Pre-Reformation Scotland* (Edinburgh: Stair Society, 1982), 79.
19. Arthur Oldham, 'Scottish Polyphonic Music', *Innes Review*, 13/1 (Spring 1962), 54. See also the recordings by Cappella Nova (www.cappella-nova.com).
20. John Purser, *Scotland's Music* (Edinburgh: Mainstream, 1992), 51–6.
21. Henry George Farmer, *A History of Music in Scotland* (London: Hinrichsen, 1947), 98.
22. *Ibid.*, 99.
23. *Ibid.*, 89
24. *Ibid.*, 90
25. *Ibid.*, 104
26. Isobel Woods, '"Our Awin Scottis Use": Chant Usage in Medieval Scotland', *Journal of the Royal Musical Association*, 112/1 (1986–7); and Stephen Allenson, 'The Inverness Fragments: Music from a Pre-Reformation Scottish Parish and School', *Music and Letters*, 70/1 (February 1989), 18.
27. David McRoberts, 'The Medieval Scottish Liturgy Illustrated by Surviving Documents', *Transactions of the Scottish Ecclesiological Society*, 15/1 (1957), 24–41.
28. David McRoberts, 'Catalogue of Scottish Medieval Liturgical Books and Fragments', *Innes Review*, 2/2 (December 1951), 49–63.
29. Farmer, *A History of Music in Scotland*, 102.
30. NLS Adv. MS 18.5.19; see also Hugh J. Lawlor, *The Rosslyn Missal*, vol. 15 (London: Henry Bradshaw Society, 1898), ix–xxvi.
31. H.J. Lawlor, 'Notes on the Library of the Sinclairs of Rosslyn', *Proceedings of the Society of Antiquaries of Scotland*, 32 (1897–8), 107.
32. John Dowden, *The Medieval Church in Scotland* (Glasgow: James MacLehose, 1910), 107.
33. J.D. Crichton, 'A Theology of Worship', in Cheslyn Jones, Geoffrey Wainwright and Edward Yarnold (eds), *The Study of Liturgy* (London: SPCK, 1978), 19.
34. T.E. Bridgett, *History of the Holy Eucharist in Great Britain*, vol. 2 (London: Kegan Paul, 1881), 142, quoting F.R. Raines, *History of the Lancashire Chantries* (Chetham Society, 1862), xx.
35. Charter of Sir William Sinclair for the Prebendaries, 1523.
36. T.E. Bridgett, *History of the Holy Eucharist in Great Britain*, vol. 2 (London: Kegan Paul, 1881), 142, quoting F.R. Raines, *History of Lancashire Chantries* (Chetham Society, 1862), xx.
37. Luciano Bernardi *et al.*, 'Effect of Rosary Prayer and Yoga Mantras on Autonomic Cardiovascular Rhythms: Comparative Study', *British Medical Journal*, 323 (22–29 December 2001), 1446–9.
38. Thompson, *The Illustrated Guide to Rosslyn Chapel and Castle, Hawthornden*.
39. James Kirk, *Patterns of Reform* (Edinburgh: T. & T. Clark, 1989), 7, 97.
40. Farmer, *A History of Music in Scotland*, 120.
41. James Kirk (ed.), *The Records of the Synod of Lothian and Tweeddale* (Edinburgh: Stair Society, 1977), i–ii.
42. David Calderwood, *The History of the Kirk in Scotland*, vol. 2 (Edinburgh: Wodrow Society, 1842), 177–8.
43. Thompson, *The Illustrated Guide to Rosslyn Chapel & Castle*, 47.
44. Kirk (ed.), *The Records of the Synod of Lothian and Tweeddale*, 17
45. *Ibid.*, 21
46. *Ibid.*, 31
47. *Ibid.*, 44

48. *Ibid.*, 48

49. *Ibid.*, 52

50. Richard Augustine Hay, *Genealogie of the Sainteclaires of Rosslyn*, ed. James Maidment (Edinburgh: Thomas G. Stevenson, 1835), 169.

51. NAS GD 164/984/1, Roslin: Account, crop 1790.

52. NAS GD 164/984/8, McKenzie Buchan: receipt, 1791; NAS GD 164/984/11, William Lamb: receipt for slating, n.d.; NAS GD 164/984/7, glazing kitchen, etc., 11 April 1791; NAS GD 164/984/2, Sir James St Clair Erskine, 11 April 1791.

53. John M. Gray (ed.), *Memoirs of the Life of Sir John Clerk* (Edinburgh: Scottish History Society, 1892), 250–1.

54. NAS GD 18/5010, Col. James St Clair to Sir John Clerk (1738–42); NAS GD 18/5111, Sir John Clerk: copy of frieze on north side of Rosslyn Chapel.

55. Gray (ed.), *Memoirs of the Life of Sir John Clerk.*

56. NAS GD 164/1013, directions for repairing Roslin Chapel, 1836.

57. Ronald Johnson, *The Earl and the Architect* (Edinburgh: R.A. Kane, 1986), 10.

58. Kenneth Clark, *The Gothic Revival* (London: Constable, 1928), 199–200.

59. *Ibid.*, 225

60. Charles L. Eastlake, *A History of the Gothic Revival*, ed. J. Mordaunt Crook (1872; New York: Leicester University Press, 1978), 240.

61. NAS GD 164/1014/1, David Bryce to Lord Rosslyn, 16 March 1859.

62. NAS GD 164/1014/5, William Burn to Earl of Rosslyn, 9 April 1861.

63. NAS GD 164/1014/6, David Bryce to Earl of Rosslyn, 4 June 1861.

64. Colin McWilliam (ed.), *Buildings of Scotland: Lothian* (Harmondsworth: Penguin, 1978), 416–17.

65. *The Scotsman*, 18 June 1861.

66. *Ibid.*

67. Aberdeen Episcopal Diocesan Library: uncatalogued MS (Edinburgh, 1892).

68. NAS RHP 46748, plan of part of the lands of Roslin proposed to be feued . . ., 1862.

69. Midlothian Local Studies: extracts from early unidentified newspaper cuttings, 16 June 1905.

70. Midlothian Local Studies: extracts from early unidentified newspaper cuttings, 23 June 1905; 17 July 1905; 15 November 1907.

71. Thompson, *The Illustrated Guide to Rosslyn Chapel and Castle*, 73.

72. This triangle of red glass forms part of the thesis in Alan Butler and John Ritchie, *Rosslyn Revealed* (Ropley: O Books, 2006); see also Claire Smith, 'Secrets in the Stone', *The Scotsman*, 28 October 2006.

73. Thompson, *The Illustrated Guide to Rosslyn Chapel and Castle*, 72.

74. NAS GD 164/1019, Andrew Kerr to the Earl of Rosslyn, 20 July 1880.

75. NAS GD 14/1019/16, Alexander Thomson Grant to the Earl of Rosslyn, 18 October 1880.

76. McWilliam (ed.), *The Buildings of Scotland: Lothian*, 413.

77. *Dalkeith Advertiser*, June 1880.

78. *Midlothian Journal*, 17 July 1914.

79. He was succeeded by Mr Taylor, who served for forty years, and his son after him, John Taylor, who became curator in the early 1940s and was still in post thirty-three years later. See Earl of Rosslyn, *Rosslyn* (Kirkcaldy: Dysart and Rosslyn Estates, 1947), 66.

80. *Midlothian Journal*, 14 March 1913.

81. NAS DD 27/656, report on Rosslyn Castle.

82. NAS DD 27/656, correspondence: M.R. Apted; Stuart Cruden, 31 January 1957.

83. NAS DD 27/656, A.L. Johnston to Secretary of the Commissioners of Works, 10 January 1951.
84. NAS DD 27/656, Peter Herd to Ministry of Works, 9 August 1951.
85. NAS DD 27/656, T. Dalrymple: report, 20 March 1957.
86. Ministry of Works (1954) Rosslyn Chapel: report on proposed further internal cleaning and preservation of stone work and ornament.
87. *Weekly Scotsman*, 11 January 1956.
88. *Dalkeith Advertiser*, 1 October 1987.
89. *The Scotsman*, 3 April 1998.
90. 'Nicholas Boyes Stone Conservation', in Kay Simpson and Brown (Architects), Rosslyn Chapel Conservation Plan, Part I: Documentary Research and Physical Evidence (draft May 2001).
91. Conservation plan contributions by Addyman and Kay Simpson and Brown (Architects) in Rosslyn Chapel Conservation Plan, Part I: Documentary Research and Physical Evidence (draft May 2001).
92. Andrew Sinclair, *The Sword and the Grail* (Edinburgh: Birlinn, 2005), 100–3.
93. *The Scotsman*, 14 September 1998. See also www.rcahms.gov.uk.
94. See Wikipedia: http://en.wikipedia.org?wiki/Cargocult (accessed 7 December 2006).

3. Visiting Rosslyn Chapel

1. Fifteen collegiate churches were erected in Edinburgh and the Lothians between 1342 and 1540. Others included the East Lothian churches of Dirleton (1444), Dunglass (1448) and Markle (1450) and, in Edinburgh, Restalrig (1487), Corstorphine and St Giles.
2. *Midlothian Journal*, 30 March 1917.
3. John Thompson, *The Illustrated Guide to Rosslyn Chapel and Castle, Hawthornden, &c.* (Edinburgh: MacNiven & Wallace, 1892), 57.
4. Ron Ferguson, *Mole under the Fence* (Edinburgh: Saint Andrew Press, 2006), 57.
5. John Macky, *A Journey through Scotland* (London, 1723), 54–5.
6. Thompson, *The Illustrated Guide to Rosslyn Chapel and Castle*, 57.
7. Colin McWilliam (ed.), *Buildings of Scotland: Lothian* (Harmondsworth: Penguin, 1978), 411.
8. William E. Addis and Thomas Arnold, *Catholic Dictionary* (London: Virtue, 1952), 23–4.
9. Earl of Rosslyn, *Rosslyn* (Kirkcaldy: Dysart and Rosslyn Estates, 1974), 16.
10. Hilda Graef, *Mary* (London: Sheed & Ward, 1963; repr. 1985), 313.
11. Madge Old, *A Short History to Celebrate the Centenary of Roslin Church* (Penicuik: Pen-y-coe Press, 1981), 2.
12. Thompson, *The Illustrated Guide to Rosslyn Chapel and Castle*, 61.
13. John Slezer, *Theatrum Scotiae* (Edinburgh: William Paterson, 1874; repr. 1893), 117. Slezer quotes Grose in saying that Roslin Castle 'became very populous, by the great covering of all ranks and degrees of visitors, that resorted to this prince, at his palace of the castle of Roslin . . . he flourished in the reigns of James I and II'.
14. Raymond E. Brown, Joseph A. Fitzmyer and Roland E. Murphy (eds), *The New Jerome Biblical Commentary* (London: Geoffrey Chapman, 1990), 27.
15. Stuart Harrison, 'Roslin Chapel Conservation Plan', in *Rosslyn Chapel*, pt 1 (Simpson Brown, May 2001), 11.
16. Robert Anderson, 'Notice of Working Drawings Scratched on the Walls of the Crypt at Roslin Chapel', *Proceedings of the Society of Antiquaries of Scotland* (1873), 63–4.
17. François Bucher, *Architector: The Lodge Books and Sketchbooks of Medieval Architects*, vol. 1 (New York: Abaris Books, 1979), 236–48.

18. *Ibid.*

19. *Ibid.*, 201–367.

20. Michael Gibson, *Saints of Patronage and Invocation* (Bristol: Avon County Library, 1982), 32.

21. Bishop of St Andrews, *St Matthew, an Example for the Church in Scotland* (Burntisland: Pitsligo Press, 1853), 6, 9, 10.

22. F.J.B. Allnatt, *The Witness of St Matthew* (London: Kegan, Paul, Trench, 1884), 11–12.

23. All the biblical quotations in this section are taken from *The New Jerusalem Bible – Reader's Edition* (London: Darton, Longman & Todd, 1990).

4. *Varieties of Speculation*

1. Dan Brown, *The Da Vinci Code* (London: Corgi, 2004), 564–70; Andrew Sinclair, *Rosslyn* (Edinburgh: Birlinn, 2005), 103. See also Simon Cox, *Cracking the Da Vinci Code* (London: Michael O'Mara Books, 2004), 145–7; Philip Coppens, *The Stone Puzzle of Rosslyn Chapel* (Enkhuizen: Frontier Publishing, 2004), 99–101.

2. R.T. Beckwith, 'The Jewish Background to Christian Worship', in Cheslyn Jones, Geoffrey Wainwright and Edward Arnold (eds), *The Study of the Liturgy* (London: SPCK, 1978), 41.

3. Peter G. Cobb, 'The Architectural Setting of the Liturgy', in Jones, Wainwright and Arnold (eds), *The Study of the Liturgy*, 474.

4. John Thompson, *The Illustrated Guide to Rosslyn Chapel and Castle, Hawthornden &c.* (11th edn, Edinburgh: MacNiven and Wallace, 1934), 42.

5. Thomas Ross, 'Rosslyn Chapel', *Transactions of the Scottish Ecclesiological Society* (1914–15), 238.

6. Andrew Kerr, 'The Collegiate Church or Chapel of Rosslyn, its Builders, Architect, and Construction', *Proceedings of the Society of Antiquaries of Scotland* (14 May 1877), 224.

7. Richard Fawcett, *Scottish Medieval Churches* (Edinburgh: HMSO, 1985), 27.

8. Ross, 'Rosslyn Chapel', 238.

9. Adrian F. Dyer, 'A Botanist Looks at the Medieval Plant Carvings at Rosslyn Chapel', *Botanical Society of Scotland News*, Nos 76–8 (March 2001–March 2002).

10. Brian Moffat, 'Magic Afoot: Rosslyn Aloes in Veritas?' *Textualities*, 1 (2006), 9–15.

11. Ross, 'Rosslyn Chapel', 240.

12. Francis Grose, *The Antiquities of Scotland* (London: S. Hooper, 1789), 44.

13. Kerr, 'The Collegiate Church or Chapel of Rosslyn', 232.

14. John Thompson, *The Illustrated Guide to Rosslyn Chapel and Castle &c.* (Edinburgh, 1892), 59.

15. Keith Cavers, *A Vision of Scotland* (Edinburgh: National Library of Scotland, 1993), 7–9.

16. Ross, 'Rosslyn Chapel', 240.

17. Conversation with author, September 2006.

18. Interviews conducted by the author, 2006.

19. Telephone call with author, 27 October 2006. For Chris Hall's work, see Ewan Mathers, *The Cloisters of Iona Abbey* (Glasgow: Wild Goose Press, 2001).

20. François Bucher, *Architector: The Lodge Books and Sketchbooks of Medieval Architects*, vol. 1 (New York: Abaris Books, 1979), 11.

21. *Ibid.*, 9.

22. *Ibid.*, 13.

23. Robert L.D. Cooper (ed.), *Genealogie of the Sainteclaires of Rosslyn* (Edinburgh: Grand Lodge of Scotland, 2002), xviii–xix.

24. *Ibid.*, xxi

25. Earl of Rosslyn, *Rosslyn Chapel* (Rosslyn: Rosslyn Chapel Trust, 1997), 50.

26. *Dalkeith Advertiser*, 24 June 1897.

27. Robert L.D. Cooper, *The Rosslyn HOAX?* (Hersham: Lewis Publishing, 2006), 153–4.

28. *Ibid.*, 244

29. Helen Nicholson, *Templars, Hospitallers and Teutonic Knights* (Leicester: Leicester University Press, 1995), 1–2.

30. Henry L. Williamson, *Preceptory of King David I at Balantradoch* (no publisher, n.d.).

31. John Edwards, 'The Knights Templars in Scotland', *Scottish Ecclesiological Society Transactions* (1912–13), 42.

32. 'Processus Factus contra Templarios in Scotia', in James Maidment (ed.), *The Spottiswoode Miscellany*, vol. 2 (Edinburgh: Spottiswoode Society, 1845).

33. Edwards, 'The Knights Templars in Scotland', 42. An extended account of the trial is also given in James Grant, *Old and New Edinburgh*, Division III (London: Cassell, 1885–7), 50–2, while the original (Latin) account is in 'Processus Factus contra Templarios in Scotia, 1309', 14–15.

34. See *Scottish Review* (July 1898) and *Scottish Historical Review* (October 1907).

35. Edwards, 'The Knights Templars in Scotland', 44–5.

36. Thompson, *The Illustrated Guide to Rosslyn Chapel and Castle*, 117.

37. Mark Dilworth, *Scottish Monasteries in the Late Middle Ages* (Edinburgh: Edinburgh University Press, 1995), 84.

38. J.C. Carrick, *The Abbey of S. Mary Newbottle*, (2nd edn, Selkirk: George Lewis, 1908), 56.

39. Robert Cochrane, *Pentland Walks* (Edinburgh: Andrew Elliott, 1908), 95.

40. NAS SP 13/50, bond of man-rent by Sir William Saintclair to Mary Queen of Scots, 1546.

5. *Contemporary Attitudes*

1. Winnie Stevenson and Veronica Meikle, *Old Roslin* (Catrine: Stenlake Publishing, 2003).

2. Bannatyne Club, *Charters of the Hospital of Soltre, of Trinity College, Edinburgh, and Other Collegiate Churches in Mid-Lothian* (Edinburgh: Bannatyne Club, 1861), v.

3. Brian Moffat (ed.), *The Sixth Report on Researches into the Medieval Hospital at Soutra* (Fala: SHARP, 1998).

4. *The Scotsman*, 10 February 1988.

5. Mary Beith, 'How Medieval Monks Quelled Sensual Desire', *Observer*, 16 September 1990.

6. Jeremy Laurance, 'Prozac, Opium and Myrrh', *Independent*, 12 September 1997.

7. Lothian Health Services Archive GB 239 LHB33.

8. As told to author, 19 July 2006.

9. Midlothian Local Studies; typescript, n.d.

10. see www.alisonkinnaird.com.

11. Joy Hendry, 'Morton's Music', *Scots Magazine* (September 1985), 591–9.

12. Robin Morton (collator), *Come Day, Go Day, God Send Sunday* (London: Routledge & Kegan Paul, 1973); Robin Morton (compiler), *Folksongs Sung in Ulster* (Cork: Mercier Press, 1970).

13. see www.templerecords.co.uk.

14. *Dalkeith Advertiser*, 9 August 1877.

15. Madge Old, *Roslin Church Centenary 1881–1891* (Roslin, 1981).

16. *Catholic Directory* (1890), 93.

17. *Dalkeith Advertiser*, 29 November 1923.

18. *Dalkeith Advertiser*, 28 July 1966.

19. Scottish Catholic Film Institute: Bert Mocogni (producer), *The Story of Margaret Sinclair* (1961), Scottish Screen Archive, ref. no. 2891.

20. 'Living in the Mystery of the Big Picture', *CAIM: Northumbria Community Newsletter*, 14 (Autumn 2000).

21. Ron Ferguson, with Mark Chater, *Mole under the Fence* (Edinburgh: Saint Andrew Press, 2006), 44.

6. Castles and Houses

1. Richard Augustine Hay, *Genealogie of the Sainteclaires of Rosslyn*, ed. James Maidment (Edinburgh: Thomas G. Stevenson, 1835), 6.

2. Gordon Donaldson and Robert S. Morpeth, *A Dictionary of Scottish History* (Edinburgh: John Donald, 1977), 57.

3. Richard Fawcett, *Scottish Medieval Churches* (Edinburgh: HMSO, 1985), 39.

4. Marcus Merriman, 'Henry's Takeover Bid', *Sunday Mail Story of Scotland* (Glasgow: Sunday Mail, 1988), 297.

5. Marcus Merriman, 'Wooing? This was Total War', *Scotland's Story*, 18 (Glasgow: Sunday Mail, 1999), 14; see also Marcus Merriman, *The Rough Wooings of Mary Queen of Scots, 1542–1551* (East Linton: Tuckwell Press, 2000).

6. Charles J. Smith, *Historic South Edinburgh*, vol. 2 (Edinburgh: Charles Skilton, 1979), 404–5.

7. Quoted in *Cassell's Old and New Edinburgh* (London: Cassell, 1880–3), 347.

8. William Anderson, *The Pentland Hills* (Edinburgh: W. & R. Chambers, 1926).

9. Alexander McCallum, *Cambridge County Geographies: Midlothian* (Cambridge: Cambridge University Press, 1912), 17.

10. Bradford A. Booth and Ernest Mehew (eds), *The Letters of Robert Louis Stevenson*, vol. 1 (London: Yale University Press, 1994), 195.

11. Robert Louis Stevenson, *Picturesque Notes on Edinburgh* (London: Seeley, 1900), 164, 170.

12. James Boswell, *The Journal of a Tour to the Hebrides with Samuel Johnson* (London: J.M. Dent, 1928), 335–6.

13. James Nasmyth, *Autobiography* (London: John Murray, 1883), 34–5, quoted in James Mackay, *A Biography of Robert Burns* (Edinburgh: Mainstream, 1992), 290–1.

14. Walter Scott, *The Talisman* (Edinburgh: Adam & Charles Black, 1871), 51–2.

15. 'Around Dalkeith, 8. Rosslyn', *Dalkeith Advertiser*, August 1877.

16. Dorothy Wordsworth, *Recollection of a Tour Made in Scotland AD 1803* (3rd edn, Edinburgh: David Douglas, 1894), 245–7.

17. Cuthbert Bede, *A Tour in Tartan-Land* (London: Richard Bentley, 1863).

18. Thomas Bonnar, *Biographical Sketch of George Meikle Kemp* (Edinburgh: William Blackwood, 1892), 8, 13.

19. *The Scotsman*, 6 December 1843.

20. John Ruskin, *Præterita*, vol. 1 (Orpington: Jon Allen, 1886), 412.

21. NAS GD 164/1017, Roslin Chapel: visitor statistics, 17 August (year unknown).

22. Hugh Jamieson, *Jamieson's Guide to Roslin and Suburban Beauties of Edinburgh* (Edinburgh: Hugh Jamieson, n.d.).

23. James Horne, *Fifteen One Day Cycle Tours from Edinburgh with Description of the Roads and Objects of Interest in the Vicinity* (Edinburgh: W. & A.K. Johnston, n.d.).

24. Harry R.G. Inglis, *Short Spins round Edinburgh* (Edinburgh: Gall & Inglis, 1897).

25. NAS GD 164/1019/16 Alexander Thomson Grant to Earl of Rosslyn, 18 October 1880.

26. *The Scotsman*, 4 October 1881.

27. *The Scotsman*, 6 April 1885.

28. *The Scotsman*, 2 April 1891.

29. *The Scotsman*, 12 September 1912.
30. *The Scotsman*, 9 March 1914.
31. *The Scotsman*, 12 October 1914.
32. VisitScotland press release, 16 October 2006.
33. *The Scotsman*, 1 October 2005.

Epilogue

1. John Thompson, *The Illustrated Guide to Rosslyn Chapel and Castle, Hawthornden &c.* (11th edn, Edinburgh: MacNiven & Wallace, 1934), app. D, quoting William Stephens, *History of the Scottish Church*, vol. 1 (Edinburgh: D. Douglas, 1894–6), 445.
2. *Ibid.*
3. *Ibid.* John Lesley, *History of Scotland*, vol. II, book viii (Edinburgh: Bannatyne Club, 1830), 54.
4. Michael Fass, *Faith and Place* (Roslin: Congregation of St Matthew's, 2003), 19.
5. Anon., 'Rosslyn Chapel and the Da Vinci Code', *Inspires* (February 2006), 5.

Index

Acho, King of Norway 36
Adamson, Robert 75, 82, 99, 207
Advocates Library 26
Albany, Duke of 43, 44
Albergati, Cardinal Nicholas 4
Alexander II, King of Scotland 36
Alexander III, 36
Alexander VI, Pope 57
Allerton, Battle of 36
aloes 138
Anderson, Robert 126, 127
Anderson, William 194
Annan, Revd William 18
Aragon, King of 42
Arbuthnot Manuscripts 66
Architectural Institute of Scotland 76
Ark of the Covenant 91
Asterius the Pict 35, 172
Augustinian Order 158

Balantradoch (Balantravach) 148, 150
Balfour, Dr Andrew 158
Balliol, King John 37
Balm Well 18
Balmoral Hotel 217
Bannockburn, Battle of 39, 150
Battlefield Band 163
Beaton, Cardinal David 176
Beattie, Stuart 216
Bell, Andrew 31
Bentley, Edward 206
Billings, Robert W. 5
Bilston Burn 37, 50
Bilston Wood 194
Bishop, Sir Henry 186
Blackadder's Crypt 47
Bodleian Library, Oxford 66

Boswell, James of Auchinleck 144, 199
Boys of the Lough 163
British Pharmacological Society 158
Brown, Dan 131, 214
Brown, Revd David 11, 12, 163, 164
Brown, Lesley Peebles 140
Brusche, Peter 179
Bryce, David 75, 76, 77, 146
Buchan, Mackenzie 73
Buchanan, George 27
Burn, William 75, 76, 78
Burnett, Revd David 19
Burns, Robert 165, 199, 200

Caithness, Earl of 30
Camden Society 75, 76
Camden, William 9
Canongate Kirk 22
Canongate Lodge, Kilwinning 144
Carden 36
Carey, Bishop Kenneth 169
Carrick, Revd J.C. 152
Carter, Ben 216
Castlelaw soutterain 198
Chapel Royal (Stirling) 63, 66
Charles II, King 20
Charles, Prince 91
Chartres 20
Chater, Mark 169
Clark, Sir Kenneth 76
Clayton & Bell, London 128
Clement V, Pope 150
Clerk, Sir John of Penicuik 73, 75, 201
College Hill House 59
Collegehill (College Hill) 39, 58, 60, 78, 91, 214
collegiate churches 56

Comyn, John 37
Constantine I, Emperor 109
Cooper, Robert L.D. 147
Corbet, Ralph 148
Covenanters, the 19, 197
Craig, Dr James 160
Crichton Collegiate Church 51, 93
Cromwell, Oliver 76
Crosier, Robert 163
crusader 152
Currie, James 23

da Vinci, Leonardo 214
Da Vinci Code, The 214, 217
Dalkeith 8, 17, 19, 61, 85, 136, 195
Dalkeith, Presbytery of 71, 72
Dalrymple, Sir John 199
Dalyell, General Tam 18
Darius, King of Persia 121, 122
Darnley, Lord Henry 69
Daubenton's bat 17
David I (of Scotland) 8, 22, 35, 36, 40, 53,
        137, 147, 176
David II (of Scotland) 155
Davidson, Revd John 61
de Clifton, Walter 150
de Honnecourt, Villard 48
de Jay, Brian 150
de Lisours, William 152
de Melville, Stephen 152
de Preston, John 194
De Quincey, Thomas 201
de Soleure, Master John 150
Death, Dance of 112
Deuchar, Alexander 155
Dickson, Revd John 57, 61, 70
Dimitri, Princess 106
Disruption, The 11, 163, 165
Divine Office (*Opus Dei*) 68
Donald (Domnall) I, King 172
Douglas, Archibald, Earl of 43, 44
Douglas, Elizabeth 46
Douglas, Margaret 58, 125
Douglas, Revd Gavin 64
Douglas, Sir James 39, 42
Drummond, James (Earl of Perth) 22, 27
Drummond, William 193, 199, 202

Dunbar, George 43
Dunkeld Music Book 62
Dunstable, John 63
Dunstaffnage Chapel 175
Dyer, Dr Adrian 138
Dyer, Revd Janet 138

Eastlake, Charles 76
Ecclesiological Society 75
Edinburgh Architectural Association 211
Edminston, Jean 183
Edward I, King of England 37, 39, 150
Edward VI, King 176
Edward VII, King 214
Eugenius IV, Pope 46
European Union 90

Fass, Revd Michael 1, 218, 219
Fawcett, Dr Richard 136
Ferguson, Revd Ron 169
feuing 53
Fife, Earl of 39
Flotterstone 197, 198
Forbes, Bishop Alexander Penrose 79
Forbes, Dr Robert 31, 115, 121
Fordun, John of 26, 27
Fort Augustus Abbey 66
Fountainhall, Lord 20
Frankfurt Lodge Book 126, 127
Fraser, Simon 37
Free Kirk 11, 164
Freemasons 142, 143, 144, 145, 146,
        147
Friends of Rosslyn 91

Gaudí, Antoni 93
General Assembly 70, 71
George IV, King 206
George V, King 213, 214
George VI, King 146
Gillies, Sir William 161, 163
Glasgow Cathedral 47, 134, 136
Glencorse Kirk 197
Glencorse Reservoir 18, 40, 198
Goose's Mound 173
Gordon, Duke of 22
Gorton, Caves of 191

Gothic Revival 75, 96
Graham, Bishop Patrick 69
Grand Lodge of Scotland 144, 147
Grant, Revd Alexander Thomson 210
Grant, Will 18
Graves, The 38
Gray, Archbishop Gordon J. 167, 169
Green Man 101, 102, 104
Gregorian chant 63, 65
Grose, Francis 139, 179
Ground-Scan Ltd 91
gypsies 113

Hall, Chris 142
Halsey, Revd John 168, 169, 170
Hamilton, Willie 175, 176
Hammermen 54
hart's tongue fern 138, 170
Hawthornden Castle 5, 191, 192, 193, 194,
    202
Hay of Barra, John 18
Hay, Fr Richard Augustine 7, 13, 18, 19, 20,
    21, 22, 23, and *passim*
Hay, John 15
Haydn, Franz Joseph 186
Henry II, King of England 36
Henry III, King of England 37
Henry VIII, King 176
Henry, Prince of Scotland 8
Herd, David 184
Herd, Peter 87
Heritage Lottery Fund 90
Hertford, Earl of 176
Hewan Bog 194
Hewitt, Richard 184
Hill, David Octavius 75, 82, 99, 207
Historic Scotland 90, 136, 140
Holloway, Bishop Richard 169
Holyrood, Abbey of 21, 40, 44, 137, 150,
    155
Holyroodhouse (Palace) 21, 113, 158
Honorius II, Pope 147
Hope, Dr John 158
Horne, James 209
How, Revd John 70
Husefleet, John of 150
Hutcheson, Revd David 57, 70

ICI Nobel 17
Illyricus, Falcius 62
Inglis, Harry R.G. 210
Irvine, William 73

Jacob's Ladder 156
James I, King (England) VI (Scotland) 70, 143
James I, King (Scotland) 4, 44, 63, 142
James II, King (England) VII (Scotland) 20,
    21, 23, 179
James II, King (Scotland) 9, 144, 176
James III, King (Scotland) 63
James IV, King (Scotland) 64
James V, King (Scotland) 60
James, Prince (Scotland) 43, 44
Jamieson, Hugh 209
Jerusalem 42, 62, 93, 147, 150
John, King (England) 36
Johnson, Dr Samuel 144, 199
Johnson, Revd Robert 62
Jonson, Ben 193, 199

Kemp, George Meikle 206
Kennedy, Bishop James 69
Ker, Mark 152, 153
Ker, Revd John 61
Ker, Sir Andrew of Cessford 152
Kerr, Andrew 59, 82, 84, 85, 91, 136, 139,
    211
Kilwinning, Lodge No. 0: 143, 144
King, Revd David 71
King's Hill 18, 40, 195, 198
Kinnaird, Alison 163
Kirk, Jordan 142
Knightfield Rig 18, 40, 195, 198
Knox, Revd John 70
Knox, Revd William 70

Lamberton, Bishop William 150
Lambeth, H.A. 186
Lang, Joe 142
Langland, William 114
Lasswade 5, 10, 61, 72, 201
Lasswade Cottage 201, 202
Lauder, Sir Harry 146
'Lay of the Last Minstrel' 204, 205
Leader Tyne Esk 90

Leith 20
Leslie, David 178
Liberton 41
Lincoln 140
Little, Commissary Clement 121
Little, Lord Provost William 121
Lombardic alphabet 122
Lothian & Tweeddale, Provincial Assembly 72
Lothian, Marquess of 153
Loughborough, Lord 213
Louis, Dauphin of France 36
Lundie, Revd George 71
Luther, Martin 67

Mabillon, Dom Jean 23, 24, 29
McCallum, Alexander 195
McDonald, Archbishop Andrew J. 167
Mackenzie, Henry 201
Mackenzie, Sir A. C. 186
Macqueen, Janet 54
Macqueen, Michael 54
McWilliam, Colin 84, 105
Magdalen Chapel 54
Maidment, James 26, 28, 29, 30, 31
Maitland-Moir, Archimandrite John 169
maize, American 138
Malcolm III, King (Scotland) 32, 33, 35
Malcolm IV, King (Scotland) 157
Malcolm the Maiden, King (Scotland) 36
Margaret, Lady 45
Martin V, Pope 46
Mary II, Queen 73
Mary of Gueldres, Queen (Scotland) 54, 66, 158
Mary, Queen (wife of George V) 213, 214
Mary, Queen of Scots 54, 69, 70, 112, 153, 176
Maxentius, Emperor 109
Maxwell, Revd James 61
Maxwell, Revd John 61
Melrose Abbey 8, 136, 139, 140
Merricks, John 15
Middleton, William of 150
Midlothian & Peebles District Asylum 160
Midlothian Council 156, 188
Midlothian County 2, 157, 158
Midlothian Ranger Service 188

Midway Cottages 56
Milbanke, Sir John 106
Milvian Bridge 109
Ministry of Works 87, 88
Mitchell, Stuart 217
Moat Pit 14
Mocogni, Bert 167
Moffat, Dr Brian 138, 158
Monck, General George 72, 105, 178
Morrison, Revd Dr E.F. 95
Morton, Robin 163
Mortonhall 18, 40, 177
Mossman, Revd James 61
Mulcahy, Abbot Columban 168, 169
Murray, Old Father 22
Mylne, Robert 26

Nasmyth, Alexander 199
Nasmyth, James 199
National Apple Register 10
National Archives of Scotland 14
National Library of Scotland 18, 26, 27, 62, 66
Navarre, Collège de 19
Neilson, Robert 14
Newbattle Abbey (Newbottle) 8, 53, 152, 153
Newman, John Henry 75
Nunraw, Sancta Maria Abbey 168

O'Brien, Archbishop Keith Patrick 169
O'Connell, Fr Denis 167
Observatory, Edinburgh 85
Oldham, Arthur 62
Orkney 36, 42, 125
Oxford Movement 75

Panthiora, Queen 172
Paton, Revd John 10
Paul II, Pope 57
Penn, William 22
Pentland 35, 60
Pentland, Old 18, 42, 71, 194, 197
Pentland Hills 2, 7, 18, 35, 39, 91, 154, 157, 188, 193, 194, 195, 207
Pentland Hills Ranger Information Centre 197
Pentland Hills Regional Park 18
Pentland Moor 39
Percy, Henry 35

Perth, Earl *see* Drummond
Philip II, King (France) 36
Philip IV, King (France) 150
Piccolomini, Aeneas Silvius 3, 4
Piers Ploughman 114
Pillar, Prince's (Apprentice) 116, 117, 120,
    121, 138, 139, 140, 141, 142
Pitt, William the Younger 10
Pius XII, Pope 167
Pollen, Patrick 127
Preston, Sir John 152
Preston, William 194
Pringle family 157
Purves, Mr 208

Ramsay, Allan 195, 197
Ramsay, Lady Margaret 152
Ramsay, Revd George 71, 72
Ramsay, Sir Alexander 13, 191, 193
Read & Son 14
recording angels 157
Reformation, Scottish 70, 105, 111, 112, 113,
    142, 155, 194
Restalrig, Collegiate Church 51, 63
Rhind, William Birnie 144, 213
Robberds, Most Revd W.J.F. 212
Robert I, King (Robert the Bruce) 18, 37, 39,
    40, 42, 58, 150, 155, 195, 198
Robert II, King (Scotland) 42
Robert III, King of Scotland 42, 155
Roberts, David 206, 207
Robertson, George 4
Robeson, Revd John 57, 70
Robin Hood and Little John 113, 183
Roger, Brother 169
Rosebery, Lord 213
Rosewell 90, 165, 166, 167
Roslin, Battle of 13, 37, 38, 173
Roslin & District Amenity Society 156
Roslin Glen 2, 6, 7, 101, 138, 188, 207
Roslin Glen Wildlife Reserve 2
Roslin Gunpowder Works 15, 156
Roslin Heritage Group 156
Roslin Heritage Society 156, 188
Roslin Inn 164, 165
Roslin/Bilston Community Council 156
Ross, Fr Anthony 29

Ross, Thomas 135, 136, 137, 141, 213
Rosslyn Castle 2, 8, 13, 172, and *passim*
Rosslyn Chapel Trust 90, 216, 220
Rosslyn, Friends of 91
Rosslynlee Hospital 158, 160
Rosslyn Missal 66
Rouen 139
Rough Wooing 176
Rounds, The 175
Royal Botanic Garden 158
Royal College of Physicians of Edinburgh 158
Ruinart, Dom Thierry 29
Rullion Green 197, 199
Ruskin, John 207

Sagrada Familia 93
St Andrews Music Books 62, 65
St Catherine in the Hopes 18, 40, 41, 44, 72,
    195, 198
St Catherine's Balm Well 41
St Clare (Santa Chiara) 29
St Giles Collegiate Church 51, 54, 64, 194,
    200
St James of Pouvins 20
St Mary's Cathedral Workshop 48, 142
St Mary's Episcopal Church, Dalkeith 85
St Matthew (Rosewell) 165, 166, 167
St Matthew's, Old 46, 50, 58
St Matthew's Well 12, 46, 60
St Nicholas Collegiate Church, Dalkeith 72,
    136
St Patrick's, Edinburgh 166, 167
St Ternan's, Arbuthnot 66
Saint-Charon 20
Sainteclaire *see* Sinclair
Sainte-Geneviève 20
Saint-Pierremont 23
Salisbury Cathedral 65
Sandilands, Sir James 153
Sang, John 79
Sarum Rite (Sarum Use) 65
Saville, Sir Jimmy 167
Schaw, William 143
Scheves, Bishop William 218
schola (*sang schule*) 61
Scone Antiphonary 62
Scot, Christiana 150, 151, 152

Scotland, Church of 71, 157, 160, 163, 197
Scots College Paris 19
Scott, Mrs Charlotte 201
Scott, Revd Alexander 61
Scott, Ridley 94
Scott, Sir Walter 5, 28, 30, 32, 150, 201, 202, 204, 206
Scott-Moncrieff, George 161
Scott-Moncrieff, Lesley 161
Scottish Ecclesiological Society 137, 213
Scottish Natural Heritage 3
Scottish Wildlife Trust (SWT) 2, 3
Seton, Lord George 57
Seton Collegiate Church 51, 93, 140
SHARP 158
Shin Bones (Shinbanes) 38
Sibbald, Revd James 66
Sibbald, Sir Robert 22, 141, 158
Siguenza Cathedral 136
Simpson, James 91
Sinclair (Sainteclaire/Saintclair/Sinclair/ St Clair)
  1st Baron Sir William St Clair (the Seemly) 35, 173
  2nd Baron Sir Henry St Clair 35
  3rd Baron Sir Henry St Clair (Cardain) 35, 36
  5th Baron Sir Henry St Clair 36
  6th Baron Sir William St Clair 36
  7th Baron Sir Henry St Clair 37, 150
  8th Baron Sir William St Clair 152
  9th Baron Sir Henry St Clair (Prince of Orkney) 42
  10th Baron Sir Henry St Clair (Prince of Orkney) 42, 46, 173, 175
  11th Baron Sir William St Clair (Prince of Orkney) 44, 45, 46, 47, 50 and passim
  13th Baron Sir William St Clair 61
  14th Baron Sir William St Clair 71, 72, 112, 176, 177
  15th Baron Sir William St Clair 183, 184
  16th Baron Sir William St Clair 177
  17th Baron Sir John St Clair 178
  18th Baron Sir James St Clair 19, 179
  19th Baron Sir William St Clair (The Last Rosslyn) 30, 31
  2nd Earl Sir James St Clair-Erskine 144

3rd Earl Sir James Alexander St Clair-Erskine 75, 79
4th Earl Francis Robert St Clair-Erskine 82, 144, 146, 212
5th Earl James Francis Harry St Clair-Erskine 144, 146
6th Earl Anthony Hugh Francis St Clair-Erskine 146
7th Earl Peter St Clair-Erskine 91, 146
St Clair, Colonel/General James Alexander 73, 75, 128
St Clair-Erskine, Hon. Alexander Fitz Roy 212
Sinclair, Aegidia 46
Sinclair, Sir Edward 70, 176
Sinclair, Henry Bishop of Ross 66
Sinclair, John Bishop of Brechin 66
Sinclair, Revd Henry 57, 195
Sinclair, Revd John 57, 195
Sinclair, Sir Oliver 69, 71
Sinclair, Andrew 91
Sinclair, Margaret 166, 167
Sinclair, Niven 91
Sinclair, Sir John 10
Slezer (Sletzer), John Abraham 22, 116, 125, 141, 183
Society of Antiquaries of Scotland 96, 139
Society of Antiquaries, London 139
Solomon, Temple of 132
'Sonnet Composed in Rosslyn Chapel' 203
Southerland, Alexander 57, 60
Southerland, Lady Marjory 57, 58
Soutra Aisle/Hospital 157, 158
Spottiswood, Jean 18
Spottiswood, Sir Henry 18
Stanks, the 173
Statistical Account, First 10
Statistical Account, Second 11
Stephen, King of England 36
Stevenson, Robert Louis 197
Stewart, Alexander 46
Stewart, Bishop James 69
Stewart, John (Earl of Buchan) 46
Straiton Burn 38
Stuart, Prince Charles Edward 13
Swanston 197
suffragettes 85, 86

Taylor, Charles 214
Taylor, Debbie 217
Taylor, James 193
Taylor, John 89, 90
Teba (Spain) 42, 152
teinds 62
Templar, Knights 147, 148, 150, 151, 152
Temple, New 148
Temple, Old 148
Temple Lands 152
Temple Records 163
Temple Village 148, 161
Thompson, Revd John 13, 23, 82, 95, 96, 105,
    106, 125, 134, 138, 140, 173, 175, 176,
    179, 182, 183, 187, 189, 191, 193, 207,
    213, 218
Thomson, George 186
Thomson, John 75, 209
Thomson, Thomas 86
Timon Films Ltd 91
Totti, Thomas 150
Transfiguration, Community of 167
Transfiguration, Hermitage of 168
Transfiguration, Houses of 169
Traquair 19
Trinity Altarpiece 63
Trinity College 54, 67, 71, 136, 158
Turner, Joseph M.W. 206
Tytler, Alexander Fraser 201

Unreason, Abbot of 113

Vanier, Jean 169

Vennel, The 213
Victoria, Queen 75, 214
Vienne, Council of 150
VisitScotland 214, 216

Wagner, Marcus 62
Wallace, Sir William 13, 37, 150
Walls, Revd Roland 99, 168, 169, 170, 171
Weet, Mrs Conwallis 210
Westmoreland, Countess of 213
Whalen, Carrick 106
Whitehead, Revd James 61
Whitekirk parish church 85
Whytock, Richard 14, 15
Widnell & Company 14
William of Orange, King 23, 72, 105, 179
William the Conqueror, King 33
William the Lion, King (Scotland) 7, 32,
    36
Wilson, Sir Daniel 5
Wilson, William 106
Wolfenbüttel 63, 65
Wordsworth, Dorothy 202, 203
Wordsworth, William 202, 203

yew tree, Rosslyn Castle 46, 182, 183
Yolande, Queen 37
York, James Duke of 20; *see also* James II and
    VII
Young, W. Drummond 145
Younger, George 90

Zorobabel 122